Species at Risk

Contents

Foreword

Once a species has disappeared from the face of the earth, it doesn't come back. Extinction is irrevocable. This indisputable fact adds importance and urgency to the work that Jason Shogren and colleagues undertake in *Species at Risk: Using Economic Incentives to Shelter Endangered Species on Private Lands*. Correctly designed market incentives can provide us with an efficient and effective set of tools to relieve and redirect pressures that are leading to the extinction or endangerment of species. By extension these same tools can enhance the habitat and natural resource base on which the country's social, economic, and environmental vitality depend.

The Endangered Species Act (ESA) was conceived with the best of intentions and, indeed, has many noteworthy achievements to its credit. It is hard to argue with the preamble to the 1973 law that identifies the goal of the legislation to conserve and protect "the ecosystems upon which endangered and threatened species of wildlife depend." Yet in practice the law has too often become polarizing and, in the view of many landowners and conservationists alike, provides perverse incentives that can work against the protection of species, especially on private land.

Although many of the act's provisions remain controversial, there is widespread agreement that promoting and encouraging more effective participation of private landowners in conservation efforts will result in better conservation of threatened and endangered species, and perhaps more important, help prevent species from getting to the point wh~ they are threatened in the first place. Numerous discussions have foc\ on this subject: the board of the Institute of Environment and Natu. Resources (IENR) at the University of Wyoming devoted its spring 1996 forum to developing a series of principles to guide policy changes to the implementation of the ESA on private property, and the Keystone Center completed a successful and broad-based dialogue identifying incentives for private landowners to protect endangered species in July 1995.

Close to 90 percent of endangered species habitat is found on private land. Any effort to conserve an endangered or threatened species or to implement an ecosystem or landscape management strategy is more likely to succeed if the private sector is a willing participant. Economic incentives have proven effective and help to address the inequity of imposing the cost of preservation on a few for the benefit of the many, but for some landowners those incentives may not go far enough. Shogren and other researchers have put their finger on something deeply significant to many landowners: they want their privacy respected, their prior and current stewardship acknowledged, and flexibility in how they manage and care for their land and their investments in the future. Some reject compensation outright for fear it will send a signal that they are not already taking good care of their land, and because compensation might invite excessive government scrutiny of activities in their own backyard.

When the IENR Board considered the ESA in 1996, it concluded: "We must all look at new, creative, bold ways to build bridges with the nation's property owners and provide incentives to them for the protection of our natural resources." This book is a direct response to that challenge. Drawing on the disciplines of economics, law, political science, history, and zoology, *Species at Risk: Using Economic Incentives to Shelter Endangered Species on Private Lands* critiques several of the approaches to species protection with proven records of success, including habitat conservation plans, safe harbors, and no-surprise policies.

The book goes a step farther, however, in identifying the limits to those approaches, suggesting additional market-based tools that could be applied to address the privacy concerns of certain landowners and, ultimately, increase the level of species conservation. In particular, the book makes a case for consideration of a market for tradable critical habitat rights, where landowners would be provided the opportunity to sell private shares of critical habitat rights on an open market.

These approaches, to be certain, are not without controversy. Some may question whether the approach affords adequate accountability of public funds expended to purchase habitat conservation measures on private lands. Others may argue that compensation of any sort is a backdoor attempt to sabotage the ESA through underfunding. To be sure, numerous technical and legal obstacles remain before such an approach could be applied, including how to measure the quality and quantity of habitat and assign it a fair market value; but this is the kind of thinking that holds potential for adding another important instrument, alongside government compensation, land trusts, purchase of development rights, technical assistance, insurance programs, and tax breaks, to build the right set of incentives for species protection.

Checking our proverbial guns at the door and engaging a healthy public debate on how to improve the alignment of our economic, environmental, and social incentives may do even more than benefit our species, our habitat, and our natural resources. It may begin to help reverse the downward spiral of trust in government and private institutions that is at the core of many of the disputes over natural resources. Bill Ruckelshaus, the first chair of the Institute of Environment and Natural Resources Board and twice the administrator of the Environmental Protection Agency, remarked during a speech at the University of Wyoming that involving citizens in the decision-making process and providing the flexibility to determine how to comply with societal goals "can begin to transform groups of people struggling with disaffection and despair into communities where energized and optimistic citizens are engaged in shaping their own future."

The stakes are high, and they go to the heart of our collective responsibility to leave this land a better place than we found it. This book is an attempt to develop and refine a workable, practical, and equitable set of incentives for preserving species and the habitat they need for survival. It seeks to engage private citizens in solving a public and, ultimately, global problem: the loss and rapid decline of species. It seeks to develop incentives for constructive action on the part of citizens. Instead of pointing the finger at government as the problem, landowners can become comfortable in being part of the solution and can act in ways that benefit the land they love while serving the interests of society as a whole.

Ambassador Mike Sullivan and the members of the board
Institute of Environmental and Natural Resources
University of Wyoming

Black-footed ferrets
crouch under hoves and dry hills.
Sunflowers tremble.
—CARA CAMPANELLA

Species at Risk

CHAPTER 1

Introduction

JASON F. SHOGREN

A sunflower named the desert yellowhead (*Yermo xanthocephalus*) is known to live on fifty acres in Fremont County, Wyoming. This rare perennial flower is a species at risk from both natural and human-caused disturbances. The U.S. Fish and Wildlife Service (USFWS) announced in the spring of 2002 that it would list the desert yellowhead as a threatened species under the Endangered Species Act (ESA) of 1973. A threatened species like the desert yellowhead is one feared to become endangered from future pressures of human activity. The ESA codifies the idea that species have "ecological, educational, historical, recreational and scientific value" unaccounted for in the course of "economic growth and development" (ESA, Sec. 2). Thirty years ago this language seemed harmless enough to the U.S. Congress, which passed the act with little or no opposition: 390–12 in the House and 92–0 in the Senate (see Mann and Plummer 1995).

Nevertheless, the ESA has proven to be controversial. First, the act broadened the scope of species protection (Bean 1999). It makes every species, subspecies, and discrete population, restricted to plants and animals, eligible for protection by being listed either as endangered or threatened. As a consequence, the list of endangered and threatened species in the United States expanded by an order of magnitude, from about 100 in 1973 to nearly 1,300 in 2002 (see Table 1.1). Plants at risk, like the desert yellowhead, make up two-thirds of the listed species. The large variety of species that might require protection under the act implies ever-increasing conflicts with on-going human demands to use and develop land (see, for example, Wilcove et al. 2000; Beissinger and Perrine 2001).

Second, the original language of the act implies that all species will be

**Table 1.1. Box Score of Threatened and Endangered Species
(as of 1 September 2003)**

Group	Endangered U.S.	Endangered Foreign	Threatened U.S.	Threatened Foreign	Total Species	Species with Plans
Mammals	65	251	9	17	342	54
Birds	78	175	14	6	273	77
Reptiles	14	64	22	15	115	32
Amphibians	12	8	9	1	30	14
Fishes	71	11	44	0	126	96
Snails	21	1	11	0	33	22
Clams	62	2	8	0	72	57
Crustaceans	18	0	3	0	21	13
Insects	35	4	9	0	48	29
Arachnids	12	0	0	0	12	5
Animal subtotal	388	516	129	39	1072	399
Flowering plants	571	1	144	0	716	574
Conifers	2	0	1	2	5	2
Ferns and others	24	0	2	0	26	26
Lichens	2	0	0	0	2	2
Plant subtotal	599	1	147	2	749	604
Grand total	987	517	276	41	1821	1003[a]

Source: U.S. Fish and Wildlife Service, Division of Endangered Species (2003).
[a] There are 555 distinct approved recovery plans. Some plans cover more than one species, and some species have more than one plan.

protected regardless of costs, which reversed the preceding doctrine that species protection would be "practicable and consistent with primary purposes" of land use. The Supreme Court upheld this view in *Tennessee Valley Authority v. Hill*, stating that "it is clear from the ESA's legislative history that Congress intended to halt and reverse the trend toward species extinction—whatever the cost." The ideal of protection at any cost creates additional conflicts because species protection must compete with other worthy public goals such as education or health care, all constrained by scarce resources and limited budgets.

Economists have not attempted to estimate what the ESA might cost the entire nation as measured by reduced opportunities due to restricted land use. They do have an estimate, however, on what federal and state agencies have spent on endangered species protection between 1989 and 1996. Table 1.2 shows that expenditures increased from $44 million in 1989 to about $270 million in 1996—out of total government expenditures of more than $1.4 trillion in 1996 (Dawson and Shogren 2001). Limited budgets and political realities also create conflicts within ESA recovery plans, in which over 50 percent of expenditures go to ten vertebrates (see Table 1.3).

Third, the ESA covers species that live on public or private land or both. The fifty acres that shelter the desert yellowhead are part of public lands managed by the Bureau of Land Management. Although not without its challenges, the protection of the sunflower is relatively straightforward; if the bureau and the USFWS can work together as sister federal agencies, they can draft a public-to-public conservation agreement. Species protection on private lands, however, is a different story. Now we are talking about creating new private-to-public agreements. The ESA prohibits private citizens from taking any threatened or endangered species on their private property, and the USFWS has interpreted "taking" to mean any action that injures or kills an endangered species or degrades its habitat. The U.S. Supreme Court has upheld that interpretation in the recent past. Most land in the United States is in fact privately owned, and since about half of the listed endangered species rely on private land for 80 percent of their habitat, the potential reach of the ESA is extensive (see Bean 1998; Brown and Shogren 1998).

Protecting nature on private lands presents both a challenge and an opportunity. The challenge is to protect both private landowner concerns and the biological needs of the environment; the opportunity is to integrate the many disciplines that fall within the natural and social sciences. Such integration offers scientists the prospect of gaining more understanding about the complexities that arise in the protection of human-dominated environments. Better integration also can help policymakers make more informed decisions about how to manage private lands by adding insight into the efficacy and efficiency of alternative choices that try to balance private rights with the public gains. Integration occurs at several different levels, ranging from accounting for feedbacks between both society and ecology within formal models to incorporating diverse methods of control to link the multiple objectives of various interest groups and people.

Table 1.2. Summary of Federal and State Endangered Species Conservation Expenditures ($1,000s)

	1989	1990	1991	1992	1993	1994	1995	1996
Federal exp.	39,638.7	96,642.5	112,684.8	160,060.3	166,885.8	217,168.0	269,345.9	255,489.2
State exp.	4,086.1	5,701.2	64,126.7	131,450.7	13,025.5	9,640.1	10,237.0	12,433.05
Total	43,724.8	102,343.7	176,811.5	291,510.9	179,911.3	226,808.1	279,582.9	267,922.21
Land exp.[a]	Inc.	Inc.	Inc.	Inc.	Separate = 42,329.0	Separate = 17,769.4	Separate = 18,093.1	Separate = 17,791.48
No. of listed species	554	591	639	728	809	914	957	Not drafted
No. of species reporting	347	477	570	679	749	819	925	Not drafted
Median exp. for species	11.95	13.15	12.20	16.00	12.94	23.00	Not drafted	Not drafted

Federal agency exp. subtotals:								
FWS	18,353.2	35,262.2	54,517.3	55,068.8	46,219.9	51,067.5	55,910.6	40,763.24
Other fed (NMFS)	21,285.5	61,380.3	58,167.5	104,991.4	120,665.8	166,100.5	213,435.3	214,725.93
								(117,111.40)
Species exp. subtotals:								
Mammals	12,936.9	29,602.4	43,124.4	58,892.2	23,592.0	23,394.7	23,593.4	23,300.03
Birds	19,683.4	49,549.1	95,098.0	141,840.9	67,111.4	68,730.1	75,766	73,406.52
Reptiles	2,345.8	7584.6	10,754.9	26,448.5	12,755.2*	13,223.7	12,435.6	13,656.08
Amphibians	62.1	232.7	197.1	573.7	278.3	660.6	801	666.86
Fish	4,947.3	10,574.4	18,108.0	47,680.6	64,010.0	103,798	144,010.4	142,872.94
Invertebrates	1,339.4	2,566.8	3,953.1	9,763.7	6,314.7	6,718.3	12,100.4	5,694.99
Plants	2,408.2	2,162.0	5,567.0	6,311.3	5,849.0	10,282.8	10,876.1	8,324.79

Source: Dawson and Shogren (2001).

a"Inc." (incomplete reporting) and "separate =" mean that before 1993, although some federal and state agencies reported land acquisitions expenditures with their conservation expenditures, FWS itself did not report its land acquisitions expenditures consistently and separately until 1993.

Table 1.3. Top Ten Vertebrate Species:
Federal Expenditures and Land Acquisitions,
1993–1996

Rank	Species	Federal Expenditures and Land Acquisitions (millions of dollars)
1	Northern Spotted Owl	55.8
2	Red-cockaded Woodpecker	38.7
3	Bald Eagle	25.2
4	Desert (Mojave) Tortoise	22.8
5	Colorado Squawfish	22.5
6	Marbled Murrelet	16.9
7	Gray Wolf	13.8
8	American Peregrine Falcon	13.0
9	Whooping Crane	10.7
10	Razorback Sucker	10.6
	Total Top Ten	232.0
	Total Vertebrate Species	484.3

A good example of the private lands challenge is the proposed listing of the black-tailed prairie dog (*Cynomys ludovicianus*) as a threatened species under the ESA. Historically, both state and local governments and ranchers have considered the prairie dog a pest, believing the rodents compete for livestock forage, create livestock hazards with their burrows, and increase soil erosion. Ranchers and government agencies have engaged in systematic programs to eliminate populations. Environmentalists and biologists, however, argue that these actions have had serious implications for grasslands, as the prairie dog is believed to be a keystone species in Great Plains ecosystems. Current biological research indicates that in addition to providing prey for various species of raptors and black-footed ferrets, the prairie dog's presence provides habitat for burrowing owls, spotted salamanders, and mountain plovers. In addition, prairie dogs rework the soil, providing nutrients for plant growth of benefit to grazing animals (Whicker and Detling 1988).

Ranchers and hunters throughout the state are understandably worried about such changes on national grasslands, but they are even more worried about the implications that actual listing of the animal would have for private land. If the prairie dog were listed as threatened, under the terms of the Endangered Species Act, ranchers would not be allowed to engage in any measures to control its population on their lands. Hunters would also not be allowed to shoot the animal for sport, an activity gaining increased commercial weight throughout the West. Furthermore, in anticipation of this possible policy change, some ranchers are currently conducting prairie dog extermination programs on their own lands to ensure that if the policy comes into effect, management of their land will not be an issue (Matthews 1999).

Once the animal is listed, a landowner with black-tailed prairie dogs will have to work with a federal agency whose basic goal is to protect species by putting explicit restrictions on how the land can be used. Strict regulatory enforcement of the ESA (or any other environmental or land-use law) may deny property owners valuable uses of their land without rising to the level of a Fifth Amendment taking—private property shall not be taken for a public use, without just compensation (e.g., Blume et al. 1984). The ESA can be used as a tool to influence actions on private lands that people believe matter to species protection. Landowners can be restricted from using their land as they once did, while still being held responsible for paying their property taxes.

Although fears of land use restrictions are real, Michael Bean (1998) argues that they are exaggerated. Bean points out that the provision of the ESA that directly affects landowners (the species takings provision) has a "far narrower sweep than either the environmentalists or landowners commonly think." The provision does not apply to plants, is not automatic for threatened animals, is not absolute even for endangered species, and is shrouded by ambiguity about whether a taking implies just a threat or the actual death or injury of the animal. The ESA is not without its bite, however, for persons caught violating the act. Of those prosecuted on criminal charges for illegal takings, one-fourth went to jail for periods of 10 to 1,170 days, one-fourth paid fines of $1,000 to $50,000, and many others were put on probation (GAO 1995).

Land restrictions are not new, and most landowners understand this. For centuries in Europe and then in Euro-America, common-law restrictions have limited what people could do to or with their property. The ESA has triggered a profound backlash, however, because private property has held a special status in the history of the United States. Many laws impose inequitable burdens on people (e.g., mountain bikers paying taxes for interstate highways), but to some people, restricting private landowner autonomy to protect obscure species seems a threat to both the economic system and broader social order.

Regarding economics, land is natural capital, and it is capital that provides people the ability to create, store, and share private wealth essential to national survival and prosperity. This classical liberal viewpoint has faith in the Hamiltonian perspective that the government should abdicate to market forces that create wealth by allowing for resources to move freely from low-valued to high-valued uses. These people follow the utilitarian view of nature promoted by John Stuart Mill and Gifford Pinchot—the resource conservation ethic is "the greatest good of the greatest number for the longest time" (Pinchot 1947).

Regarding social order, many agree with James Madison's argument within the *Federalist Papers* that "the wide diffusion of independent property rights . . . was the essential foundation for stable republican government" (McEvoy 1998). The fear is that unjustifiable restriction of private land use for species protection without just compensation is another step down the slippery slope that would undo much of what is good about America (see Epstein 1985, 1995). Gail Norton, the current Secretary of the Interior, supports this view: "The goal of government must be to empower people to be citizen conservationists while respecting the need to make a living off the land" (Norton 2002). The idea that private landowners hold the key to species protection, however, is neither new nor novel. Aldo Leopold argued in the 1930s that conservation "ultimately boil[s] down to reward the private landowner who conserves the public interest" (see Bean 1997).

Others disagree. The romantic-conservation ethic promoted in the United States by Ralph Waldo Emerson, Henry Thoreau, and John Muir is a good example. The preservationists, as they came to be called, believed that land had other uses than just for human financial gain. Landowners would be free to pursue private profits provided they behaved as responsible social citizens too, because by definition land is already in public service. All land uses should be viewed as "harm-preventing" rather than as "public good providing." As Sagoff (1997, p. 845) puts it: "The conviction that the freedom to wring the last speculative penny from one's land is of a piece with one's most fundamental civil, political, and personal liberties seems to be grounded less on argument than on assumption." Based on recent Supreme Court decisions (e.g., *Lucas v. South Carolina Coastal Council, Dolan v. City of Tigard*), the Fifth Amendment takings clause is not applicable to all ESA restrictions. These decisions have established that a regulation related to the public purpose will require compensation only if it singles out a vulnerable minority, deprives a landowner of all viable uses of his property, or physically invades or occupies the property (Sagoff 1997). Most landowners affected by the ESA arguably do not satisfy any of those three criteria.

Although the courts have ruled that the government does not need to compensate for endangered species protection, it does not answer the question of whether the government *should* compensate private landowners (see Innes et al. 1998). Michael Bean (1998), who has studied the ESA–private lands–compensation triangle for years, believes that "without positive incentives, the act's goals are unlikely to be achieved." This argument reflects Leopold's evolutionary-ecological land ethic, which emerged in the 1940s, in part out of frustration with the other two views. Leopold (1949) based his ethic on the scientific notion that nature is not a collection of separate parts but an integrated system of actions, reactions, and feedbacks. This more scientific notion focuses on defining the natural system within the context of human interaction and well-being. Within this mind-set of integrating natural science and social science, one can promote more understanding between mind-sets by working together to define a set of evaluative criteria that reflects the range of ethical views. For the private lands challenge, the criteria should address perceived biological needs, landowner incentives, and regulatory power and control.

Regulatory approaches do exist to offer compensation to landowners for the costs of protecting species on their land. Providing landowners with incentives for better practices relies on the carrot of financial reward, rather than the stick of prosecution for violating ESA's prohibition on harming listed species or their habitat (Eisner et al. 1995; Shogren et al. 1999). Since the benefits of protecting endangered species accrue to the entire nation, should the public use incentive methods to compensate private landowners who pick up a sizable share of the costs? If not, why not? If so, how should these compensation schemes be designed to maximize protection to species and maximize the rights of self-determination? How should we determine the value of the compensation, the value of private land use lost due to species protection, or the public nonmarket value of land as species habitat? (See Farrier 1995; National Research Council 1995; Innes et al. 1998; Thompson 1997.)

Policymakers have addressed the compensation question in part by offering up voluntary incentive programs to landowners to increase their incentives for private species protection and biodiversity conservation. The idea is to transform an environmental liability into a marketable asset (Bayon 2002). The USFWS and more than a thousand nonprofit land trusts promote habitat conservation by using voluntary incentive mechanisms to elicit the cooperation of private landowners. Mechanisms include conservation easements, leases, habitat banking, habitat conservation planning, safe harbors, candidate conservation agreements, and the no-surprises policy (see Bean 1999).

The Defenders of Wildlife (2002) recently reviewed incentive-based approaches currently being used to encourage habitat conservation on private land across the United States. Based on a survey of state incentive programs, they found that about four hundred incentive programs enrolling some 70 million private acres exist in the fifty states, 50 percent of which were created within the last decade. The typical state offers four to six conservation incentives, usually in some form of direct payment and easement with tax relief. About 28 percent of the states make direct payments, 22 percent provide education and technical support, 20 percent give tax relief, and 13 percent use property-right tolls like easements and deed restrictions. Market institutions for species protection were used in about 3 percent of the programs.

Despite the existence of many incentive systems, internal rifts within the landowner and ESA-supporter communities continue to cloud the compensation question. Some landowners want compensation; those who complain about the high costs of complying with the ESA demand compensation for compliance. Ranchers and farmers say they will retire acres for habitat or will put up with large predators (e.g., grizzly bears, wolves) provided they are compensated. Those landowners willing to consider compensation demand a very fine level of detail about the program, need to see a local precedent, and need some basic reassurances to overcome an instinctual distrust of the regulatory aspects of the government (Korfmacher and Elsom 1998).

Some ESA defenders agree that compensation is needed; they see compensation as a pragmatic way to bring private land into the fold of species protection. Compensation would reduce a landowner's incentive to wipe out the potential environmental value of land, thereby avoiding any potential ESA restrictions. The Defenders of Wildlife, for example, have paid out more than $64,000 for nearly 100 grizzly depredations since 1997, and more than $200,000 to about 180 ranchers for livestock losses to wolves since 1987.

Other landowners do not want to be paid to protect species. They say they want nothing to do with a compensation policy for they fear further public erosion of their autonomy and private control. They also fear that any contracts they enter with federal agencies will be unenforceable (see Melious and Thorton 1999). They see compensation as a set of golden handcuffs, in which more and more will be required of them and taken from them. Their view is that sometimes compensation is not enough; landowners want their privacy respected, their prior steward-ship efforts acknowledged, and their ability to protect their investments flexible. As one rancher put it, "It sounds to me like you're basically sell-ing the state or federal government the right to control, not necessarily your land, but down the road it seems to me that the government then has control of private lands" (as quoted in Korfmacher and Elsom 1998).

Some proponents of the ESA also think compensation is a bad idea, although for a different reason. They view compensation payments as a tool to paralyze the ESA through continual congressional underfunding of budget sources. They fear that mandatory compensation that is not coupled with the necessary federal funding would in effect gut the ESA.

The compensation question has helped stall ESA reauthorization for over a decade. Congress has proposed several bills; none has passed. A good example is the Endangered Species Recovery Act (ESRA) intro-duced into the House of Representatives numerous times by Represen-tative George Miller (D-CA) and others. The ESRA encourages habitat planning by allowing for multispecies, multilandowner conservation plans. The act would expand opportunities for public participation and help landowners through tax incentives, technical assistance, and a streamlined permitting process. The act is silent, however, about direct compensation to landowners who shelter species. Another bill intro-duced from the opposite view is the Penalties Liability Reform Act (H.R. 1404), which affirms as a legitimate defense the case in which a land-owner did not respect an endangered or threatened species because he or she did not know, nor could reasonably have known, that the species was endangered or threatened. To date, neither the ESRA nor the Lia-bility Reform Act has been passed, and neither have any other bills falling to the left or right.

No one sees a quick end to the ESA controversy. Society is faced with difficult economic choices, choices that affect and are affected by bio-logical needs and political realities. Working through this tangle requires more explicit attention to how economic incentives might affect private landowners, ESA supporters, and policymakers. People can point to vol-untary programs that have worked to encourage some landowners to protect endangered species on their private property. These programs offer a regulatory safeguard to promote cooperation; some use explicit economic incentives such as payments for easements. Examples exist in which private landowners have voluntarily become partners in positive and proactive plans to protect and enhance natural resources on their land. Turner and Rylander (1998), for instance, describe several examples in which incentives have worked to protect species like the Louisiana black bear and the red-cockaded woodpecker.

Other observers remain skeptical of voluntary incentive programs within the ESA. They question whether economic incentives will work and what we know about the opportunities and challenges of using such schemes to promote proactive measures on private property. Although their concerns are legitimate, the cooperation of private landowners still remains vital to the preservation of endangered species. One can attempt to compel their cooperation through command and control mandates, or one can attempt to induce cooperation through flexible incentives that reward landowners for their good stewardship of habitat and species. A variety of such flexible compensation schemes are possible: direct compensation from the government to owners of land; conservation banking and tradable rights in habitat, under which those who wish to develop land would buy permits from those who would then not be able to develop; insurance programs under which landowners are compensated if endangered species impose costs on them, like the fund created by Defenders of Wildlife; estate tax relief to allow large chunks of land to be preserved, rather than broken up to pay federal estate taxes, or tax deductions for conservation expenses.

All incentive systems present opportunities and challenges. No incentive tool or approach is a panacea. The type of species, landowner, and land configuration problem can affect each incentive system. Aligning the incentives for unique landowners with society's desire for protection of certain species is not a one-size-fits-all proposition. Assessing and integrating how each incentive system works for each landowner and species and habitat will require a case-by-case process. This book primarily focuses on the abstract ideas underlying incentives because these issues cut across people, species, time, and space. Several case studies are presented to help make the abstract more concrete.

Compensation for private landowners can be subject to shaky claims and extensive litigation. Trading habitat requires ways of measuring what quantity and quality of habitat is equivalent—not a simple task. Although the government can provide the institutional framework within which people make trades for goods of value, widespread use of the insurance mechanism may be curtailed because of the costs of ascertaining the losses to property owners. It is not obvious that tax breaks for preserving large estates would generate more benefits than buying the land, or allowing it to be sold with some sort of easement, and the political attractiveness of providing additional tax breaks to wealthy landowners is questionable.

Plus, buyers of species protection will have to find willing sellers, those landowners who will sell or lease their property rights to habitat. In addition, determining a value for habitat requires independent and confidential biological and economic appraisals of habitat. Private companies are now also playing a role. The goal of the developers Greenvest, for example, is to develop land to balance "the goals of profit maximization and the creation of unique and aesthetically pleasing residential communities and commercial developments."

Creative suggestions on how to generate and use public monies more effectively are also welcome, even those with low odds of short-term political success. One wide-reaching proposal offered up by Gregg Easterbrook (1998) is that Congress should codify a "build-and-save" plan. For each and every acre developed, another acre of habitat must be purchased and conserved for species protection. The idea is to align developers' and conservationists' interests such that if the economy grows, so do our national parks and forests and grasslands. Over the last decade about 1.5 million acres of new development has occurred each year; therefore, a development fee of $1,000 an acre would generate a conservation fund of about $1.5 billion per year.

Such schemes have appeal, but a more likely approach in the short run is to find more creative ways to use compensation in conjunction with existing programs in the government. The difficulties of implementing new programs might suggest that one could fund conservation through existing programs, such as the Wetlands Reserve Program run by the USDA Natural Resource Conservation Service. The WRP, a nationwide voluntary program, offers payment based on agricultural value for wetlands that have been drained and converted to agricultural uses. Another USDA incentive is the Wildlife Habitat Incentive Program, which provides cost-sharing to assist landowners who use their habitat to protect wildlife and threatened and endangered species. In addition, Title II of the new farm bill (the Farm Security and Rural Investment Act of 2002) has budgeted about $17 billion for incentives for conservation on agricultural lands, including the newly created Conservation Security Program. The CSP pays producers who adopt and maintain conservation practices on private lands. Contracts run five to ten years, and annual payments range from $20,000 to $45,000. The CSP uses an initial Secretary's bonus to encourage people to sign up.

Another imaginative bonus scheme that could be incorporated into these existing incentive options is an agglomeration bonus. Suppose the dual goal is to maximize species protection cost-effectively and minimize private landowner resentment. The agglomeration bonus mechanism pays a bonus for every acre a landowner retires that borders on any other retired acre (see Parkhurst et al. 2002). The mechanism provides an incentive for adjacent landowners to create a contiguous reserve across their common border voluntarily, resulting in the single large habitat usually desired for effective conservation. A government agency's role is to target the critical habitat, to integrate the agglomeration bonus into the compensation package, and to provide landowners the unconditional freedom to choose which acres to retire.

Oregon's Conservation Reserve Enhancement Program (CREP) illustrates the idea of an allied land retirement bonus scheme. The CREP pays an extra bonus to enrollees along a stream if at least 50 percent of the stream bank within a 5-mile stream segment is enrolled in the U.S. Department of Agriculture's Conservation Reserve Program. The bonus is a one-time payment equaling four times the annual rental rate for each acre enrolled. Note that the CREP does not require retired acres to be contiguous, which might not create a single large habitat (see USDA 1998). Such targeted bonuses could also reduce the risk of a piecemeal approach that spreads conservation dollars too thinly among too many scattered landowners or programs (see Wu and Boggess 1999).

This book addresses the challenges and opportunities to use economic incentives as compensation for protecting species at risk on private property. Extending our first volume, which explored the challenges and opportunities of protecting species on private property (Shogren 1998), we have assembled a collection of essays by lawyers, economists, political scientists, historians, and zoologists who have examined the role of economic incentive schemes for species protection. Each chapter considers the promise of and the trepidation over economic incentives. The authors raise questions about whether landowners should be provided the opportunity to sell private shares of critical habitat rights on the open market without opening themselves up to public access. The goal is to form a better understanding of how incentive schemes can be both more cost-effective and socially acceptable given alternative views toward the nature of opportunity costs, legal standing, biological effectiveness, moral appropriateness, and social context. Each essay offers a different perspective on how we got here, what options we have, and what pitfalls confront us as we try to provide more species protection at less cost.

Overview of the Book

Some main points raised in the book are highlighted in Part I, an overview of existing and future options for incentives. In Chapter 2, law professor Debra Donahue examines the history of the Endangered Species Act and the current set of tools available for species protection. She examines the current programs offered by the USFWS to landowners for maintaining some financial uses of their land. These programs aim to reduce regulatory uncertainty for the landowner while protecting species at risk. The programs include habitat conservation planning (HCP) with no surprises, safe harbors, and candidate conservation agreements with assurances (CCA). HCPs with no surprises are useful for landowners who already have ESA-driven land use restrictions in place and who want to regain some financial uses on other portions of their land. For landowners who want to undertake land practices that increase the quality of habitat on their land but are hesitant to do so because of the actual or potential threat of increased ESA restrictions, the safe harbors and CCA programs assure a regulatory ceiling. Safe harbors apply to listed species; CCA is applicable to species that are candidates for listing.

The HCP program has been characterized as win-win; the landowner reduces the ESA land use restrictions on her land, which increases the landowner's expected profits, and the USFWS ensures a level of species protection. But is it win-win? From the landowner's point of view, she is a loser if her expected profits prior to ESA restrictions are compared against expected profits after completion of the HCP process. The landowner can be considered a winner when comparing her expected profits after ESA restrictions with her expected profits on completion of the HCP process. The landowner is still faced with the incentive to avoid initial ESA restrictions. Safe harbors are similar, in that landowners with land uses already restricted by ESA regulations can benefit. As of 2000, five safe harbor programs exist in the United States.

In Chapter 3, Gregory Parkhurst and myself review a set of economic incentive mechanisms designed to protect species on private land. We explore the pros and cons of eight incentive mechanisms for conserving habitat. These incentive mechanisms range from command-and-control, in which the government establishes a standard that landowners must satisfy, to voluntary incentive mechanisms that compensate the landowner. Each incentive mechanism has good and bad points as measured by economic, biological, and political criteria. No one incentive mechanism is the all-inclusive solution. The incentive mechanism that performs best under any given situation depends on the regulator's objectives, the budget, available land, how land qualities vary, landowner dispositions toward conservation, and the information available to the regulator.

As economists, we focus our pro-con discussion primarily on economic criteria. We acknowledge and appreciate that other scholars and policymakers use alternative social criteria to judge the pros and cons of these incentive mechanisms, including justice, fairness and equity, control, power, authority, and public participation in environmental protection. Part II explores the idea of incentives from a broader context. These chapters address the challenges facing the use of economic incentives for species protection. In Chapter 4, professors Frieda Knobloch and McGreggor Cawley examine endangered species protection and ways of life beyond our current narrow perspective of economics and ecology. They argue that extending the ESA to private property creates a conflict between preserving species and preserving a community's way of life. The way of life consists of all the values of the people of the community. Financial incentives are but one value. The effects of financial incentives should not be considered alone. They should be viewed by acknowledging how compensation affects all other individual values and obligations that define the community. When protecting species is in conflict with a community's way of life, financial incentives may be insufficient. Here Knobloch and Cawley suggest that protecting species must be aligned with people's way of life, so that compensation is combined with land management techniques that provide for the long-term reconnection of "people's livelihoods and ways of life" with "environmental health and stability."

Debra Donahue returns in Chapter 5 to evaluate the role of economic incentives for conservation. She argues that the use of financial incentives to protect species has four major pitfalls: funding is insufficient, individual efforts often lead to fragmented habitat, failure will occur unless the incentive policy is backed with enforced penalties for noncompliance, and landowners may not develop a land ethic that protects species long-term because they expect to be compensated for every lost land use. The chapter considers the details at work in her fourth pitfall, how landowners, looking to be compensated when land uses are restricted, do not establish a land ethic that employs adaptive management techniques for species preservation. Donahue argues that financial incentives should be tied to a stewardship ethic, thus altering the attitudes of landowners toward conservation, making species protection an asset, and changing land use expectations permanently, perhaps redefining property rights to include the obligation of maintaining and enhancing the land's biota. Donahue further asserts that for a financial incentive policy to be effective in promoting a stewardship ethic, the underlying regulation should have teeth.

Biologists Steven Buskirk and Samantha Wisely address the challenges associated with appraising the conservation value of private lands in Chapter 6. They develop a bioappraisal process that assesses the conservation value of land by describing and documenting land characteristics and attributes that affect the conservation value of the land. The relevant land characteristics and attributes (and hence the land parcel's conservation value) are dependent on the objectives of the regulator or conservator. A short list includes a description of the property and the types and frequencies of habitat and species, how the land parcel's habitat relates to the habitat on surrounding properties, and the extent to which habitat quality and species viability can be enhanced through active management.

Though a system of bioappraisals is not established today, conservation valuation approaches have been used in implementing the ESA and the National Forest Management Plan. Those approaches lack the comparability that is obtained through the use of the bioappraisal process suggested by Buskirk and Wisely. The bioappraisal process will need to establish a common language, in the form of a certification process that may need to be species- and region-specific. Bioappraisals might also require a professional association that can define standards and transfer information between buyer and seller. The process must be defined by contract law as it applies to appraisals. Implementing any method that measures and quantifies biodiversity has similar needs.

In the next chapter, economist Thomas Crocker addresses whether people can create actual markets for conserving biodiversity habitat in principle or in practice. Crocker argues that the current command-and-control policy for achieving the goals of the ESA on private lands is an inefficient approach to species conservation. Efficiency, or achieving habitat conservation at lower costs, can be enhanced with the use of markets to transfer the responsibility of conservation to those who can afford it best because of lower opportunity costs or higher values for conservation or both. A standard approach of tradable habitat credits is suggested, but in the ESA setting, the regulator sets a minimum amount of land conservation that must be achieved, and as such, each landowner benefits by the other landowners' conserved acres. This creates a positive externality between landowners, which reduces each landowner's willingness to conserve land and makes tradable habitat credits less than efficient. Tradable habitat credits combined with a tax subsidy mechanism can achieve the ESA land conservation objective at the lowest cost.

The final chapter in Part II considers the role of information in designing conservation incentives for property owners. Rodney Smith, John Tschirhart, and myself consider how financial incentives that align landowner objectives with those of the ESA are embodied in a policy of voluntary participation. The argument is that in designing a cost-effective voluntary incentive mechanism the regulator should account for landowners' private information regarding their alternative land use values as well as the conservation value of their land. In accounting for information shortages, the regulator establishes a menu of alternatives that combine subsidy payments with specific conservation acre set-asides, which exposes each landowner's type through self-selection of program alternatives. To insure that each landowner type chooses the appropriate alternative, low-value landowner types are overcompensated. Compensation that exceeds the landowner's private land use value is called information rent and is the cost to the regulator of purchasing private landowner information. (For a more technical investigation see Smith and Shogren 2002.)

Greg Parkhurst and I close the book by evaluating the set of economic incentive options. Based on the discussions from earlier chapters in the book, we consider three sets of criteria to assess how each incentive can address a set of biological needs, landowner interests, and government or regulatory concerns. We offer our evaluation as a broad starting point; specific applications will have different success rates depending on the specific combination of species, landowners, and habitat type.

Concluding Remarks

The logic of Jim Berger, the former president of the Wyoming Stock Growers Association, that the "best wildlife management we can have is a local game warden, a rancher, and a cup of coffee" (Kruckenberg

2000), rings true for many people. Species are local, and politics are local, which makes the political economy of species protection local. Many others might add that a fat checkbook would be helpful too. This book addresses whether this ESA checkbook makes sense from several vantage points, and if so, how much compensation should be paid to landowners who protect endangered species on private land. Reauthorization of the Endangered Species Act has been blocked for a decade in part by this issue, which leaves undefined the scope of species protection and the method by which species will be protected. Central to the discussion is who should bear what fraction of the costs to protect listed species on private lands: the landowners or the general public. In the past, implementation of the ESA on private lands has asked the landowner to pay most of the costs to preserve species and their habitat through the loss of profitable land uses (some costs are financial but most take the form of forgone opportunities). Landowners want to avoid these costs if possible and might even take actions to avoid them. Landowners who fear that the government will not keep its word and will impose future ESA land use restrictions have an incentive to alter or develop habitat, if they believe their personal investments to create and store wealth will be left unprotected.

Private lands do matter for successful ESA implementation (Bean and Wilcove 1997). Attempts to reauthorize the act have focused on altering the incentives to private landowners by creating financial incentives that shift the burden of conserving habitat from the landowner to a government agency or a private organization. Financial incentives for landowners have proponents and opponents on both sides of the debate. Some landowners and activists will buy and sell habitat and species protection; others want no part of this transaction. The authors in this volume examine the issues behind compensation to expose the elements that have promoted or impeded the success of such incentive programs. Key issues are the necessity of gathering better information provided by methods to measure habitat value (biological, social, and economic) and the need to respect landowners' privacy and provide assurances against future regulations. In the end, if compensation plans are to work cost-effectively, they should be voluntary for private landowners, be flexible enough to accommodate the species' biological needs in a single large reserve or several small habitat reserves, provide incentives for the landowner to profit from his or her private information about the land (biological and economic), and account for the opportunity costs of the funds used to compensate for acre set-asides.

All this suggests that to succeed at protecting species at risk cost-effectively, incentive mechanisms will have to be used in combination. Combining incentives into a cohesive strategy for species protection can be complex, depending on the target and desired degree of efficiency. We have to ask ourselves the basic questions: how much of a risk do we face, what will the solution cost, how much better will the solution make things, and what else could we spend our money on. Making the cost of achieving species protection goals cheaper increases the demand to achieve these goals and reduces the resistance to achieving them. The essays in this book illustrate how academic insight can significantly lower the cost of doing society's business. Although the authors differ about the advisability and application of economic incentive systems, the question of which compensation package is the *best* for species protection is here to stay. Evaluating the range and mix of incentive options that exist within the context of government regulation and stakeholder-participation processes can allow all of us to enjoy more species protection at the best price possible. Although my bias is obvious, I agree with the recent remark by commentator Bill Moyers: "If you want to fight for the environment, don't hug a tree; hug an economist."

References

Bayon, R. 2002. A bull market in . . . woodpeckers? *Milken Institute Review* (first quarter): 30–39.

Bean, Michael J. 1997. Review of "Private property and the Endangered Species Act: Saving habitat, protecting homes." *BioScience* 49:825.

———. 1998. The Endangered Species Act and private land: Four lessons learned from the past quarter century. *Environmental Law Reporter* 28: 10701–10710.

———. 1999. Endangered species? Endangered act? *Environment* 41:12–38.

Bean, M., and D. Wilcove. 1997. The private-land problem. *Conservation Biology* 11:1–2.

Beissinger, S., and J. Perrine. 2001. Extinction, recovery, and the Endangered Species Act. Pp. 51–71 in *Protecting endangered species in the United States: Biological needs, political realities, economic choices,* edited by J. Shogren and J. Tschirhart. New York: Cambridge University Press.

Blume, L., D. Rubinfeld, and P. Shapiro. 1984. The taking of land: When should compensation be paid? *Quarterly Journal of Economics* 100:71–92.

Brown, Gardner Jr., and Jason Shogren. 1998. Economics of the Endangered Species Act. *Journal of Economic Perspectives* 12:3–20.

Dawson, D., and J. Shogren. 2001. An update on priorities and expenditures under the Endangered Species Act. *Land Economics* 77:527–532.

Defenders of Wildlife. 2002. *Conservation in America: State government incentive for habitat conservation.* Washington, D.C. March.

Easterbrook, G. 1998. Getting around the takings problem. *PERC Reprints* (Bozeman, Mont.) 16, no. 2 (June). Originally published in *New Republic,* 2 March 1998.

Eisner, T., J. Lubchenco, E. O. Wilson, D. Wilcove, and M. Bean. 1995. Building a scientifically sound policy for protecting endangered species. *Science* 268:1231–1232.

Epstein, R. 1985. *Takings: Private property and power of eminent domain.* Cambridge, Mass.: Harvard University Press.

———. 1995. *Simple rules for a complex world.* Cambridge, Mass.: Harvard University Press.

Farrier, D. 1995. Conserving biodiversity on private land: Incentives for management or compensation for lost expectations? *Harvard Environmental Law Review* 19:303–408.

General Accounting Office (GAO). 1995. *Endangered Species Act: Information on species protection on nonfederal lands.* Washington, D.C. GAO/RCED-95-16 (Dec. 1994).

Innes, Robert, Stephan Polasky, and John Tschirhart. 1998. Takings, compensation, and endangered species protection on private lands. *Journal of Economic Perspectives* 12, no. 3: 35–52.

Korfmacher, K., and E. Elsom. 1998. Voluntary incentive for farmland preservation in Central Ohio: What do farmers think? Working paper 98-4, Center for Agriculture in the Environment, American Farmland Trust. DeKalb, Ill.: Northern Illinois University.

Kruckenberg, L. 2000. A conservation crystal ball. *Wyoming Wildlife,* February.

Leopold, A. 1949. *A Sand County almanac, and sketches here and there.* New York: Oxford University Press.

Mann, C., and M. Plummer. 1995. *Noah's choice: The future of endangered species.* New York: Knopf.

Matthews, M. 1999. Standing up for the underdog. *High Country News,* 16 August.

McEvoy, A. 1998. Markets and ethics in U.S. property law. Pp. 94–113 in *Who owns America? Social conflict over property rights,* edited by H. Jacobs. Madison: University of Wisconsin Press.

Melious, J., and R. Thornton. 1999. Contractual ecosystem management under the Endangered Species Act: Can federal agencies make enforceable commitments? *Ecology Law Quarterly* 26, no. 3: 489–542.

National Research Council. 1995. *Science and the Endangered Species Act.* Washington, D.C.: National Academy Press.

Norton, G. 2002. Helping citizens conserve their own land—and America's. *New York Times,* 20 April.

Parkhurst, Gregory, Jason Shogren, Chris Bastian, Paul Kivi, Jennifer Donner, and Rodney Smith. 2002. Agglomeration bonus: An incentive mechanism to reunite fragmented habitat for biodiversity conservation. *Ecological Economics* 41:305–328.

Pinchot, G. 1947. *Breaking new ground.* New York: Harcourt, Brace.

Sagoff, M. 1997. Muddle or muddle through: Takings jurisprudence meets the Endangered Species Act. *William and Mary Law Review* 38:825–993.

Shogren, Jason F., ed. 1998. *Private property and the Endangered Species Act: Saving habitat, protecting homes.* Austin: University of Texas Press.

Shogren, J. F., J. Tschirhart, T. Anderson, A. W. Ando, S. R. Beissinger, D. Brookshire, G. M. Brown Jr., D. Coursey, R. Innes, S. M. Meyer, and S. Polasky. 1999. Why economics matters for endangered species protection. *Conservation Biology* 13:1257–1261.

Smith, Rodney B., and Jason F. Shogren. 2002. Voluntary incentive design for endangered species protection. *Journal of Environmental Economics and Management* 43:169–187.

Thompson, Barton S. Jr. 1997. The Endangered Species Act: A case study in takings and incentives. *Stanford Law Review* 49:305–376.

Turner, J., and J. Rylander. 1998. The private lands challenge: Integrating biodiversity conservation and private property. Pp. 138–144 in *Private property and the Endangered Species Act: Saving habitat, protecting homes,* edited by J. Shogren. Austin: University of Texas Press.

U.S. Department of Agriculture (USDA). 1998. *Conservation Reserve Program: Oregon State Enhancement Program.* Farm Service Agency. Washington, D.C.: Government Printing Office.

Whicker, A. S., and J. K. Detling. 1988. Ecological consequences of prairie dog disturbances. *BioScience* 38:778–785.

Wilcove, D., D. Rothstein, J. Dubow, A. Phillips, and E. Losos. 2000. *Precious heritage: The status of biodiversity science in the United States.* New York: Oxford University Press.

Wu, J. J., and W. Boggess. 1999. The optimal allocation of conservation funds. *Journal of Environmental Economics and Management* 38:302–321.

PART I

CURRENT AND PROPOSED INCENTIVE OPTIONS FOR SPECIES PROTECTION ON PRIVATE LANDS

CHAPTER 2

The Endangered Species Act and Its Current Set of Incentive Tools for Species Protection

DEBRA DONAHUE

The purposes of the Endangered Species Act, or ESA, are to "provide a means whereby the ecosystems upon which endangered species and threatened species depend may be conserved," to establish a "program for the conservation of such" species, and to take action to accomplish the goals of certain international agreements (Endangered Species Act 1996).

The act contains four key requirements designed to achieve its purposes. First, the secretary of the interior is directed to list species in need of protection. Second, federal agencies must conserve the populations and habitats of listed species and may not take any action that would "jeopardize the continued existence" of any listed species. ("Conserve" is defined by the act to mean, essentially, the use of all methods that are necessary to improve the condition of threatened and endangered species so that they can be removed from the list.) Third, all federal agencies must (under section 7) consult with the U.S. Fish and Wildlife Service (USFWS) or, in the case of marine species, the National Marine Fisheries Service (NMFS) on any of their activities that may adversely affect listed species. Finally, all persons are prohibited (by section 9) from "taking" endangered fish or wildlife.

The ESA also authorizes various other measures aimed at protecting threatened or endangered species and their habitats. For instance, the USFWS is directed to designate critical habitat when it adds species to the list, and it may enter into conservation agreements, called habitat conservation plans, with other agencies and private parties. The act also implements U.S. treaty obligations concerning threatened and endangered species by, among other things, restricting imports of protected species. It establishes penalties for violations of the ESA and any regulations adopted by the USFWS or NMFS. Citizen suits are included among the act's enforcement provisions. Citizens may sue to prevent any person from violating the ESA by, for example, taking a threatened or endangered species. Citizens may also sue the interior secretary to compel him to enforce the act's prohibitions, to list a species as threatened or endangered, or to designate critical habitat.

Administration of the ESA is the responsibility of the secretary of the interior, acting through the USFWS, and, to a lesser extent, the secretary of commerce, acting through the NMFS (referred to jointly herein as the "services"). Responsibility for conserving marine species and anadromous fish belongs to the NMFS; the USFWS bears responsibility for all other species. The USFWS and NMFS determine whether species should be added to the list of threatened or endangered species, prepare biological opinions in the consultation process, develop habitat conservation plans and recovery plans, and enforce the ESA.

The effects (and perceived effects) of the ESA on owners of private land are among the most contentious aspects of the act's implementation. The implications of this issue are significant and far-reaching for both property owners and species at risk. As of 1993, 80 percent of listed species (609 of 781) had some or all of their habitat on private lands. A significant number occur solely on private lands. In Texas, for instance, nearly all lands are private; the number of listed species found there is among the highest of all states (GAO 1995, 4–6; Bean 1998).

Wildlife law authority Michael Bean recently examined the successes and failures of ESA implementation on private lands. His examination (Bean 1998) yielded the following "four lessons": (1) Section 9's taking prohibition "has a far narrower sweep than either environmentalists or landowners commonly think." (2) Fear of section 9's impact on them has "prompted some landowners to manage their lands in ways designed to prevent endangered species from ever occurring on them." (3) Amendments to the act that would establish "positive incentives for landowners to conserve endangered species could significantly improve prospects for the Act's success." (4) "Finally, in the absence of new incentives, the only hope for effectively addressing many of the threats that lie beyond the reach of the taking prohibition is the creative use of the Act's provisions relating to habitat conservation." [1]

In our view, Bean's assessment is well taken. The purposes of this chapter are to develop and learn from his lessons 3 and 4 (although in reverse order). In its first section, the chapter examines the most significant provisions of the act and regulations relating to private property: the habitat conservation planning (HCP) process, no-surprises policy, and the recently adopted safe harbor and candidate conservation agreement (CCA) programs. Some experiences with and criticisms of these provisions are also considered. The second section examines how the enhanced use of incentives, some of which may require additional legislative authority, could promote conservation goals on private lands. The final part discusses the potential risks in carrying an incentives-based approach to species conservation too far.

Section 9: Prohibition against Taking

The driving force behind private land endangered species protection efforts and issues is section 9 of the Endangered Species Act of 1973. Section 9 makes it unlawful for any person to take an endangered species. Section 3 defines "take" to mean "to harass, harm, pursue, hunt, shoot, wound, kill, trap, capture, or collect, or to attempt to engage in any such conduct." The USFWS has extended that prohibition, by regulation, to all threatened species as well. Another USFWS regulation (*U.S. Code,* vol. 50, sect. 17.3) defines the word "harm" (used in the statutory definition of "take") to mean "an act which actually kills or injures wildlife. Such act may include significant habitat modification or degradation where it actually kills or injures wildlife by significantly impairing essential behavioral patterns, including breeding, feeding, or sheltering." Landowners may be subject to penalties under the ESA for taking a threatened or endangered species if they modify habitat (e.g., by cutting timber or cultivating or developing the land) in a way that would result in the actual death or injury of a threatened or endangered animal.

Landowner fear of section 9 stems significantly from this perceived enlargement of the act's taking prohibition. In *Babbitt v. Sweet Home Chapter of Communities for a Great Oregon* (1995), the U.S. Supreme Court upheld the USFWS definition of "harm" against a challenge that it exceeded the agency's authority under the act and improperly constrained private landowners' ordinary use of their property. In a 6–3 decision, the court decided that both the ordinary meaning of "harm" and the legislative history of the ESA supported the regulatory definition, and it rejected the argument that harm must involve direct or intentional action. While the rule is written broadly and might be applied in a particular case to forbid conduct that Congress had not intended to regulate, the court intimated, such issues must be decided on a case-by-case basis.

The court founded its decision in part on the 1982 amendment of the

ESA, which authorized permits for the "incidental" and unintentional taking of endangered species. This provision, the court said, suggests that Congress believed that section 9 prohibits "indirect as well as deliberate takings," and that indirectly harming a species, such as by modifying its habitat, is unlawful unless permitted under section 10 (*Babbitt v. Sweet Home*, 700).

According to the three dissenting justices (Rehnquist, Scalia, and Thomas), the harm rule violates established legal principles of foreseeability and proximate cause. It has this effect, they argued, by rendering private landowners strictly liable for ordinary activities, such as growing crops or harvesting trees, where those activities "fortuitously injure protected wildlife, no matter how remote the chain of causation and no matter how difficult to foresee." The dissenters charged that the majority's decision "imposes unfairness to the point of financial ruin—not just upon the rich, but upon the simplest farmer who finds his land conscripted to national zoological use." The majority, however, seemed to assume that traditional notions of causation and foreseeability would apply when the federal government seeks to enforce the harm regulation (*Babbitt v. Sweet Home*, 697–714).

As Michael Bean put it, the *Sweet Home* decision "upheld the regulation, but did not resolve what it means." Courts since *Sweet Home*, he says, "have been all over the lot in their attempts to decipher" the harm rule. Some courts and most commentators have concluded that the rule does retain traditional notions of causation and foreseeability, as well as proof standards. In other words, although a farmer would harm and consequently take an endangered frog if he drained a marsh known to harbor it, he would not violate the harm regulation for downstream, attenuated effects of his use of pesticides on his crops. Interpreted as such, the rule will not produce the unfair or absurd results that the dissenters and the *Sweet Home* plaintiffs apparently envisioned (Bean 1998).[2]

Other courts have taken a more liberal view of the rule. A Ninth Circuit appellate panel ruled that "habitat modification which significantly impaired the breeding and sheltering of a protected species amounts to 'harm' under the ESA," implicitly concluding that the habitat modification was, itself, the injury referred to in the harm regulation (*Marbled Murrelet v. Babbitt* 1996). At least two circuits, the First and the Eighth, have held that the regulatory acts of governmental entities can cause takes of protected wildlife. In *Strahan v. Coxe*, the First Circuit Court of Appeals ruled that a state agency caused takings of the endangered right whale because it "licensed commercial fishing operations to use gillnets and lobster pots in specifically the manner that is likely to result in violation of [the ESA]." In *Defenders of Wildlife v. Environmental Protection Agency,* the Eighth Circuit held that the EPA caused takes of the endangered black-footed ferret through its "decision to register pesticides" even though other persons actually distributed or used the pesticides.

In *Strahan,* Massachusetts law prohibited fishing companies from using gillnet and lobster pot fishing equipment without a license. A state agency issued the licenses and, through regulation, restricted the use of the fishing equipment only in certain areas. According to the National Marine Fisheries Service, "entanglement with fishing gear is one of the leading causes of the depletion of the [endangered] Northern Right whale population." A conservationist sued the state agency under the ESA, alleging that its continued licensing of fishing equipment caused harm to the right whale. The district court granted a preliminary injunction. It found a sufficient causal connection between the agency's licensing of fishing equipment and the alleged harm to whales, noting that "[f]ishing vessels *cannot,* legally, place gillnets and lobster gear in Massachusetts waters without permission from [the agency]." The district court further found that the agency's "commercial fishing *regulatory scheme* likely exacted a taking in violation of the ESA," considering it "irrelevant that [the agency's] permitting of commercial fishing gear is only an indirect cause of whale entanglement" (*Strahan v. Coxe* 1997, pp. 159, 163; emphasis added).

On appeal, the First Circuit affirmed the district court's interpretation of the ESA. First, the court held that "a governmental third party pursuant to whose authority an actor directly exacts a taking of an endangered species may be deemed to have violated the provisions of the ESA." Second, the appellate court affirmed the district court's finding of causation, stating that "while indirect, [the harm] is not so removed [from the agency's regulatory action] that it extends outside the realm of causation as it is understood in the common law." Finally, the court rejected the agency's analogy that its fishing equipment licensure "does not cause the taking any more than [the state's] licensure of automobiles and drivers solicits or causes federal crimes, such as interstate drug trafficking." The First Circuit reasoned that unlike the licensing of automobiles, the licensing of fishing equipment "does not involve the intervening independent actor [as] a necessary component" because "it is not possible for a licensed commercial fishing operation to use its gillnets or lobster pots in a manner permitted by the [state agency] without risk of violating the ESA by exacting a taking."

In contrast, a federal district court in Florida refused to hold Volusia County liable for takes of protected sea turtles caused by beach lighting, where the county had passed and was enforcing an ordinance prohibiting artificial lighting on the beach, but where violations of the ordinance by beach area residents were harming the turtles. Like the state agency in *Strahan,* the county in *Loggerhead Turtle v. County Council* was alleged to be a "governmental third party pursuant to whose authority an actor directly exacts a taking of an endangered species." Just as the agency in *Strahan* was "vested with broad authority to regulate fishing" under state law, Volusia County was "vested with broad authority to regulate" artificial beachfront lighting. But the county contended, and the court agreed, that its ordinance did not permit an act otherwise unlawful, in contrast to the situation in *Defenders of Wildlife v. Environmental Protection Agency,* nor did it expressly license an act in a manner likely to result in an ESA violation, as in *Strahan.* In fact, the county's sea turtle ordinance was drafted specifically to be consistent with the ESA. The court rejected the contention that the county, by voluntarily regulating beach lighting, was responsible for the ESA-violative conduct of its residents under an "implied permission" theory. According to the court, forcing the county to assume liability for the acts of its private citizens under these circumstances "would frustrate the intent and purpose of the Act's cooperative agreement provisions."

These opinions suggest that when a governmental agency authorizes and regulates activities that result in a take of a listed species, it may be liable equally with the person actually causing the take. This result seems consistent with the common law doctrine that any person responsible for (that is, in a position to control) activities of another may be held equally responsible for any harm that results therefrom. The clearest example is that of an employer's responsibility for actions of his employees.

Furthermore, as a practical matter, ESA enforcement depends largely on the USFWS's (or the NMFS's) ability to prove that a taking has occurred. Draining the only known wetland habitat of an endangered amphibian, for example, almost certainly would take the protected animal by harming its habitat. On the other hand, farmers who allow irrigation water containing pesticides to flow off croplands, contributing to downstream levels that pose risks to a threatened fish, almost certainly would not be prosecuted for taking the fish. The requirement that the federal government prove harm, as defined by the rule, helps to assure that it will not bring cases involving long or tenuous chains of causation.

Since the ESA was enacted, no court has ruled that ESA regulation has resulted in an unlawful taking of private property in violation of the U.S. Constitution (Parenteau 1998, p. 282). Nevertheless, the *perception* that enforcement of the USFWS harm rule could restrict unduly private property owners' use of their land can have consequences for both landowners and species conservation. It can reduce the market value of property and induce landowners to take steps to prevent the colonization or use of their land by listed species or species proposed for listing.

Section 10: Incidental Taking Permits and Habitat Conservation Plans

A 1982 amendment to section 10 of the ESA authorizes unintentional, incidental takings of listed species, if approved in advance by the USFWS. Section 10(a)(1)(B) of the act provides: "The Secretary may permit, under such terms and conditions as he shall prescribe, . . . any taking otherwise prohibited by [U.S. Code section 1538(a)(1)(B)] if such taking is incidental to, and not the purpose of, the carrying out of an otherwise lawful activity." The issuance of an incidental take permit (ITP) is subject to several conditions, specifically:

(a)(2)(A) No permit may be issued by the Secretary . . . unless the applicant submits to the Secretary a conservation plan that specifies—
(i) the impact which will likely result from such taking;
(ii) what steps the applicant will take to minimize and mitigate such impacts, and the funding that will be available to implement such steps;
(iii) what alternative actions to such takings the applicant considered and the reasons why such alternatives are not being utilized; and
(iv) such other measures that the Secretary may require as being necessary or appropriate for purposes of the plan.
(B) If the Secretary finds, after opportunity for public comment, with respect to a permit application and the related conservation plan that—
(i) the taking will be incidental;
(ii) the applicant will, to the maximum extent practicable, minimize and mitigate the impacts of such taking;
(iii) the applicant will ensure that adequate funding for the plan will be provided;
(iv) the taking will not appreciably reduce the likelihood of survival and recovery of the species in the wild; and

(v) the measures, if any, required under subparagraph (A)(iv) will be met; and he has received such other assurances as he may require that the plan will be implemented, the Secretary shall issue such permit. The permit shall contain such terms and conditions as the Secretary deems necessary or appropriate to carry out the purposes of this paragraph, including, but not limited to, such reporting requirements as the Secretary deems necessary for determining whether such terms and conditions are being complied with.

The section provides further that issuance of a permit must be "consistent with the purposes and policies" of the ESA.

The plan required by section 10 has become known as a habitat conservation plan, or HCP. According to the federal agencies in chapter 1 of the *Habitat Conservation Planning and Incidental Take Permitting Handbook* (the *HCP Handbook*), "HCPs are evolving from a process adopted primarily to address single developments to a broad-based, landscape level planning tool utilized to achieve long-term biological and regulatory goals." The services clarify that the purpose of HCPs and ITPs "is to authorize the incidental take of threatened or endangered species, not to authorize the underlying activities [e.g., logging or land development] that result in take." Section 10 implementing regulations "reiterate ESA requirements and provide a framework for issuance and management of permits. Beyond that it is Service policy to promote 'flexibility and ingenuity' in working with permit applicants and developing HCPs." The *HCP Handbook* observes, "While species conservation is of course paramount, the section 10 process recognizes the importance of both biological and economic factors." The agencies interpret the ESA as *not* allowing them to "mandate that HCPs contribute to recovery," but applicants are "encouraged to develop HCPs that produce a net positive effect on a species." [3]

HCPs often take the form of an agreement entered into by private landowners, local government entities, the USFWS, and occasionally other federal agencies. An HCP allows a permittee to proceed with development or land use activities under the plan, despite the incidental taking of protected species, in exchange for long-term conservation commitments. In other words, in exchange for taking steps to mitigate the effects of his activities and otherwise conserve the species' habitat, the developer is insured against prosecution or civil penalties imposed under the ESA for actions that incidentally harm a threatened or endangered species.

As long as the proposed activity or land use involves no federal permitting or funding, the ESA does not require landowners or developers to initiate preactivity contact with the USFWS or NMFS or to undertake any proactive conservation measures on behalf of listed species that may be present on the land. (The act imposes duties to consult and affirmatively to conserve species only on *federal* agencies.) Still, the landowner must consider the risks of proceeding without an incidental take permit if his activities could harm a listed species. He also must weigh against that risk the burdens of developing a satisfactory HCP prerequisite to obtain a permit. Some lenders and business partners may insist that the property owner secure a permit, or at least contact the regulatory agency, before proceeding. On the other hand, a landowner might choose instead to self-permit, by "designing the project so as to minimize or substantially reduce overt intrusions into protected species' habitat." This approach, however, will not "provide legal protection if the project later is determined to have caused take" (Ruhl 1999).[4]

The popularity of HCPs got a boost during the Clinton administration largely through the efforts of former USFWS director Mollie Beattie. Beattie encouraged greater use of long-term habitat conservation planning under the ESA as a means of conserving whole ecosystems, including both listed and unprotected species, and of avoiding future listings. For the process to work, she said, state and local officials and landowners would have to "come to the table" with USFWS officials and "agree on long-term conservation." She called this approach to management "anticipatory and aggressive." Between 1983 and 1992 only 14 incidental take permits (and associated HCPs) were approved. By August 1996 the number had increased to 179, with another 200 in development. More than 200 HCPs and incidental take permits had been issued by early 1999. HCPs are also covering larger areas. Of the 218 HCP permits issued by August 1997, at least 18 encompassed more than 500,000 acres (including one of more than 1.6 million acres), 25 involved 100,000 to 500,000 acres, and 25 were greater than 10,000 acres. "To cope with this growing section 10 workload," the services announced in the *HCP Handbook* plans to "streamline the HCP process to the maximum extent practicable and allowed by law" (Salzman and Ruhl 2000, p. 648, n. 105).[5]

In general, the permitting process involves three stages: developing an HCP, formal permitting, and implementating and monitoring the HCP. Applicants are responsible for compliance with ESA sections 9, 4(d), and 10(a), as well as for preparing and implementing the HCP. The responsible regulatory agency (USFWS or NMFS) publishes notice of the permit application in the *Federal Register* and begins the process of reviewing the application. Issuing an ITP is a federal action subject to both the National Environmental Policy Act (NEPA) and to ESA section 7. The applicant is responsible for preparing the HCP; usually, it or its consultant prepares the required NEPA documentation, as well. The USFWS or NMFS must determine compliance with the ESA (both sections 7 and 10) and with NEPA. Depending on the breadth and predicted impacts of the HCP, NEPA compliance may be achieved in one of three ways. First, an activity with minimal impacts may qualify for a categorical exclusion, that is, be excused by regulation from NEPA compliance. Most HCPs, however, require preparation of an environmental assessment and a finding of no significant impact. In some cases, a full environmental impact statement (EIS) is required. In any event, the services combine the HCP and NEPA documentation development processes into what they describe as one "streamlined" analysis.[6]

In response to the increasing popularity of HCPs, a simplified approach was developed for small projects with limited impacts (considered prior to implementation of any mitigation). Low-effect HCPs are those "involving: (1) minor or negligible effects on federally listed, proposed, or candidate species and their habitats covered under the HCP; and (2) minor or negligible effects on other environmental values or resources." Similarly, low-effect ITPs "individually and cumulatively have a minor or negligible effect on the species covered in the HCP." Low-effect permits and plans often, but not necessarily, apply to geographically small-scale projects. The relevant factors are the expected effects of the proposed activity on the listed species' distribution or numbers (*HCP Handbook*, ch. 1, p. 8).

The services consider each permit application and proposed HCP individually. If an activity qualifies for low-effect treatment, it will also be categorically excluded from NEPA. Processing requirements include an HCP, notice publication in the *Federal Register*, formal section 7 consultation, and agency findings. No implementing agreement is required, although an applicant may request one. All other HCPs include those requirements plus an environmental assessment or EIS, an implementing agreement (which may be optional), and review by the interior solicitor's office. Compliance with section 7 and compliance with section 10 are now considered "concurrent, integrated processes" rather than "independent analyses." To "avoid possible biases," however, the federal official who conducts the section 7 consultation "should not be the section 10 biologist providing technical assistance to the applicant." According to the services, the level of NEPA analysis required is the most variable requirement in HCP permitting. Target processing times (for applications deemed complete) are less than three months for categorically excluded low-effect HCPs, three to five months for HCPs requiring an environmental assessment, and ten months or less for HCPs with an EIS (*HCP Handbook*).[7]

Segmenting is not allowed; that is, proposed activities cannot be divided into pieces or phases to qualify for low-effect HCP permitting. On the other hand, the services encourage regional or multispecies HCPs, pointing out their numerous potential benefits, including greater flexibility and options for mitigation, reduced burdens on individual landowners as a result of distributing conservation and planning burdens among multiple parties, better coordinated decision-making with consequent benefits for species, long-term assurances for landowners, and reduced regulatory compliance burdens for affected parties. The *HCP Handbook* recommends that the services "strongly encourage applicants to include as many proposed and candidate species as can be adequately addressed and covered by the permit," to "provide more planning certainty to the permittee" and to "increase the biological value of the HCPs," but it acknowledges, "ultimately the decision about what species to include in the HCP is always the applicant's." This reflects the fact that the ESA imposes on private landowners no affirmative incentive to conserve either listed or unlisted species.[8]

In early 1997 an HCP (at the time the largest ever approved for forest lands) was finalized in Washington. The plan, which involves the Washington State Department of Natural Resources and four timber companies, encompasses 2.135 million acres, including 1.6 million acres of state-managed forests, and has a time span of 70 years. The area contains habitat for northern spotted owl and several species of salmon and trout. The plan provides for harvesting a set amount of timber (650 million board feet) despite any future changes in federal ESA regulations, in exchange for managing the covered lands as an integrated ecosystem. Later in the same year South Carolina applied for a statewide incidental take permit, which would authorize the take of red-cockaded woodpeckers on all lands enrolled in a proposed safe harbor program, developed as part of an HCP (South Carolina 1997). (Safe harbor agreements are described later in this chapter.) A similar HCP was approved for red-cockaded woodpeckers in Georgia (Hood 1998).[9]

The three HCPs described above are examples of what the USFWS refers to as "programmatic HCPs." Programmatic HCPs should address a group of well-defined, similar activities, which "occur within a described geographical area or at similar points in time." The targeted applicants are county and state governments. Another form of HCP is known as a habitat-based HCP. Prime examples are the HCPs in southern California developed in conjunction with the Natural Community Conservation Planning program. Instead of addressing one or more species, these HCPs protect one or more habitat types, including all species therein. Use of the no-surprises policy (discussed in the next section of this chapter) avoids the need to amend the HCP when a candidate or proposed species is subsequently listed. Both habitat-based and programmatic HCPs are relatively new, and the USFWS reports that it is exploring these approaches carefully (*HCP Handbook,* ch. 3 pp. 37–39).[10]

The largest HCP to date, known as the Sonoran Desert Conservation Plan, is now being developed in Arizona. This Pima County (Tucson area) HCP will encompass nearly 6 million acres, or 9,000 square miles. It is designed to protect about 100 species, 16 of which are endangered, while also allowing development. The plan is being developed by a 90-member steering committee; cooperating agencies include several federal and state agencies, the City of Tucson, three towns, and the county. Components of the plan include riparian area restoration, habitat corridor conservation, and conservation of sensitive and critical habitats. Although environmentalists have criticized similar large-scale plans in other metropolitan areas (e.g., San Diego, San Bernardino, and Austin) as ineffective and unduly influenced by development interests, some national and local environmental groups reportedly have high expectations for the Sonoran Desert plan (Henry 2000).[11]

Information on specific HCPs is available from a variety of sources, including the federal agencies' own documents and reviews, such as the Defenders of Wildlife's *Frayed Safety Nets* (Hood 1998, app. C). Readers interested in a detailed explanation of the section 10 permitting process are encouraged to consult the federal *HCP Handbook* and J. B. Ruhl's insightful article "How to Kill Endangered Species, Legally." Some specific requirements are outlined here, however, so that the impacts of the ESA on private landowners can be better understood. First, every HCP submitted to support an ITP application must contain the following information: the likely impact resulting from the proposed taking; measures to be taken (and the funding available) to monitor, minimize, and mitigate impacts; procedures for dealing with unforeseen circumstances; alternative actions for avoiding the impacts and the reasons why they were rejected; and additional measures required by the service. Identifying impacts necessitates delineating the HCP boundaries (including, potentially, mitigation areas), collecting and synthesizing biological data, identifying the activities that are likely to result in take, and quantifying the anticipated take (Endangered Species Act, sect. 10; *HCP Handbook*, ch. 3).

Applicants must consider both direct and indirect impacts of their proposed activities; however, the services recognize the difficulty of tracing "a causation chain of indirect effects," particularly for large-scale projects. With that in mind, the *HCP Handbook* offers the following guidance: "If a species is likely to be jeopardized as a result of the indirect effects of activities proposed in an HCP, the services may not issue the permit unless these effects are adequately addressed. However, before an HCP is required to contain additional requirements to adequately address indirect effects under section 7: (1) the risk of jeopardy should be clear and reasonably certain to occur; and (2) the indirect effects in question must be reasonably foreseeable and a proximate consequence of the activities proposed in the HCP" (ch. 3, pp. 16–17). This advice reflects both the services' obligation to avoid jeopardy and their belief that "assigning responsibility for all potential subsequent effects to the originator of a particular action may not be justified or practical."

Although ESA sections 7 and 10 are similar, the services explain, "section 7 and its regulations introduce several considerations into the HCP process that are not explicitly required by section 10—specifically, indirect effects, effects on federally listed plants, and effects on critical habitat." In other words, once the HCP-ITP process is undertaken, the distinctions between the act's requirements on federal agencies and private landowners are lessened or at least blurred. For example, the act does not protect listed plants located on private lands. Nevertheless, HCP applicants are encouraged to take plants into account in their plans because, under section 7, an incidental take permit may not be granted (or an HCP approved) if it would jeopardize the continued existence of a listed plant species. Applicants are advised to "ensure that actions proposed in the HCP are not likely to jeopardize any federally listed plant species." Similarly, a permit may not be issued if proposed HCP activities would alter or destroy critical habitat "to the extent that the survival and recovery of affected species would be appreciably reduced" (*HCP Handbook*, ch. 6, pp. 12–18).[12]

Nevertheless, the services assure applicants that in most cases they "will not actually experience a significant increase in responsibilities under the HCP because of the services' associated section 7 responsibilities. This is because there are relatively high thresholds under section 7 (i.e., jeopardy), and many of the same relevant biological considerations are already integrated into the HCP process." For instance, section 10's "not appreciably reduce" standard is considered functionally equivalent to "no jeopardy" under section 7. In other words, "if the Services and the applicant work together to develop an adequate HCP . . . then a 'no-jeopardy' biological opinion at the close of the section 7 consultation should be virtually assured." [13] Likewise, the services continue, critical habitat considerations are not likely to add to the HCP applicant's burden because the ITP issuance criteria prohibit reducing appreciably the "likelihood of the survival and recovery of the species in the wild." The *HCP Handbook* asserts unambiguously: "It is possible to approve an HCP that authorizes land use or development activities within an area designated as critical habitat" (ch. 7, p. 4). Applicants are given the further assurance that the services will work closely with them and provide technical advice to them to ensure that HCPs will meet section 7 requirements. An approved HCP and ITP provide "long-term assurances that [the landowner's] activities will be in compliance with" the ESA (ch. 1, p. 7).

Perhaps the biggest sources of uncertainty in developing and obtaining approval for HCPs are the nature and extent of mitigation that will be sufficient to satisfy the act—and the service. There is no cookbook approach to mitigating impacts on threatened or endangered species (though, as explained below, once an HCP is approved, the risks inure to the protected species or to the government, not to landowners). The ESA itself directs only that the HCP applicant "minimize and mitigate" the impacts of incidental takings and that permit issuance not "appreciably reduce the likelihood of survival and recovery of the species in the wild" [sect. 1539 (a)(2)]. Nor does the *HCP Handbook* "establish specific 'rules' for developing mitigation." Rather, it "sets forth some fundamental standards" and "suggests some broad mitigation strategies." For instance, the *HCP Handbook* calls for mitigation that is "based on sound biological rationale," "practicable," and "commensurate with the impacts" addressed. It also calls for consistency in mitigation requirements (ch. 3, pp. 19, 23).[14]

Development of specific mitigation programs is the responsibility of ITP applicants, with the help of service personnel. Private landowners will, understandably, be concerned about cost, but as Professor Ruhl notes, the "ESA does not prohibit take at all costs." He explains that the "to the maximum extent practicable" standard requires a balancing of benefits to the species of additional conservation measures against the costs to the applicant. Still, the test will be applied, he cautions, "in a way that pushes the project applicant to the limit of economic feasibility." Accordingly, Ruhl advises applicants to include in the proposed HCP a discussion explicitly "link[ing] project economics with the proposed minimization and mitigation program" (Ruhl 1999, pp. 382–383).

As tentatively amended by a 1999 draft addendum, the *HCP Handbook* requires every HCP to include "specific biological goals and objectives." Biological goals are "the rationale behind the minimization and mitigation strategies." According to the services, developing "biological goals and objectives for individual HCPs will help to focus the conservation programs of HCPs on cumulatively achieving landscape level conservation." The goals and objectives "should be commensurate with the specific impacts and duration of the HCP applicant's proposed action." The services offer an example:

> [T]he overall goal could be to ensure population viability by maintaining habitat contiguity. The specific measurable objective to achieve this goal may be to conserve an adequate number of acres of habitat in a certain configuration, so that a viable corridor is maintained. The conservation measures could specify the number of acres and configuration. If [they] were not determinable, an adaptive management strategy could be used, and the HCP . . . could list a series of incremental steps to be taken within an agreed upon range of management adjustments for determining and securing a viable corridor.

Goals must be based on the best scientific information available; relevant sources include recovery plans, state conservation strategies, candidate conservation plans, and various state and federal scientific experts (Draft Addendum 1999).

As a general matter, mitigation involves avoiding, minimizing, rectifying, reducing or eliminating, or compensating for impacts to species. HCPs often involve several of these strategies. Although the services interpret the act as not requiring HCPs to recover, or contribute to the recovery of, listed species, "recovery is an important consideration in any HCP effort," they insist, and "contribution to recovery is often an integral product of an HCP." Whenever "feasible," the services "encourage HCPs that result in a net benefit" to species or "contribute to recovery plan objectives." Conversely, "plans that are not consistent with recovery plan objectives should be discouraged" (HCP Handbook, ch. 3, pp. 20–21).

Habitat mitigation, that is, compensating for habitat loss or disturbance, is acceptable and can be accomplished by acquiring or protecting onsite or offsite habitats. (The latter generally should be as similar and as close as possible to the habitat in question.) Chapter 3 in the *HCP Handbook* lists these specific examples: using habitat banks and mitigation credit systems, establishing mitigation funds, acquiring existing habitat, protecting existing habitats through conservation easements or similar legal devices, enhancing or restoring degraded or former habitats, managing habitats "to achieve specific biological characteristics," and creating new habitats. The services caution that restoration and creation methodologies should be "proven and reliable or, if relatively new, that contingency measures or adaptive management procedures [be] included to correct for failures." The scope of mitigation should generally be commensurate with the scope of impacts; for example, if impacts include permanent habitat losses, mitigation lands should be protected permanently. Funding research is generally not a "preferred mitigation strategy," but providing money for habitat restoration activities, recovery plan implementation, or conservation measures on public lands may be acceptable.

In practice, adaptive management provisions are frequently incorporated in HCPs. Adaptive management concepts are seen as helping to compensate for gaps in knowledge about species' needs, especially long-term conservation requirements. Employing adaptive management allows those responsible for implementing HCPs to adjust mitigation strategies to accommodate changed conditions or to improve their ability to accomplish plan goals or objectives. Use of adaptive management requires that (1) testable hypotheses and measurable "thresholds for review" be established for HCP mitigation strategies, (2) mitigation activities be monitored and analyzed for effectiveness, and (3) appropriate changes be instituted when plan goals are not being achieved. Adaptive management "provisions must be linked to measurable biological goals and monitoring." All requirements should be specified in the approved plan (Draft Addendum 1999).

Applicants are required by regulation to monitor the effectiveness of HCP mitigation measures, even if the plan does not incorporate adaptive management. (Where adaptive management is employed, monitoring is indispensable to its effectiveness.) Monitoring requirements should be specific, monitoring should be performed and reported regularly, and monitoring plans should contain "target milestones" throughout the life of the plan. Requirements will vary and should be commensurate with the size and scope of the HCP. All requirements should be spelled out in the plan, including who will be responsible for collecting and analyzing monitoring data and the acceptable protocols and parameters for those collections and analyses. A qualified, identified person other than the permittee may conduct the monitoring. In addition, the USFWS or NMFS is responsible for monitoring compliance with the terms of the HCP and the effectiveness of the mitigation. Technical review teams may be established for the purpose of reviewing and ensuring compliance with large-scale HCPs.

Although controversial, the services allow ITP applicants to conduct development activities before replacement habitats are secured, so long as legal or financial assurances (e.g., letters of credit, escrow accounts, or mitigation funds) are provided up front. Such mechanisms are useful to small landowners but may be opposed by environmental or conservation interests concerned that habitat losses, which precede mitigation, might ultimately never be addressed. The federal government considers mitigation funds and habitat banks effective mechanisms for mitigating the cumulative impacts of small-scale, low-effect projects and enabling their proponents to participate in larger-scale HCPs. According to Ruhl (1999, p. 396), "the HCP applicant and the permitting agency can explore and negotiate creative minimization and mitigation options so long as local consistency is maintained and a solid record of the bases for the program is established." [15]

"Ensuring mitigation consistency is essential," the *HCP Handbook* maintains, while conceding that it is also a challenge, especially when species' habitats encompass multiple offices or regions. Mitigation standards for the same species should differ only for "biological or other good reasons" and only if "clearly explained." Consistent mitigation policies help streamline HCP development and provide assistance, especially to applicants for small-scale HCPs. The *HCP Handbook* contemplates that USFWS regional and field offices will develop consistent habitat-based mitigation requirements (by area and species) as the agency gains experience with habitat conservation planning. Ruhl suggests that the use of ratios or other standards may become more common. For example, he writes,

[a USFWS] office might "rank" the quality of a protected species' habitat into categories such as prime, fair, suitable, and buffer. The agency then might assign replacement or enhancement mitigation habitat ratios based on the quality of the lost habitat and the quality of the mitigation habitat. An acre of lost prime habitat, for example, might require three acres of prime habitat or seven acres of fair habitat as mitigation.

Ruhl warns applicants (and correctly so) that "challenging the agency's bases for habitat mitigation ratios will require superior biological theory and field research"—a decidedly difficult proposition (Ruhl 1999, pp. 394–395).[16]

Another source of uncertainty and confusion in developing and obtaining approval for HCPs is the section 10 requirement that applicants describe "alternative actions to such taking." According to the *HCP Handbook* the most common alternatives examined are "any specific alternative" that would reduce incidental take below levels predicted for the proposed project, and the "no action" alternative. For low-effect HCPs, the latter may be sufficient. The applicant must explain why the alternative was not adopted. "Economic considerations" are permissible, but if they are the reason for rejecting an alternative, "data supporting this decision must be provided to the extent that it is reasonably available and non-proprietary" (ch. 3, pp. 35–36). The services have no authority to impose an alternative on an applicant but will advise applicants if an alternative is unlikely to satisfy permit issuance requirements.

Implementing HCPs poses several issues. First, the most appropriate applicant for an HCP permit might not always be the landowner or project proponent. (It could be the homeowners' association for the planned residential development, for instance.) Relevant considerations include the kinds and duration of mitigation measures that are likely to be required, how mitigation will be funded, and whether (and how) future permit transfers should be provided for. This "dilemma" prompted Ruhl to urge that "where possible, and especially where the developer wishes above all else to be removed from long-term obligations, mitigation should take the form of measures that can be completed early." Options include funding recovery plans or acquiring mitigation habitat and transferring ownership to a conservation organization or land trust. Ruhl adds: "It may also be desirable, even if it means increasing front-end mitigation burdens, to avoid project design measures that require continuous enforcement, such as lot development limits [or predator control requirements]." The tradeoff, of course, is between up-front capital expenditures and the costs of long-term administration. Choosing the front-end approach would help the service to "reasonably conclude that the HCP permit will not be routinely violated." Funding mechanisms (e.g., for conservation measures and monitoring) must be established prior to permit approval; permit transfer issues also should be decided at the time the permit is being developed (Ruhl 1999, pp. 396–404).

No Surprises

The habitat conservation planning program received its biggest boost from the Clinton administration's no-surprises policy. From adoption of the policy in 1994 through 1997, about 225 HCPs were approved and another 200 were being developed; only 14 were approved between 1982 and 1992. (See Parenteau 1998, p. 292, and GAO 1992.)

According to the services' notice promulgating the no-surprises policy, a "driving concern" behind the policy was "the absence of adequate incentives for non-Federal landowners to factor endangered species conservation into their day-to-day land management activities." The policy's purpose is to assure nonfederal landowners "that no additional land restrictions or financial compensation will be required from an HCP permittee for species adequately covered by a properly functioning HCP in light of unforeseen or extraordinary circumstances." The policy was an attempt to reconcile the tension between developers' preference for certainty and the possibility of changed circumstances necessitating the reconsideration of mitigation measures in an HCP agreement. The 1994 policy was challenged as improperly promulgated under the Administrative Procedure Act and subsequently published as a proposed rule. It was finalized in 1998 (USFWS and NMFS 1998). (See Ruhl 1999, p. 403, n. 200.)

In support of the policy, the services cite the legislative history of the section 10 amendments, which reveals that Congress intended HCPs to contain provisions for dealing with changed circumstances. Congressional concerns, however, encompassed both species and HCP proponents (U.S. House 1982). Accordingly, the services recognize the "potential tension between two primary goals of the HCP program: (1) adequately minimizing and mitigating for the incidental take of listed species, and (2) providing regulatory assurances to section 10 permittees that the terms of an approved HCP will not change over time, or that necessary changes will be minimized to the extent possible" (*HCP Handbook*, ch. 3, p. 28). Achieving insurance against the uncertainty of future regulation is a strong motivation for private parties' participation in HCPs, but failing to adapt HCPs to environmental or other changes could diminish or negate their ability to achieve the desired conservation benefits. The services' no-surprises policy, as well as the safe harbor and candidate conservation policies, is designed to minimize the risks and uncertainty to both landowners and species. Once a policy is engaged by an approved agreement, the remaining uncertainty and risks rest chiefly on the target species or on persons other than the private parties to the agreement (e.g., on federal agencies; Bean 1998, p. 10701, n. 67).

Although the USFWS reserves the right to amend HCPs, safe harbor agreements, and candidate conservation agreements if necessary, any revisions must now be consistent with the assurances provided to the permit holders under each of these agreements, as well as with the regulations governing these agreements (USFWS and NMFS 1999a).

Essentially, the no-surprises policy provides that the USFWS may seek additional compensation or mitigation measures, *other than* land, water, or financial compensation or land use restrictions, from HCP permittees, only in "unforeseen circumstances." Any additional measures required must be limited to the original conserved habitat areas and to the HCP's "operating conservation program." (The services do not indicate what forms such additional compensation or mitigation may take.) For example, chapter 3 of the *HCP Handbook* offers,

> if a developer had agreed to dedicate a certain amount of funding annually in support of a particular conservation program (e.g., habitat restoration) but subsequent research demonstrated that greater conservation benefits could be achieved by redirecting funding into depredation control, and extraordinary circumstances warranted such a shift, the No Surprises policy would allow the modification.

Moreover, any such changes to the terms of an HCP are to be limited "to the maximum extent possible." Under the policy, the primary obligation to take additional mitigation measures will rest not with a permittee who is properly implementing an approved HCP, but with the USFWS itself, other governmental entities, private conservation organizations, or other private landowners who are not participating in an HCP. (Of course, HCP permittees may consent to or voluntarily undertake additional responsibilities not prescribed in the HCP.)

The no-surprises assurances apply only to species that are adequately covered in an HCP. "Adequately covered" refers to any listed or unlisted species that is addressed in an HCP that meets ESA permit issuance criteria; in other words, adequately covered unlisted species are treated as if they were listed species. The net result is that HCP permittees are guaranteed that the land and financial costs of mitigation, as well as the land use restrictions, agreed to in the original HCP will not change. This is so even with respect to adequately covered unlisted species that may later be listed. In this way, voluntary, front-end commitments by landowners can allow them to avoid restrictions that would otherwise apply as a result of further species listings in the future. (See also *HCP Handbook* ch. 3, p. 30, and ch. 4, p. 4.)

The services distinguish between "unforeseen [formerly, extraordinary] circumstances" and "changed circumstances." The latter, which include the listing of new species or changes in HCP activities such as monitoring plans, "can reasonably be anticipated and planned for." The former, in contrast, are those that "were not or could not be anticipated by HCP participants and the Services." They may include catastrophic events, such as fires or earthquakes. HCPs should address both types of changes. A plan's discussion of "unforeseen circumstances," however, is limited to describing how such changes, if they arise, will be dealt with, and it must be consistent with the no-surprises policy.

"Unforeseen circumstances means changes in circumstances affecting a species or geographic area covered by a conservation plan that could not reasonably have been anticipated by plan developers and the Service at the time of the conservation's plan and development, and that result in a substantial and adverse change in the status of the covered species" (*HCP Handbook,* ch. 3, pp. 30–31). The *HCP Handbook* and the regulations contain criteria to assist the services in determining whether and when extraordinary circumstances necessitate amending an HCP. These criteria are presumably relevant to the unforeseen-circumstances inquiry called for by the 1998 regulations. They include size of the species' current range, percentage and ecological significance of range affected by the HCP, and whether failure to adopt additional conservation measures would appreciably reduce the species' likelihood of survival and recovery. The "primary focus of the inquiry" will generally be the "level of biological peril to species covered by the HCP" and "the degree to which the welfare of those species is tied to a particular HCP." Although the services have discretion in determining whether unforeseen circumstances exist, the regulations clearly place on them the burden of demonstrating such a turn of events, using the best scientific and commercial data available.[17]

The federal government may, as a last resort, revoke an HCP permit "in the unlikely situation in which an unforeseen circumstance results in likely jeopardy" to a covered species and "the Service has not been successful in remedying the situation through other means." Of course, the services remain free to undertake additional mitigation at their own expense at any time (USFWS and NMFS 1999a).

Finally, according to the *HCP Handbook,* where an HCP (1) was designed to provide an overall net benefit to the species, (2) contains measurable criteria for measuring its success, and (3) is "properly functioning," the HCP permittee shall not be required to provide any additional mitigation. "Properly functioning" means simply that the HCP's provisions are being (or have been) fully implemented by the permittee and that the permittee is in full compliance with the conditions of the permit. This policy is not part of the final rule; it is unclear whether it remains in effect (*HCP Handbook,* ch. 3, pp. 30–31).

According to Bean (1998, p. 10701, nn. 52–54), the no-surprises policy enjoys broad support among both landowners and environmentalists; it "has won praise in both *Audubon* magazine and *Farm Bureau News.*" Its "only virulent critics," Bean asserts, come from "the far fringes of the Wise Use Movement," but in fact the policy has attracted criticism, suspicion, or scorn from some environmental groups, numerous scientists, and others. Law professor Patrick Parenteau, for instance, calls the policy "bad science" and "bad law." He sees it as an unauthorized administrative effort to "reform" the ESA, which violates the agencies' affirmative conservation obligation under section 7 as well as section 10's mandate that take permits not appreciably reduce the likelihood of a listed species' recovery. He also argues, with some force, that the policy "runs directly counter" to the policy in favor of adaptive management. No Surprises may make the HCP program "fair," Parenteau says, but it undermines the ESA goal of species recovery (Parenteau 1998, pp. 291–308).[18] Bean himself conceded that given the no-surprises assurances, "there is no going back" if mitigation measures in an approved HCP "prove inadequate" (Bean 1998, p. 10701, n. 67).

Safe Harbor Agreements with Assurances

Safe harbor agreements with assurances are described by the services as "a means of providing incentives to [nonfederal] property owners to restore, enhance, or maintain habitats and/or populations of listed species that result in a net conservation benefit to these species." Implemented by regulation in 1999 (USFWS and NMFS 1999b), the safe harbor program is allegedly authorized by ESA section 10(a)(1)(A), which (in relevant part) authorizes the secretary to permit "any act otherwise prohibited by [U.S. Code 16, sect. 1538] . . . to enhance the propagation or survival of the affected species." [Recall that ITPs and HCPs are governed by section 10(a)(1)(B).] Safe harbor incentives consist of technical assistance offered to nonfederal property owners in developing voluntary agreements, and assurances (in approved agreements) that additional land, water, or natural resource use restrictions will not be imposed as a result of the agreed-to conservation actions. When all terms of an agreement are met, the "Services will authorize incidental taking of the covered species [via an "enhancement of survival" permit] at a level that enables the property owner ultimately to return the enrolled property back to agreed upon baseline conditions." The intent, however, is to "ensure that the protection provided to covered listed species is not eroded below current levels." (See also South Carolina 1997, p. 679.)[19]

The safe harbor policy is founded on two beliefs: (1) that "a collaborative stewardship approach to the proactive management of listed species involving government . . . and the private sector is critical" to achieving the ESA's goal of recovering species, and (2) that species recovery can be promoted by "short-term and mid-term enhancement, restoration, or maintenance" of habitats on nonfederal property (USFWS and NMFS 1999b).[20]

Review and permitting mechanisms for safe harbor agreements are set forth in the regulations; additional details concerning the safe harbor policy were published in the *Federal Register* on the same date as the new rules and will be provided by the service to interested persons (USFWS and NMFS 1999a,b). Agreements must meet seven specific requirements, in addition to satisfying all requirements of section 10, to qualify the landowner for an "enhancement of survival" incidental taking permit. (Some of these requirements include identifying the species or habitats covered, specifying management actions, describing any incidental take, and providing for monitoring.) The issuing agency is required to engage in a section 7 consultation on the proposed permit and meet NEPA requirements. (The latter will generally be satisfied by a categorical exclusion.) The time period of an agreement depends on the time required to accomplish the conservation actions included in the agreement and the landowner's wishes. The assurances in the agreement, including the incidental take authorization, run with the land and remain in effect as long as the owner of the enrolled tract (the original owner or any successor) complies with the agreement and the permit.

The USFWS considers this "long-term certainty" a "major incentive for property owner participation." In addition, agreements may be terminated before the end of their term for reasons outside the landowner's control, and the land returned to baseline conditions, even if the net conservation benefits have not been achieved.

Landowners who have complied with the terms of an agreement retain the right to use their land in a manner different from its original use, without incurring additional restrictions under the act, as long as baseline conditions are maintained. If the new use would result in incidental take that is inconsistent with baseline conditions, an ITP would be required. But if baseline conditions were zero (that is, the habitat initially was unoccupied) and the habitat became occupied as a result of activities carried out under the agreement, no further ESA authorization would be required. In other words, the landowner could take (incidentally) all the newly established individuals. The services would work with the landowner, however, to relocate the animals or to extend the agreement.[21] The baseline conditions documented in an agreement may be revised to reflect changes outside the control of the landowner (e.g., loss of nest trees due to storm damage).

According to the services, safe harbor agreements are not appropriate in all situations, for example, where a property owner needs an immediate ITP or where the "net conservation benefit" standard would not be met. (The services note, by way of illustration, that the "net conservation benefit" requirement would not be met where a landowner proposed "translocating individuals from a habitat preserved in perpetuity to a site with zero baseline condition." The reason: the relocation site could later be "altered or destroyed, which would put the species at risk.") Net conservation benefits can be achieved in numerous ways, for example, by connecting fragmented habitat, maintaining or increasing populations, buffering protected areas, or creating areas for testing and implementing new conservation measures. In the services' view, net benefits contribute to the recovery of species, "but this contribution . . . may be of varying duration and not permanent in nature." Even if short term, the cumulative benefits from these agreements are seen as contributing to recovery over time. The services concede, however, that delisting decisions should not be based solely on safe harbor agreements, given the participating landowners' right to return their properties to baseline conditions (USFWS and NMFS 1999b, pp. 32718–32720).

The safe harbor policy was developed principally to deal with situations involving individual landowners. (The first three safe harbor agreements, considered the models of the draft plan, involved Attwater's prairie chicken and the aplomado falcon, both in Texas, and the red-cockaded woodpecker in North Carolina.) As finally promulgated, however, the rules allow for programmatic permits if appropriate. The USFWS is also developing a process to coordinate safe harbor agreements with landowner agreements under other federal programs, such as Farm Bill or Partners for Wildlife programs. The objective will be "to provide assurances on a programmatic basis" to participating landowners, "as long as a net conservation benefit is achieved for listed species covered by the Agreements."

Federal funds for developing safe harbor agreements come from the USFWS's recovery activities budget. (The service predicts that most participating properties will be family-owned farms and ranches. If this proves true, relatively little financial support can be expected from the private sector.) Their limited budget has led the service to focus on agreements that seem to promise the greatest contribution to recovery and on those for which sufficient information is available to enable development of biologically sound conservation strategies. The USFWS budget for fiscal year 1999 included $11.7 million for developing both safe harbor and candidate conservation agreements. About $2.5 million of this was expected to be used for "financial assistance incentives" to landowners participating in safe harbor agreements. The services were urged (during the rule-making process) to include tax incentives and monetary payments to landowners as components of the safe harbor policy. The agencies agreed that such financial incentives would be effective in encouraging voluntary conservation efforts, but explained that they currently lack authority to implement such measures.

Some legal scholars argue that the government lacks authority to enter into safe harbor agreements, pointing to the lack of any relevant language in the act or evidence of congressional intent to allow the agencies to "enter into long-term contracts waiving the government's regulatory authority in this fashion" (Parenteau 1998, pp. 287–288). The policy is also disparaged for not assuring that the "habitat will be there when the species needs it" (Kostyack 1998, p. 22). A report prepared for Defenders of Wildlife lists three concerns about these agreements, namely, how baseline responsibility will be determined, whether landowners could intentionally degrade habitat to achieve a lower baseline, and how the appropriate circumstances for using the agreement will be determined (Hood 1998). Still, one critic conceded that "carefully drawn" safe harbor agreements "can provide benefits to species that strict enforcement of the ESA might not," and some scientists agree (Parenteau 1998, p. 288).

Candidate Conservation Agreements with Assurances

Final rules for safe harbor agreements and for candidate conservation agreements (CCAs) were promulgated simultaneously (USFWS and NMFS 1999a,b,c). The rules reflect similar policies and incorporate nearly identical mechanisms; both are available to all nonfederal property owners, although the primary participants are expected to be family farms and ranches. Both agreements involve a section 10(a)(1)(A) "enhancement of survival" permit, although the effective date of the permit accompanying a CCA will be keyed to the date of any subsequent listing of a covered species. Both agreements are subject to section 7 consultation and NEPA documentation requirements.

The chief difference between the two forms of agreement is the species targeted. Safe harbor agreements are designed to benefit listed threatened or endangered species; CCAs provide conservation benefits exclusively to candidate, proposed, and other species not yet added to the federal lists. (Another difference is that the term "net benefit" relates to safe harbor agreements but not to CCAs.) The goal of CCAs is "to remove enough threats to the covered species to preclude any need to list them as threatened or endangered." The services compare this with a "recovery standard." The services assert that the "substantive requirements of [CCAs], if undertaken on a broad enough scale by other property owners similarly situated, *should be expected to* preclude any need to list the species covered by the Agreement" (USFWS and NMFS 1999a; emphasis added).[22]

The Endangered Species Act has been widely criticized for its reactive, rather than proactive, approach to conserving species at risk. Issuance of the CCA policy attempted to address this deficiency, but at the same time it drew criticism that the services lack authority to adopt regulations aimed at unlisted species. The services responded by citing ESA sections 2, 7, and 10. Section 2 points out the importance of "encouraging the States and other interested parties, through Federal financial assistance and incentives, to develop and maintain conservation programs," to safeguard "the Nation's heritage in fish, wildlife, and plants." Section 7 requires the services to "utilize" the programs they administer "in furtherance of the purposes" of the ESA. Although section 10 refers expressly only to listed species, the legislative history of the 1982 amendments reveals that Congress plainly contemplated that HCPs appropriately could include conservation measures for candidate species, proposed species, and other unlisted species (U.S. House 1982; see also *HCP Handbook,* p. i, ch. 1 p. 2, ch. 4 p. 1).

About 40 CCAs without assurances, benefiting more than 200 species, were being implemented as of 1999. These agreements, which the services claim had allowed them to avoid listing some species, had involved principally other federal agencies.[23] The new policy, CCAs with assurances, was adopted to assuage nonfederal property owners' fears that conservation efforts undertaken now could lead to ESA restrictions later if species attracted to their land were ultimately listed. CCAs, like safe harbor agreements, in other words, provide both proactive protection for species and offer regulatory certainty to landowners.

The rules for CCAs, like those for safe harbor agreements, set forth the review and permitting mechanisms but not the substance of the agency's policy. That policy was published in the *Federal Register* on the same date and will be provided by the service to persons interested in entering into a CCA. Consistent with the agencies' conviction that "collaborative stewardship" can significantly enhance early conservation efforts for declining species, the policy authorizes the services to enter into agreements with individuals as well as programmatic agreements with appropriate tribal, state, or local entities, such as fish and wildlife or land management agencies. The agreements will specify the assurances and take allowances that may be distributed among individual, participating landowners (USFWS and NMFS 1999a, p. 32708).

To enter into an agreement, the services must "determine that the benefits of the conservation measures implemented . . . , when combined with those benefits that would be achieved if it is assumed that conservation measures were also to be implemented on other necessary properties, would preclude or remove any need to list the covered species." The government calls this convoluted, seemingly theoretical requirement "essentially a recovery standard." It is tempered somewhat by the agencies' statement (USFWS and NMFS 1999c, p. 32728) that they will not enter into a CCA unless:

> the threats to and the requirements of the covered species are adequately understood so that the Services can determine that the agreed upon conservation measures will be beneficial to the covered species; and the effects of the agreed upon conservation measures are adequately under-

stood so that the Services can determine that they will not adversely affect [i.e., jeopardize] listed species or adversely affect critical habitat or (2) any information gaps relating to the requirements of the covered species or the effects of the conservation measures on the covered species or listed species can be adequately addressed by incorporating adaptive management principles into the Agreement.

The CCA policy and implementing regulations prescribe "general requirements" with which CCAs should or must comply. In addition, the USFWS's draft *Candidate Conservation Agreement Handbook* includes a "list of conditions under which [CCAs] would most likely be successful." Although those conditions were developed for CCAs without assurances, the service considers them applicable as well to agreements with assurances (p. 32730).

The services assured commenters that CCAs with assurances would not be used to replace recovery plans or to avoid or delay listing a species if listing is warranted.[24] (The agencies are required by statute and regulation to meet certain time limits in rendering listing decisions.) Conversely, the agencies believe that it will be possible, in some cases, to complete the development of CCAs and thus "remove the need to list before a final listing determination could be made" (USFWS and NMFS 1999c, p. 32735).

Like safe harbor agreements with assurances, CCAs would allow a landowner who exceeds the conservation goal specified in the agreement subsequently to reduce the level of benefits (to, but not below, the agreed upon level), and the associated "enhancement of survival" permit would excuse the incidental take (of ultimately listed species) that accompanied this reduction of benefits. The service would be given an opportunity first to relocate individuals of the covered species.[25]

The CCA rules provide an early-out option for participating landowners who, "for good cause," choose to terminate their participation in an agreement before its expiration date (USFWS and NMFS 1999c, p. 32736). Early termination is available as long as baseline conditions are maintained and the service is given the opportunity to relocate individuals of covered species (a conservation strategy about which some environmentalists and the National Research Council have expressed concerns). The USFWS predicts, based on its experience with other voluntary habitat management programs (such as Partners for Wildlife), that very few participants will invoke this option.

The services have committed to providing "the necessary technical assistance to develop Agreements," and "may assist or train property owners to implement conservation measures." The estimated processing time and federal cost to develop either a safe harbor or candidate conservation agreement with assurances (along with the accompanying permit) are one month and $15,000. The agencies did not estimate costs to participating landowners. The USFWS noted, however, that because the agreements are voluntary, the regulations are not expected to have adverse effects or increase costs or prices for consumers, individual industries, or governments. Nor is a significant impact expected on "small ownerships," given that most "costs are on a per acre basis" and relatively few agreements will be developed and approved in any given year.

To function usefully, CCAs will have to be based on sound biological data and be more detailed than prelisting agreements have been to date. According to Professor Parenteau (1998, p. 289), several federal courts have noted that such agreements "lack substance"—indeed, they "contain more wishful thinking than concrete solutions."

Summary and Conclusions

An incidental take permit under section 10(a)(1)(B) is the appropriate mechanism when a property owner wishes to engage in some land use or other activity that is likely to harm a listed (threatened or endangered) species. The application for an incidental take permit must include a habitat conservation plan, which must address all listed species that may be affected and which may address any unlisted (proposed candidate or other) species. The no-surprises policy then essentially protects the permittee from any additional, future obligations with respect to any listed or unlisted species "adequately covered" by the plan.

"Enhancement of survival" permits under section 10(a)(1)(B) are appropriate when no immediately planned land use or activity poses a threat to a listed species. On the contrary, the landowner may wish to undertake some activity that could enhance the habitat of one or more listed species or attract individuals of species not currently present. If listed species might be attracted, or if their habitat could be enhanced, the landowner may wish to enter into a safe harbor agreement with assurances and obtain an incidental take permit. A safe harbor agreement can cover listed as well as unlisted species. On the other hand, if no listed species are present or likely to be attracted, the appropriate approach is a candidate conservation agreement with assurances. An approved CCA will be accompanied by an incidental take permit, whose effective date will be that of any subsequent listing of a covered species.

Congress and the services have attempted to strike a balance between accommodating the concerns of landowners and meeting the needs of threatened or endangered species and their habitats on nonfederal lands. The federal agencies have announced their policy to promote "flexibility and ingenuity" in working with private landowners and permit applicants (*HCP Handbook,* ch. 1, p. 3). At least one knowledgeable commentator has concluded that the "HCP program suggests sufficient flexibility and force to accommodate both real estate development and species conservation goals" (Ruhl 1999, p. 404). In the past ten years, many more and larger, more comprehensive, HCPs have been approved. Yet in spite of these policy strides and the short-term progress, critics on both sides argue that additional efforts and more creative techniques are needed, if endangered species conservation is to function effectively and fairly, for species and property owners (Bean 1998; Parenteau 1998).

Enhancing the ESA's Effectiveness for Species Protection and Its Palatability to Property Owners

Despite (or, some would say, because of) the ESA, more threatened or endangered species are declining than improving (National Research Council 1995, p. 197). Perhaps expanded habitat conservation planning efforts, along with the related policies described above, will stem or even reverse the tide. It may simply be too early to tell. It is more probable, however, that additional, innovative conservation strategies will be needed.

Some techniques currently in use are new and have little track record as yet. Mitigation banking is one example. Mitigation banks are gaining popularity in several contexts. Federal guidance for wetland mitigation banking was issued by the U.S. EPA and Army Corps of Engineers in 1995. This form of banking involves the creation, enhancement, or restoration of wetlands in advance of damaging or destroying other wetlands pursuant to a Clean Water Act section 404 permit or the federal Swampbuster program. The created or restored wetlands are banked, and that account can be debited later to provide the mitigation required by a section 404 permit, or the banked wetlands can be sold to other section 404 permit applicants. Recent bills to reauthorize and amend the Clean Water Act have contained mitigation banking provisions, and the

1996 Farm Bill approved a pilot mitigation banking effort for the Swamp-buster program. Many public or private banks have been established; at least twenty states have or are developing mitigation banking policies. Neither the ESA nor the implementing regulations directly address mitigation banking, but the *HCP Handbook* (ch. 3, p. 23) touts the advantages of habitat conservation banks, especially for assisting property owners and developers with mitigating the impacts of small-scale projects. Legal scholars and some biologists have also encouraged the creation of habitat banks (Ruhl 1998, p. 85; Salzman and Ruhl 2000). As a result, habitat banks have been created or proposed and are beginning to be used by developers, particularly in California, to meet ESA mitigation requirements.

For example, after the California gnatcatcher was listed in 1993 as a threatened species,[26] the city of Escondido was restricted in its ability to approve future development projects in or affecting coastal sage scrub habitat. The city and six other North County cities developed the Multiple Habitat Conservation Program as a subregional effort to prepare a comprehensive HCP under the Natural Community Conservation Planning program. Daley Ranch, the largest undeveloped property within Escondido, was considered a potentially valuable contributor to this program, because of its size, location adjacent to undeveloped county lands, and the diversity of species (including the gnatcatcher) found on the property. Negotiations involving the Trust for Public Lands, the California Department of Fish and Game, and the USFWS, as well as the city and property owner, led to the purchase of Daley Ranch by the city (in January 1997) and creation there of a habitat preserve and mitigation bank. The 3,058-acre Daley Ranch conservation area is to be managed in perpetuity for the preservation of a biologically unique and diverse habitat area of regional importance. It constitutes approximately 15 percent of the overall Multiple Habitat preserve system and more than 34 percent of the total public lands contributed by the seven participating cities.

A critical component of the negotiations was the ability to establish a habitat conservation bank. The property owner (a major developer) would benefit as a recipient of some of the conservation bank credits, as well as from the city's assurance that it would not transfer the property to another developer. The city would benefit by conserving the land in perpetuity, thereby eliminating some infrastructure and service demands, while meeting a substantial portion of its conservation responsibilities under the Multiple Habitat program. The city also created a potential revenue source through the future sale of conservation credits. As a result of lengthy negotiations with the state and federal wildlife agencies, the majority (2,842 acres) of Daley Ranch was set aside as an approved conservation bank. The implementation agreement with the wildlife agencies allows the city to sell credits from the bank for mitigation to offset the impacts from development projects within western San Diego County.

Another example is the ITP application and proposed HCP submitted in 1999 by proponents of concrete production facilities in San Bernardino County, California. The proposed action would directly impact the endangered Delhi Sands flower-loving fly by removing about 65 acres of habitat on the 96-acre parcel. The applicants propose to dedicate about 30.5 acres of fly habitat to a land manager or conservation organization to be managed and preserved in perpetuity. The proposal includes a 5-acre mitigation bank, established within the 30.5-acre conservation area. Proceeds from the sale of credits would offset the management endowment cost. This action would compensate for the loss of habitat resulting from the project and would benefit the long-term conservation of the endangered fly (USFWS 1999).[27]

The Lake Mathews Multiple Species Habitat Conservation Plan and Natural Community Conservation Plan also relies in part on the use of a habitat bank. The plan affects nearly 6,000 acres owned by the Southern California Metropolitan Water District around Lake Mathews in northwestern Riverside County. (In *San Bernardino Valley Audubon Society v. Metropolitan Water District,* the project was challenged by a local Audubon chapter over the failure to prepare an environmental impact report.) The plan involves creation of a mitigation bank consisting of lands owned by the water district and the Riverside County Habitat Conservation Agency. The water district would use its share of the mitigation bank to obtain ESA authorizations and for mitigation needs (under the California Environmental Quality Act) for its future projects and activities around Lake Mathews. The county agency would acquire conservation easements over areas occupied by Stephen's kangaroo rat in the mitigation bank and would "be given conservation credit toward a future multiple species plan for the other biological values of the habitat."

Habitat banks are an example of a conservation strategy allowed, but not mandated or expressly promoted, by current law. Many other conservation options exist, though some strategies may be outside the law or beyond the capabilities (or at least inclinations) of property owners and local governments because of legal or budgetary limitations.

Many persons, from congressional leaders to governors to conservation biologists to private landowners, have urged the enactment or funding of federal incentives to encourage private land conservation efforts on behalf of threatened, endangered, and declining species (Thompson 1997; Hood 1998; National Wildlife Federation n.d.).[28] Recall Michael Bean's conclusion that "positive incentives for landowners to conserve endangered species could significantly improve prospects for the Act's success." The 1997 Chafee-Kempthorne ESA reauthorization bill, which was believed to have nearly universal support but still failed, would have allowed landowners who donate land for conservation purposes to deduct the full value of the land (exclusive of ESA restrictions on its use or development), allowed the deferral of estate taxes on land subject to a conservation easement, and afforded additional capital gains tax relief to persons who transfer land to qualified conservation organizations. Another recent bill, introduced by Congressman George Miller (D-Calif.), also contained several economic incentives (Donahue 1998, pp. 88–89; Parenteau 1998, pp. 302–303).

A wide variety of economic conservation incentives have been proposed; some are being used at the local and state levels. This book considers several of these incentive-based approaches that hold promise for promoting Endangered Species Act goals. Gregory Parkhurst and Jason Shogren examine these approaches in detail from an economics perspective in Chapter 3. Chapter 5 reviews their feasibility and usefulness.

Notes

1. Bean was the author of the original (1977) treatise on wildlife law, the third edition of which (entitled *The Evolution of National Wildlife Law*) was released in 1997 with co-author Melanie J. Rowland. He is a senior attorney with the Environmental Defense Fund in Washington, D.C. Some idea of the sweep of section 9 can be gleaned from the General Accounting Office's 1994 audit of ESA implementation. The GAO reported that over six fiscal years (1988–1993), 4,230 ESA violations were adjudicated. Of those, only 126 (3 percent) involved illegal takings. Of those 126, 86 involved criminal charges. Fines were levied in 59 instances; jail sentences were rendered in 18 cases. Over approximately the same period (1 Jan. 1988 through 30 Sept. 1993), 321 investigations of illegal takings on nonfederal lands resulted in 100 prosecutions, 32 convictions were obtained, and 29 cases were still in litigation. Only 7 of the 32 convictions were based on habitat modification (GAO 1995, pp. 11–13).

2. See, e.g., *United States v. West Coast Forest Resources Ltd. Partnership,* WL 33100698 (D. Ore. 28 July 1997) granting temporary injunction, WL 298707 (D. Ore. 13 Mar. 2000) denying permanent injunction; *Defenders of Wildlife v. Bernal,* CV-98-120-TUC-FRZ, slip opinion (D. Ariz. 8 May 1998), affirmed, 30 ELR 20403 (9th Cir. 2000). For instance, the dissenters in *Sweet Home* asserted that the majority's ruling regarding the meaning of harm "requir[es] us to accept that a farmer who tills his field and causes erosion that makes silt run into a nearby river which depletes oxygen and thereby 'impairs [the] breeding' of protected fish has 'taken' or 'attempted to take' the fish" (799). Justice O'Connor countered: "The farmer whose fertilizer is lifted by a tornado from tilled fields and deposited miles away in a wildlife refuge cannot, by any stretch of the term, be considered the proximate cause of death or injury to protected species occasioned thereby" (713).

According to one commentator, very few court opinions explicitly apply proximate cause or foreseeability to the ESA's take prohibition or harm regulation. Doyle (1996) recommended that *Sweet Home* be treated merely "as a statutory construction case that upheld the validity of an agency's regulation," and that courts should look to other take and harm case law, such as *Palila v. Hawaii Dep't of Land & Natural Resources,* 852 F. 2d 1106 (9th Cir. 1988), in analyzing the element of causation. (In *Palila* the plaintiff proved causation by showing that feral sheep ate particular vegetation, in its immature stages, on which the endangered palila bird relied in its mature form.)

3. The absence of any "legal requirement that HCPs be consistent with species recovery" is a source of great concern to environmentalists and of criticism for the HCP program. See, e.g., the introduction to Hood 1998 ("because FWS and NMFS do not require HCPs to advance recovery, the plans may actually undermine it") and p. 294 in Parenteau 1998, rejecting the services' view and arguing that section 10 "plainly states that the Secretary cannot issue an ITP unless he finds that the HCP 'will not appreciably reduce the likelihood of the survival and recovery of the species.'" See also Farrier 1995, noting that the HCPs "that have been approved involved significant compromise in terms of loss of habitat for listed species" (p. 376). Note that the federal agencies explain that the *HCP Handbook* is "intended primarily as internal agency guidance," but that it is "fully available for public evaluation and use, as appropriate." Moreover, "nothing in this handbook is intended to supersede or alter any aspect of Federal law or regulation" (*HCP Handbook,* ch. 1, pp. 1–3).

4. Ruhl points out that as more and more activities are brought under the section 7 consultation requirement, the instances in which self-permitting is possible will become fewer (p. 364).

5. See also www.nceas.ucsb.edu/projects/hcp for a summary of HCPs approved by USFWS.

6. Note, however, that the service may prepare the environmental assessment, as it did in the case of the Angelus Block Company's application for an ITP and HCP (USFWS 1999). In some cases, an environmental assessment will suffice, when an EIS would otherwise be required, if mitigation measures (which reduce impacts to less-than-significant levels) are part of the original proposal or HCP and are enforceable (*HCP Handbook,* ch. 5, pp. 3–4).

7. Compare these target processing times to the range of actual processing times, four months to three years, reported by USFWS to the GAO in 1994 (GAO 1995, p. 9).

8. Chapter 4 of the *HCP Handbook* provides suggested language for covering unlisted species for inclusion in permits.

9. Oliver Houck (1997, pp. 965–971) describes the Plum Creek Timber Company's 200,000-acre, 100-year HCP in Washington's Cascade Mountains.

10. Section 4(d) of the ESA, which gives the services greater flexibility in their regulatory approaches to recovering threatened species, provides authority for programs such as the NCCP. For a description of the NCCP, see Houck 1997 or Hood 1998.

11. The Sonoran Desert plan would appear to be a hybrid between a habitat-based and a programmatic HCP. It is worth noting that HCPs have been the object of little litigation, but Professor Ruhl (1999) predicts "that is likely to change," pointing to a recent case (*Sierra Club v. Babbitt*) that overturned two HCPs for the endangered Alabama beach mouse.

12. Professor Ruhl has opined that "just when FWS and NMFS are devoting increased attention to the HCP permit program, the universe of real estate development projects for which HCP permits are the appropriate incidental take authorization vehicle is rapidly shrinking." He noted in particular the debate over whether the ESA consultation requirement (i.e., the requirement that federal agencies consult with the services regarding the likely impacts of their proposed actions) also applies to exercises of federal authority delegated to states or tribes. For example, are state water pollution authorities obligated to consult before they authorize development activities under construction general permits, issued pursuant to their delegated authority under the federal Clean Water Act (CWA)? (EPA would consult before it issued such a permit.) If the answer to that question is yes, Ruhl says (referring to a CWA National Pollutant Discharge Elimination System general permit, recently reissued by EPA, which authorizes certain land development projects to discharge stormwater), a "significant universe of projects formerly thought to be . . . in a position to evaluate the desirability of ESA incidental take authorization without federal oversight, could disappear" (Ruhl 1999, pp. 364–372).

According to the EPA (2001), however, although states and tribes must provide the services with notices of draft CWA permits, the ESA consultation duty applies only to federal agencies, not to states or tribes. Under the CWA, however, EPA may object to a draft permit issued by a state or tribe, and it will object to any draft permit that it "determines is likely to cause the extinction of a listed species." See also *American Forest & Paper Ass'n v. EPA,* 137 F. 3d 291 (5th Cir. 1998).

13. Plainly, the USFWS may not grant an ITP if it determines the HCP would jeopardize a species, but jeopardy opinions are uncommon and seldom halt proposed actions. Although more than 100,000 consultations were conducted between 1989 and 1995, only 54 projects were terminated as a result of jeopardy opinions (Donahue 1998, pp. 246–247).

14. Ruhl (1999) identifies three "difficult issues": the interpretation of the section 10 phrases "to the maximum extent practicable," "ensure adequate

funding," and "not appreciably reduce." The USFWS's past record on "consistency" is vulnerable to criticism. Hood (1998, sect. 2, part 1) notes that a 1992 USFWS manual called for maintaining only half as much red-cockaded woodpecker foraging habitat on private land as a 1985 agency document required on federal lands.

15. As an example of nonhabitat-based mitigation, Ruhl cites Federal Fish and Wildlife Permit No. PRT-782829, issued to Beth Morian, Davenport Limited, which required the permittee to make cash payments to the USFWS's "designee for specified Geographic Information System (GIS) entry work benefitting the golden-cheeked warbler." The permit expressed the take as the "removal or alteration of 112 acres of habitat for the species."

16. Systems for ranking or classifying habitat according to its importance to species, communities, or biodiversity generally have been proposed, which might be adaptable to serving ESA goals. See, e.g., O'Connell and Noss 1992, pp. 441–448.

17. The federal *HCP Handbook* provides sample no-surprises assurances, which can be adapted for inclusion in HCP implementing agreements. The no-surprises rule can be found at 50 C.F.R. sec. 17.22(b)(5)-(6) and 17.32(b)(5)-(6).

18. Parenteau questions the policy at length, citing criticisms from other sources, including Defenders of Wildlife and the National Science Foundation. The NSF study looked at 208 HCPs, 44 in detail. The chair of the study team stated that a "huge number of HCPs . . . probably should not have been written" (Schoch 1998). See also Kostyack 1998, p. 22, describing a letter in which 167 scientists stated that the no-surprises policy "does not reflect ecological reality and rejects the best scientific knowledge and judgment," and Hood 1998, executive summary, summarizing concerns regarding policy; but compare Ruhl 1999. Parenteau's argument regarding no surprises and adaptive management notwithstanding, a strong argument can be made that adaptive management provisions can and should be included in HCPs to deal with changed circumstances, even if not applicable to unforeseen circumstances (Ruhl 1999, pp. 402–403).

19. The services had previously provided safe harbor assurances under other provisions of the ESA, but ultimately "determined that the 10(a)(1)(A) 'enhancement of survival' permit provisions provide the best mechanism to carry out a permanent Safe Harbor policy" (USFWS and NMFS 1999b, p. 32718). The "safe harbor" term itself can be misleading. It refers more accurately to landowners than to species covered by a safe harbor agreement.

20. The final safe harbor policy was implemented jointly with the final policy for candidate conservation agreements with assurances, described in the next section of this chapter. Both policies are codified in 50 C.F.R. part 17.

21. The definition of baseline conditions offered later in the notice, however, would seem to contradict the example of zero baseline conditions in the text. "Baseline conditions" is defined as "population estimates and distribution and/ or habitat characteristics and determined area of the enrolled property *that sustain seasonal or permanent use* of the covered species at the time the Safe Harbor Agreement is executed" (USFWS and NMFS 1999b, p. 32722; emphasis added). The services "clarify" this muddle by explaining that where no occupa-

tion by covered listed species is documented, baseline conditions will be deemed to be "zero" (p. 32724).

22. In the final policy document (p. 32727), the USFWS offered this rather circular explanation of its belief:

> The Services must determine that the benefits of the conservation measures implemented . . . , when combined with those benefits that would be achieved if it is assumed that conservation benefits were also to be implemented on other necessary properties, would preclude or remove any need to list the covered species. "Other necessary properties" are other properties on which conservation measures would have to be implemented in order to preclude or remove any need to list the covered species.

It seems to me that the answer to this inquiry would always be yes, except in those cases when no conservation measures could avoid the conclusion that a species is in fact threatened or endangered (and should be listed as such). At best, it is difficult to see how the services will apply such a standard.

23. The notice was ambiguous as to how many species listings were believed to have been avoided by existing CCA agreements (USFWS and NMFS 1999c, p. 32729). Chapter 4, p. 2, of the *HCP Handbook* acknowledges that "primary jurisdiction over unlisted species rests with the affected state."

24. Parenteau (1998, pp. 288–289) asserts that CCAs "can become an excuse not to list a species that should be" and cites a "string of court cases holding that pre-listing agreements were unlawful."

25. The policy document also includes this cryptic, apparently contradictory, explanation: "[I]n the event the [covered] species is listed in the future, incidental take authorization enables property owners to continue current land uses that have traditionally caused take, provided take is at or reduced to a level consistent with the overall goal of precluding or removing any need to list" (USFWS and NMFS 1999c, pp. 32733–32734). How can take be "consistent with . . . removing any need to list" when the species has already been listed?

26. At the time of its listing, the California gnatcatcher had lost 80 to 90 percent of its habitat to real estate development (Houck 1997, p. 961).

27. Other alternatives considered included participation in a multiple-species plan for the entire San Bernardino Valley (which would have required applicants to delay construction until the multiple-species HCP is complete) and development of 83 acres, dedication of a 13.4-acre conservation area, habitat restoration, and an endowment fund for maintenance and management of the conservation area.

28. See Bowles et al. (1998) for a concise survey of economic incentives, tax policies, and other "economic instruments" that could be used to promote biodiversity conservation.

References

Babbitt v. Sweet Home Chapter of Communities for a Great Oregon, 515 U.S. 687–714 (1995).

Bean, Michael J. 1998. The Endangered Species Act and private land: Four lessons learned from the past quarter century. *Environmental Law Reporter* 28:10701–10710.

Bowles, Ian, David Downes, Dana Clark, and Marianne Guerin-McManus. 1998. Economic incentives and legal tools for private sector conservation. *Duke Environmental Law and Policy Forum* 8:209–243.

Defenders of Wildlife v. Administrator, Environmental Protection Agency, 882 F. 2d 1294, 1300–1301 (8th Cir. 1989).

Defenders of Wildlife v. Bernal, CV-98-120-TUC-FRZ, slip opinion (D. Ariz. 8 May 1998), affirmed, 30 ELR 20403 (9th Cir. 2000).

Donahue, Debra L. 1998. *Conservation and the law: A dictionary.* Santa Barbara, Calif.: ABC-CLIO.

Doyle, Andrew J. 1996. Note: Sharing home *Sweet Home* with federally protected wildlife. *Stetson Law Review* 25:889–924.

Draft Addendum to the HCP Handbook. 1999. Questions and answers. Notice of availability of a draft addendum to the final handbook for habitat conservation planning and incidental take permit processing. *Federal Register* 64 (9 March): 11485–11490.

Endangered Species Act. 1996. *U.S. Code,* vol. 16, secs. 1530–1540.

EPA. 2001. Question 5. Draft memorandum of agreement regarding the Clean Water Act and the Endangered Species Act: Questions and answers. The final MOA was published in *Federal Register* 66 (22 Feb. 2001): 11202.

Farrier, D. 1995. Conserving biodiversity on private land: Incentives for management or compensation for lost expectations? *Harvard Environmental Law Review* 19:303–408.

General Accounting Office (GAO). 1992. *Endangered Species Act: Types and number of implementing actions.* GAO/RCED-92-131BR (May 1992).

———. 1995. *Endangered Species Act: Information on species protection on nonfederal lands.* Washington, D.C. GAO/RCED-95-16 (Dec. 1994).

HCP Handbook. 2000. *Habitat conservation planning and incidental take permit processing handbook,* 4 November 1996 (updated 9 February 2000). Washington, D.C.: U.S. Fish and Wildlife Service and National Marine Fisheries Service. http://endangered.fws.gov/HCP/ hcpbook.html.

Henry, Natalie M. 2000. Arizona crafts largest habitat conservation plan. *Land Letter* 19 (14 March): 1–2.

Hood, Laura C. 1998. *Frayed safety nets: Conservation planning under the Endangered Species Act.* Washington, D.C.: Defenders of Wildlife.

Houck, Oliver A. 1997. On the law of biodiversity and ecosystem management. *Minnesota Law Review* 81:869–979.

Kostyack, John. 1998. Surprise! *Environmental Forum* 15:19–22.

Loggerhead Turtle v. County Council of Volusia County, 92 F. Supp. 2d 1296 (M.D. Fla. 2000).

Marbled Murrelet v. Babbitt, 83 F. 3d 1060, 1067 (9th Cir. 1996), cert. denied sub nom., *Pacific Lumber Co. v. Marbled Murrelet,* 117 U.S. 942 (1997).

National Environmental Policy Act. 1969. *U.S. Code,* vol. 42, sections 4321–4370d.

National Research Council. 1995. *Science and the Endangered Species Act.* Washington, D.C.: National Academy Press.

National Wildlife Federation. n.d. Habitat conservation plans. www.nwf.org/ nwf/endangered/hcp/index.html.

O'Connell, Michael A., and Reed F. Noss. 1992. Private land management for biodiversity conservation. *Environmental Management* 16:435–450.

Parenteau, Patrick. 1998. Rearranging the deck chairs: Endangered Species Act reforms in an era of mass extinctions. *William and Mary Environmental Law and Policy Review* 22:227–311.

Ruhl, J. B. 1998. Taming the suburban amoeba in the ecosystem age: Some do's and don'ts. *Widener Law Symposium Journal* 3:61–86.

————.1999. How to kill endangered species, legally: The nuts and bolts of Endangered Species Act HCP permits for real estate development. *Environmental Lawyer* 5:345–405.

Salzman, James, and J. B. Ruhl. 2000. Currencies and the commodification of environmental law. *Stanford Law Review* 52:607–694.

San Bernardino Valley Audubon Society v. Metropolitan Water District of Southern California, Calif. Ct. Apps., 4th Dist., Div. 2, filed 14 April 1999 (Super. Ct. 274844).

Schoch, Deborah. 1998. New approach to protecting fragile habitats criticized. *Los Angeles Times,* 20 July.

Sierra Club v. Babbitt, 15 F. Supp. 2d 1274 (S.D. Ala. 1998).

South Carolina. 1997. South Carolina statewide incidental take permit. *Federal Register* 62:51678.

Strahan v. Coxe, 939 F. Supp. 963–985 (D. Mass. 1996), aff'd in part, vacated in part on other grounds, 127 F. 3d 155–164 (1st Cir. 1997), cert. denied, 525 U.S. 830 (1998), and cert. denied sub nom., *Coates v. Strahan,* 525 U.S. 978 (1998).

Thompson, Barton S. Jr. 1997. The Endangered Species Act: A case study in takings and incentives. *Stanford Law Review* 49:305–376.

U.S. EPA and Army Corps of Engineers. 1995. Wetland mitigation banking guidance. *Federal Register* 60 (18 Nov.): 58605.

USFWS. 1999. Applications for incidental take permits for the Delhi Sands flower-loving fly. *Federal Register* 64:37807.

USFWS and NMFS (U.S. Fish and Wildlife Service and National Marine Fisheries Service). 1998. Habitat conservation plan assurances ("no surprises") rule (final rule). *Federal Register* 63:8859–8861.

————. 1999a. Safe harbor agreements and candidate conservation agreements with assurances (final rule). *Federal Register* 64:32706–32716.

————. 1999b. Final safe harbor policy. *Federal Register* 64:32717–32726.

————. 1999c. Final policy for candidate conservation agreements with assurances. *Federal Register* 64:32726–32736.

————. 1999d. Safe harbor agreements and candidate conservation agreements with assurances (final rule, correction). *Federal Register* 64:52676.

U.S. House. 1982. H.R. Report 835, 97th Congress, 2d Session 29.

CHAPTER 3

An Economic Review of Incentive Mechanisms to Protect Species on Private Lands

GREGORY M. PARKHURST AND JASON F. SHOGREN

Most economists believe that economic incentives help guide human behavior, even when dealing with nonmarket goods like endangered species and biodiversity. Endangered species inhabiting private land can be better protected if economic incentives encourage landowners to preserve their property. Currently, the Endangered Species Act (ESA) provides some regulatory incentive for landowners to cooperate with species conservation policy through habitat conservation plans (plans that allow a landowner to alter habitat under certain management restrictions), but current financial incentives may induce landowners to prevent government biologists from looking for listed species on private property, or to destroy habitat for listed species, or to take listed and potentially listed species. These actions may result in direct harm to listed species, destroy or reduce the value of habitat, and increase the costs of designating habitat and species recovery. Agencies or private parties can attempt to prevent such actions by providing incentives for landowners to cooperate through compensation for takings, rather than through permits or criminal penalties.

The previous chapter defined where the ESA is now. The next important task in the ESA reform debate is to examine whether and how the net benefits can be increased if an amended act provides economic rewards to landowners for good stewardship of actual and prospective habitat and species thereon. Reducing risks to species depends on the cooperation of private landowners, since about half of the listed endangered species rely on private land for 80 percent of their habitat. Without their cooperation, landowners have incentive to minimize the risk of economic loss to a taking under the act by hindering the gathering of information about species on their land or, at the extreme, by destroying potential habitat overtly before the species are listed and covertly afterward. For instance, Brown and Shogren (1998) discuss the following example. An owner of 7,200 acres of timber had to forgo harvest on about 1,500 acres to protect a dozen colonies of red-cockaded woodpeckers. The owner threatened to "start massive clear-cutting" to avoid creating any additional habitat, thereby avoiding further restriction if the woodpeckers expanded to new territory.

A variety of compensation schemes are possible: direct compensation from the government to owners of land that is taken; tradable rights in habitat, under which those who wish to develop land would buy permits from those who would then not be able to develop; insurance programs under which landowners are compensated if endangered species impose costs on them, like the fund created by Defenders of Wildlife under which ranchers are compensated when wolves destroy livestock; or tax breaks to allow large chunks of land to be preserved rather than broken up to pay federal estate taxes.

This chapter reviews eight incentive mechanisms from an economics perspective: zoning, impact fees, subsidies, tradable development rights, conservation banking, fee simple acquisition, and conservation easements in the form of either purchased development rights or donations for tax relief. Examples exist of nearly all these incentive options that use compensation, and none are simple or straightforward to implement. We describe each incentive mechanism and sort through their pros and cons. We see that compensation schemes for private landowners are subject to concocted claims and possibly litigation. Trading habitat requires researchers to develop methods to measure what quantity and quality of habitat are equivalent. Tax breaks for preserving large estates might not generate more benefits than buying the land outright or preventing certain uses through an easement. We now consider the underlying economics behind each incentive mechanism.

Zoning

As a comparative benchmark for understanding the usefulness of flexible economic incentive mechanisms, we first discuss the standard approach to land use questions on endangered species: zoning. Local governments, by exercising their police power of command and control, influence activities on private property through zoning ordinances. These ordinances either specify allowable land uses or they enjoin particular activities for specific land regions (USFWS 2000). We use zoning as our comparative benchmark because it has been the standard, status quo approach for decades.

Governments have traditionally used zoning to restrict development and other land uses to protect attributes and characteristics of the environment that the government, acting in the interest of the public, deems desirable (Miller 1999). Governments use zoning to guide development toward existing infrastructure and away from environmentally sensitive areas. Zoning has also been engaged to protect scenic views, open space, vegetation and trees, and river corridors (Utah CLCC 1997).

Pros. Many people see zoning as a useful conservation mechanism because it targets both specific properties and attributes of the landscape to accomplish conservation goals. Zoning also can hit desired targets with minimum financial cost to the local government (Boyd et al. 1999; USFWS 2000), because it is the landowners whose property rights are restricted who pick up the tab for the public good.

Political pressure for more flexibility has forced many land use planning agencies to become more creative about how to make land use regulations more responsive to landowners and developers. Two examples of flexible zoning include cluster zoning (the land is divided into a high-density development cluster and an open space cluster) and performance zoning (a developer provides a certain level of conservation prior to approval of the development plan). Because of the project-by-project review process, flexible programs usually increase the administration costs to the local government and subject the developer to more governmental control (Miller 1999; Utah CLCC 1997). Flexible zoning can reduce the cost of road construction, maintenance, and infrastructure because less land is developed and it is often developed closer to existing infrastructure.

Cons. Zoning has five main problems. First, many critics depict zoning as rigid, static, and inflexible. Most attempts to increase the flexibility in zoning laws usually increase governmental administrative costs, increase costs due to time delays and application processes to the developer, and increase government control resulting from project-by-project review and discretion of developer plans (Kayden 1992; Miller 1999). This inflexibility is the main driver for the use of economic incentive mechanisms, in which landowners and developers have the freedom to find creative ways to lower their costs to hit a conservation target.

Second, zoning is an effective and noncontroversial tool when the restrictions represent a win-win situation, but inflexible regulation of land uses rarely results in mutual gains. It is more a question of a redistribution of wealth from traditional sectors like agriculture to newer sectors like recreation. The more typical outcome is that a small fraction of society bears a disproportionate amount of the costs to provide a public good. The threat of restricting development rights without compensation creates an incentive for landowners to develop their land to avoid suffering possible losses from future regulation (Miller 1999; Epstein 1996; Boyd et al. 1999).

How opportunity costs fall across industries has been estimated for critical habitat designation in a few cases like the Virgin River basin. Several conclusions emerge from these studies. The difference in economic output for a county with and without critical habitat designation is relatively small, often measuring in the range of one-fiftieth of a percentage point (Brown and Shogren 1998). The impact of critical habitat designation on regional income, tax revenues, and employment is similar. The real consequence is a transfer of wealth to recreation and environmental interests from agriculture in the region.

Third, zoning has been criticized for its susceptibility to political pressure and rent seeking, which can cause a community to waste scarce resources fighting over how an economic pie is divided up rather than using these resources to produce a bigger pie. Political pressure can guide land use decisions away from the more science-based "best land management" techniques (Miller 1999; Kayden 1992). Rent seeking is intensified by the lack of permanence of zoning schemes and the court system. Private ownership gives rational landowners incentive to expend resources seeking changes in zoning laws to provide them greater returns from their land. Conservationists also have incentive to use resources fighting over how rigid the zoning laws will or should be. Both sides expend valuable resources battling over the degree of flexibility of a zoning scheme, a conflict that could be avoided with a more flexible system of economic incentives (see for instance Settle et al. 2001).

Fourth, zoning does not guarantee that the land with the largest net benefit to society is the land that is conserved. Government would need to obtain private information regarding landowners' land use values to minimize the cost of conservation efforts to society as a whole. This is because of what economists call information rents; private information about a landowner's economic circumstances causes the regulator to pay more than necessary to achieve a given target. (This is discussed at length in Chapter 8.) If the regulator cannot distinguish between landowners, it will have to pay top dollar to them all, which means the cost of conservation is not minimized. Zoning, like most forms of command and control, does not have an instrument to accomplish this task (Boyd et al. 1999).

The more flexible rules like cluster and performance zoning, because of the project-by-project scrutiny, can be designed to leave the highest-valued conservation land undeveloped. But this must be done on a project-by-project basis. For example, it is possible that society's interests would be best served by conserving one landowner's entire landholdings while developing the property of a second landowner. Zoning instruments alone, however, do not allow such land use patterns and therefore can create the fragmented habitat that puts species recovery at risk (Saunders et al. 1991).

Fifth, zoning has high monitoring and enforcement costs, with or without a habitat conservation plan in place (Boyd et al. 1999). The opportunity costs to monitor and enforce the ESA include the forgone opportunities due to restrictions placed on the use of property as a result of listings, designation of critical habitat, and recovery plans. Opportunity costs also include the reduced economic rents from restricted or altered development projects, agriculture production, timber harvesting, minerals extraction, recreation activities, wages lost by displaced workers who remain unemployed or who are re-employed at lower wages, lower consumer surplus due to higher prices, and lower capital asset value.

The costs without an HCP involve trying to gain access and monitor private property to ensure the landowner is complying with the ESA and potential land use changes. This is a challenge since landowners have to be assumed innocent until proven guilty. The government cannot just enter private property without just cause, which takes resources to establish. If a landowner has an HCP in place, then the private transaction costs for dealing with the act include the time and money spent applying for permits and licenses, redesigning plans, and legal fees. Estimates of these costs for the act do not exist. As a crude comparison, the Comprehensive Environmental Response, Compensation, and Liability Act of 1980, or Superfund, generates private party transaction costs of about 30 cents on the dollar (Brown and Shogren 1998). The ESA does not have the same liability system as Superfund, which suggests its transaction costs should be lower.

Impact Fees

An impact fee is a cash or in-kind payment by a developer to a government as a precondition to receive a development permit. Governments often require developers to expend resources to create a local public good like a park, as a precondition to receiving the necessary permits for development. These expenditures are called exactions, and they take the form of either a cash payment or a land donation, public parks, streets, or other public goods (Altschuler and Gomez-Ibanez 1993). Regardless of whether the land use exaction is a cash payment or an in-kind transfer, the developer assigns a cost to receiving the development permit— the impact fee.

Impact fees have become popular in the last two decades. The goal of an impact fee is to offset the negative consequences of development to the surrounding environment and existing infrastructure. Developers pay an impact fee, for instance, as a condition for receiving permits for new projects that would otherwise increase the demand for existing public goods and services. The revenues received from impact fees finance the provision of new public goods such as parks, recreational facilities, and open space and the improvement of roads and telecommunications (Altschuler and Gomez-Ibanez 1993; Utah CLCC 1997).

Local governments can also issue bonds as an alternative financial tool to fund the acquisition and construction of public goods to satisfy the increase in demand that results from new development. The bonds, upon maturity, are typically paid for through the community's general tax fund, which places the burden of funding on all local residents. In contrast, impact fees are usually paid when the developer obtains a permit, which allows the new public goods to be created before completion of the development project. Impact fees have the additional attribute that those creating the new demand for public goods pay for that demand, allowing existing residents to maintain a level of public good provision by requiring development to pay its own way (Brueckner 1997).

A local government's right to assess an impact fee on new development rests in its regulatory authority, which is authorized by the state. This use of police power by local governments has encountered its share of conflict, and litigation has resulted in court rulings that specify that a "rational nexus" between the impact fee and the development's negative impact on the community must exist. To be legal, the impact fee must exhibit a direct relationship between the externalities caused by the developer's activities and the purpose for which the fees are used. (See

Altschuler and Gomez-Ibanez 1993 and Miller 1999 for further discussion.) Establishing such a cause and effect requires an accurate forecast of future demand for a public good, which is always a challenge because of the imprecision of economic information.

Another alternative to impact fees for mitigating adverse environmental effects of new development projects is performance bonds, deposits that developers pay prior to initiating a project to ensure that predetermined onsite quality levels are met. The developer must pay up-front the costs as they arise and must oversee the project to ensure that standards are met. Once the regulator determines that the developer has met the contract conditions, the performance bond is refunded (Hanley et al. 1997). In contrast, impact fees are paid when the developer purchases his permit, are generally not refundable, and are used for offsite projects that benefit society as a whole. The municipality determines how, where, and for what the impact fees are to be spent, but these projects must be reasonably related to the development and be justified by the community's general plan. (See Altschuler and Gomez-Ibanez 1993, pp. 49–54.)

Pros. Impact fees have the benefit of restricting development to those efficient cases in which the land will be developed only if the expected profit from development exceeds the impact fee assessed the developer. The regulator could also try to quantify society's benefits from development control, compare them with the costs faced by the developer (i.e., expected profits forgone), and adjust the impact fee so that the incremental gains just equal the incremental costs. Although challenging, setting the impact fee at that level allows a local government to maximize the net benefits to society by limiting development to only that land that provides a net benefit.

To determine this optimal development level, however, the regulator still needs to know the value of the landowner's alternative uses and the value society puts on conservation—information rarely available to regulators. Because of the uncertainty about landowners' incremental costs and society's benefits, the calculation of an impact is at best an educated guess, affected as much by politics and economics as it is sound science; therefore, it is unlikely that society would maximize its net benefits with the initial selection of an impact fee. The hope is that over time, the push and pull of the political arena would help move the impact fee toward a level that would balance society's desires for affordable housing and protected habitat.

The use of impact fees increased rapidly among local governments during the last half of the twentieth century, from a rarity before 1960

SAN JOAQUIN KIT FOX
Vulpes macrotis mutica

Status: The San Joaquin kit fox was designated as an endangered species in March 1967. The kit fox is found in California and is considered a keystone species within its ecosystem. Protecting habitat for the kit fox also provides critical habitat for numerous other threatened and endangered species (e.g., California jewelflower, Hoover's wooly-star, and the Tipton kangaroo rat).

Habitat: For survival the kit fox requires large expanses of grassland and scrubland. It depends on its surrounding area to provide an abundance of prey, primarily nocturnal rodents, hares, and squirrels. As is the case for many other species, the reproductive success of this fox is tied to the effort necessary to forage for food. As prey become scarcer, the kit fox must expend more effort to hunt for food, and the fox's reproduction diminishes.

Threats: The initial threat to the kit fox was agricultural, industrial, and urban development, which reduced the stock of habitat and also fragmented the remaining habitat into smaller habitat areas. More recently, natural occurrences such as starvation, flooding, drought, and both natural and human-induced predation have been the primary threats to the kit fox's existence (http://arnica.csustan.edu/esrpp/).

Incentive mechanisms: Impact fees, fee simple acquisition

The Metropolitan Bakersfield Habitat Conservation Plan Trust Group oversees the implementation of this habitat conservation plan. The plan requires landowners to pay an impact fee when developing their land. The impact fee is based on a flat rate applied to the acreage of the development project ($1,250 per acre in 1994). The funds are used to acquire and manage habitat. Since 1994 more than 4,000 acres of habitat have been protected. The trust group determines what habitat to purchase and monitors development activities (www.ci.bakersfield.ca.us/cityservices/).

to nearly 60 percent of all communities in the United States by 1980. Although some communities determine impact fees according to a formula, the most common method is for the developer and the local government to negotiate the amount of the impact fee. On average, impact fees accounted for approximately 5 percent of development costs, with an average fee of $12,000 for a three-bedroom, single-family home of 2,000 square feet and between $5 and $7 per square foot for nonresidential structures (Altschuler and Gomez-Ibanez 1993).

DuPage County in Illinois illustrates the ability of impact fees to limit development. DuPage County, which consists of 29 municipalities, was estimated by the U.S. Census Bureau to be the fastest-growing county in Illinois from 1970 to 1990. Each municipality varied in the use and timing of impact fees. Researchers collected time-series data over the two decades and used statistical tools to correct for inherent differences across the counties. Their empirical results suggest that impact fees significantly decreased residential development over the fifteen years from 1977 to 1992 (Skidmore and Peddle 1998).

Cons. Impact fees have three main problems. First, a regulator interested in using the fee to achieve economic efficiency should have reasonable information on the relative sensitivity of the benefits and costs to each additional unit (acre) of conservation. This means the regulator should understand how many extra benefits go to society from one more acre of conservation and how many extra costs accrue to developers from that extra acre. If the regulator is uncertain about the benefits to society or the cost to developers, using an impact fee can lead to unpredictable conservation efforts. For instance, suppose the regulator knows the benefits but does not know the costs. Here the effectiveness of the impact fee depends on the sensitivity of benefits to extra acres. If each parcel conserved provides a constant benefit to society, the regulator equates the impact fee to this fixed benefit per unit of conservation. The landowner conserves his land if the expected profits from development are less than the impact fee, or he develops the land if the expected profits are at least as great as the impact fee; either case leads to the greatest net benefit to society.

Alternatively, if people demand nearly the same amount of conservation at any price, the effectiveness of the impact fee diminishes. Again a regulator tries to set the impact fee at the level where the incremental benefits equal the expected incremental costs of conservation. If the regulator underestimates the actual costs, the impact fee is set too low and some landowners develop land best used for conservation. If the actual costs are overestimated, the impact fee is set too high and too much land is conserved. Society would be better off if more land was developed. The more the estimated costs deviate from actual costs, the worse the outcome of the impact fees, providing either too much or too little conservation (Hanley et al. 1997, pp. 65–66; Boyd et al. 1999).

Second, land parcels differ in the benefits they provide to the public (Boyd et al. 1999). It may be that the land with the greatest developed value is also the land with the greatest conservation value, in which case, an impact fee mechanism may decrease social welfare (i.e., fewer net benefits to society). To maximize social welfare, a mechanism to control development should have a component targeted to develop land that provides the largest net benefit to society—a component generally absent from impact fee schemes. With an impact fee, the decision to develop depends on the difference between expected profits and the costs of the fee. The land will be developed, regardless of its conservation value, when the profits exceed the total costs, including the impact fee. A more effective impact fee scheme for conservation would be tailored to individual properties, which leads us to another problem.

Third, tailoring an impact fee to an individual property requires the regulator to acquire and verify land-specific data about species populations and other biological information. Even if the needed data can be acquired, assigning a conservation value to the land parcel remains a formidable task; no agreed-upon method currently exists for determining that value (Polasky et al. 1997; this question is also examined in Chapter 6). Finally, if controversy surrounds the conservation value of the land parcel, such that a direct relationship between the impact fee and the public good for which it is assessed is questionable, the landowner can seek relief through legal actions, which increases the regulator's monitoring and enforcement costs (witness the litigation over natural resource damage assessment).

Assume for a moment that a noncontroversial method exists for assessing the land's conservation value. If so, the impact fee is set at that value relative to the development benefits. Land parcels assessed an impact fee greater than the developed value are conserved; those less than the developed value are developed. Because impact fees are typically assessed on the developer when the developer seeks a building permit, basing impact fees on the conservation value of land provides the developer more incentive to decrease the value of the impact fee by destroying the habitat quality of his land prior to applying for permits (see Innes et al. 1998; Innes 1997).

Of course, not all developers follow through with this temptation, but the incentive still exists to destroy the habitat before listing occurs (known as the "shoot, shovel, and shut up" strategy). The print media routinely report cases of habitat destruction triggered by an anticipation of listing (Brown and Shogren 1998). For example, ten days before the Fish and Wildlife Service listed the golden-cheeked warbler, a firm owned by Ross Perot hired migrant workers with chain saws to destroy hundreds of acres of oak and juniper warbler habitat (Mann and Plummer 1995). Wilcove et al. (1996) cite this incentive as "one reason why

GOLDEN-CHEEKED WARBLER
Dendroica chrysoparia

Status: The golden-cheeked warbler was listed as endangered in May 1990 because of a significant decline in its population and a continuing reduction in its nesting habitat. This warbler winters in Mexico and Central America but migrates for breeding to the cedar brakes of the Texas Hill Country from the early part of March to the end of August.

Habitat: For nesting habitat the golden-cheeked warbler requires a combination of mature Ashe junipers and hardwoods in a closed-canopy woodland, a habitat that occurs solely in Texas, where 97 percent of all land is privately owned.

Threats: The primary source of habitat loss was tree clearing for fence building and to improve pasture for cattle. More recently urbanization has contributed significantly to habitat loss. Also, as habitat is lost, fragmentation results in greater edge effects, which increase the threat to the warbler from natural nest predators, such as cowbirds, raccoons, blue jays, and feral cats.

Incentive mechanisms: Subsidy, cost sharing, and technical support

The Environmental Defense Fund initiated a program in which landowners are provided subsidies, cost sharing, and technical support. Landowners are paid to restore land as nesting habitat, remove invasive juniper species, conduct prescribed burns, and trap cowbirds. Landowners are protected from increased land use regulations under Environmental Defense's safe harbor agreement. As of February 2001, more than 58,000 acres had been enrolled by 25 landowners in Texas.

so many species are teetering on the very brink of extinction by the time they receive protection."

Subsidy

Subsidies are financial assistance offered to landowners by regulators. Subsidies can be used to create an incentive that encourages landowners to maintain their land in an undeveloped state or to mitigate the environmental impact of development by helping the landowner meet maintenance and restoration costs of environmentally sensitive areas. Subsidies usually take the form of grants, loans, cash payments, or tax allowances that are offered by federal, state, or nonprofit organizations

(Hanley et al. 1997). Subsidy programs are funded by numerous methods, including tax revenue, lottery funds, and special permits. Four examples serve to illustrate how subsidies are used in species protection.

Example 1. Tax Benefits
California's Timber Tax Credit

The California Department of Fish and Game (CDFG) administers a subsidy program called the Timber Tax Credit Program. The program induces private landowners to undertake conservation projects voluntarily to improve habitat, along with the probability of survival of the coho and chinook salmon and the steelhead trout. It provides a tax credit of up to $50,000 to a landowner on completion of the approved project. Approved projects include the restoration of the stream banks or other improvements to the flow of the stream, revegetating the habitat with indigenous plants, and performing upland work to reduce sediment runoff and to improve the timing and distribution of water returning to the stream. Many projects decrease the speed of the flow of the stream and cool the temperature of the water (CRA 2000).

A landowner who is interested in participating in the program submits an application listing the applicant's personal information, a brief description of the proposed project, an estimate of total and qualified project costs, location, directions to the proposed project, estimated time frame, type of fish that will likely benefit from the project, and the tax credit recipient's name and I.D. number. This tax credit information is accompanied by two more pieces of information: a detailed description of the proposed project and a detailed estimate of the project costs.

Upon receipt of the application and attachments, the CDFG determines if the proposed project complies with state and federal law. Projects in compliance are given an initial onsite inspection and then can be approved for tax credit. A final inspection of the project is conducted within 30 days of completion, and if the project satisfies the inspection, a tax credit certificate is issued within 90 days (CRA 2000).

Tax credits can be up to 10 percent of the estimated qualified costs of the proposed project (labor, materials, and in some instances rental of heavy equipment). The costs must be incurred for purposes that directly increase the survival rate of salmon and steelhead. Costs associated with the installation of water pumps, well drilling, permanent roads and buildings, and services rendered by professional engineers do not qualify. At the end of the year, the CDFG sums the estimated qualified costs for all of the completed approved projects and then divides $500,000 by that summed number to obtain the tax credit percentage, which cannot exceed 10 percent. The estimated qualified costs are then multiplied by the tax credit percentage, and the landowner is issued a tax credit in that amount. This tax credit is levied against the net tax, and if not completely used in the year issued, the remaining credit can be applied to tax liabilities in future years. The timber tax credit is funded by a tax placed on timber sales outside the United States and receives approximately $500,000 a year, which is entirely issued in credits. The costs of administering the program are covered by a nondedicated preservation fund (CRA 2000).

Example 2. Cost Share
Idaho's Habitat Improvement Program

Idaho's Department of Fish and Game (IDFG) is the administrator of the Habitat Improvement Program, a cost-share program that allocates funds for improvements on both private and public lands. Idaho recognizes the role that private landowners play in providing habitat for both upland game and wild birds. The primary objective of the program is to encourage private landowners to invest in habitat restoration and enhancement projects that will increase the populations of wild birds (IDFG 2000). The IDFG introduced the program because changes in agricultural production practices (both new forms of irrigation and more use of marginal land) affected bird populations.

The IDFG attributes the increased attrition of wild birds, in part, to farmers' decreased dependence on water canal systems. New irrigating technologies, such as sprinkling systems, make canals obsolete. As a result, farmers have lined irrigation ditches with concrete or removed them completely, thereby eliminating habitat areas that provided wild game birds with winter homes and nesting areas necessary for reproduction. The other threat to the population of wild birds is the increased use of land by farmers, as they employ land that was previously idle and often occupied by wild birds.

Landowners interested in participating in Habitat Improvement can contact the local office of the IDFG, which will provide a habitat biologist to evaluate the land and design the habitat restoration project so that it will benefit upland game and wild birds. Not all landowner requests are funded. For those projects that are funded, IDFG personnel assist the landowner in locating indigenous vegetation and provide other technical information. Accepted projects can encompass revegetating or creating riparian areas, erecting fences to keep livestock away from wild game habitat, creating water sources, establishing windbreaks, or providing wild animals with winter forage. Projects that provide a benefit to the local wildlife can be implemented on land parcels of all sizes and shapes, and in conjunction with other government programs such as the Conservation Reserve Program (IDFG 2000).

Landowners with accepted projects enter into an agreement with the IDFG that documents the project plan and specifies the landowner's requirement to maintain the land, which typically extends for a period greater than ten years. The IDFG reimburses up to 75 percent of the landowner's costs, 37.5 percent for projects on lands enrolled in the Conservation Reserve Program, with a maximum of $2,000 per project. The IDFG encourages, but doesn't require, project participants to allow public access to their land, and landowners can leave the program at any time by returning the cost-share funding (IDFG 2000).

Example 3. Cost Share
Washington's Salmon Recovery Funding Board

The Salmon Recovery Funding Board administers a program whose purpose is to "support salmon recovery by funding habitat protection and restoration projects and related programs and activities that produce sustainable and measurable benefits for fish and their habitat." The board consists of ten members, five appointed by the governor of the state of Washington, one of which is a representative of the governor's cabinet. State agency directors from the departments of Ecology, Game and Fish, Natural Resources, and Transportation and the State Conservation Commission make up the remaining five board members. Only the five appointed board members are given the right to vote on the procedures and policies associated with obtaining salmon recovery funding (SRFB 2000b).

Funds are made available to private landowners, state agencies, cities, counties, conservation districts, special purpose districts, Native American tribes, and nonprofit organizations. The funds are obtained through a two-step process. Step one has the landowner or other interested party submit its proposed projects to the local lead entity, which can be a nonprofit organization, local government, or tribal government but must be agreed on by the cities, counties, and tribes within the region the lead entity is to serve.

The requirements the lead entities place on the applicant vary from region to region, but they must include several board-mandated criteria. The minimum cost of a project must be at least $5,000, and the board requires the applicant to provide matching funds of 15 percent of the requisitioned funds to increase the probability of the project being completed. Next, the proposal should specify the exact location of the project, unless the applicant can prove that the project could be located anywhere within a specified region.

Finally, to be eligible for funding, the project must be one of eight types: (1) Acquisition of land in its entirety or acquisition of a "purchased development rights" easement. (2) Improvements to fish migration up- and downstream. (3) Creation of screening to keep fish away from in-stream diversions, such as dams or headgates, or creation of a fish bypass. (4) Improvements to the habitat below the high-water mark, including increasing or decreasing the amount of gravel, rocks, wood, and plants in the streambed, along the stream banks, or in the floodplain. (5) Improvements in the quality of the riparian area, including planting indigenous habitat, removing invasive plants, fencing the area off from livestock, repairing stream crossings, or improving the quality of the water supply. (6) Improvements to the area outside the riparian area, or upland, that decrease the sediment runoff, provide shade for cooling the water, and affect the time it takes for water to reach the stream. (7) Projects that are a combination of any of the above, in particular those projects that provide for both the acquisition and restoration of salmon habitat. (8) Evaluations, studies, and reports can be funded if they are justified as needed to improve the administration of the program (SRFB 2000b).

Step two requires the lead entities across the state to submit a prioritized list of projects to the board. This list is then scrutinized according to the board's funding policies and a scientific evaluation and assessment of each project. Each project must be accompanied by a standard application, which includes general information such as the project type, organization type, name, address, phone number of both the organization and the contact person, a description of the project, requested funding, how the requirement for the matching contribution is to be met, project cost estimates, and a biological assessment that addresses species information, habitat factors, necessary permits, and measurement information (SRFB 2000a).

To aid the board in evaluating projects, each project on the list must also answer three threshold questions and six evaluation questions. The

HOOD CANAL SUMMER-RUN CHUM SALMON
Oncorhynchus keta

Status: The Hood Canal summer-run chum salmon was listed as a threatened species on 2 August 1999.

Habitat: These salmon spawn in tributaries to the Hood Canal. In 1994 the summer-run chum spawned in seven of the twelve streams that were identified as recently supporting spawning populations. In six of the seven remaining spawning beds, the salmon populations were declining. Of particular concern was the decrease in the Discovery Bay and Sequim Bay fisheries.

Threats: The primary threats to the existence of the Hood Canal summer run are diminishing habitat quality, harvesting, low stream flows, and competition with the fall chum salmon.

Incentive mechanisms: Conservation easement, fee simple acquisition

The Jefferson Land Trust, in cooperation with the Washington Department of Fish and Wildlife, Jefferson County Conservation District, North Olympic Salmon Coalition, Wild Olympic Salmon, Trout Unlimited, and Jefferson County, received a $400,000 grant from the Salmon Recovery Funding Board to protect streams that provide habitat for the Hood Canal summer-run chum salmon. The Jefferson Land Trust will protect the streams by purchasing conservation easements or buying the land through fee simple acquisition (Land Trust Alliance, www.lta.org).

threshold questions address how the project is to be monitored for effectiveness, the long-term plan for managing and maintaining the project, and whether the proposed project is already legally required to be undertaken. The evaluation questions provide the board with information concerning the expected benefit of the project to the survival of salmon, how well the project complements other projects or programs for salmon recovery, the scientific basis or conservation plan that supports the project, the cost effectiveness of the project, the ability of the project coordinator to complete the proposed project, and the reason that the project should be undertaken (SRFB 2000a,b).

After receiving the applications and other relevant information, a technical panel of people with experience and expertise in various scientific fields and employees of the USFWS and NMFS evaluate the projects. The evaluation specifies whether the project has a high benefit to salmon, the level of certainty the project exhibits, and the importance of the project on a regional scale. Based on the evaluation, recommendations are presented to the board in the form of a report, which is used in the decision-making process. Once decisions are made, the recipients of funding deal directly with the board and the Office of the Interagency Committee for Outdoor Recreation, who are responsible for monitoring and enforcing agreements. Funding is provided on a reimbursement basis and cannot exceed the requested funding allotment (SRFB 2000b).

Example 4. Conservation Leasing
The USDA's Conservation Reserve Program

The Conservation Reserve Program (CRP) was established when Congress passed the Food Security Act of 1985, with its initial goal to reduce the amount of soil erosion by paying farmers to idle highly erodible lands (Environmental Defense Fund 2000). The program was reauthorized under the Food, Agriculture, Conservation, and Trade Act of 1990, and its goals were extended to include environmental concerns and improvements in the quality of water, along with the previous goal of reducing soil erosion (Farm Service Agency 2000).

In 1994 the priority placed on environmental considerations increased, and the program was redirected to enlist land that provided for greater environmental benefits. To increase the enrollment of environmentally sensitive lands, the U.S. Department of Agriculture announced that owners of less sensitive lands—lands not "devoted to high-priority conservation practices" or lands over 100 feet away from rivers, streams, and other bodies of water—were allowed an early release from Conservation Reserve contracts. Lands that opted out were replaced with lands along riverbanks or other riparian areas, or lands that served as filter strips. The USDA paid extra for environmentally sensitive lands to encourage landowners possessing the more desirable land to enroll (Farm Service Agency 1997c).

The passage of the Federal Agricultural Improvement and Reform Act of 1996 confirmed the environmental focus of 1994. Under the 1996 law, the enrollment of conservation reserve lands was capped at 36.4 million acres, and the program was to be extended through the year 2002. As of 1996, nearly 33 million acres had been taken out of production as a result of program enrollment, with an average annual subsidy of roughly $50 per acre and a total cost of around $1.8 million per year (Farm Service Agency 1997a).

Landowners or land tenants interested in enrolling their land in the program have two options. The first option is to wait for a program sign-up period, when an interested landowner or tenant may submit a bid that meets certain eligibility criteria to the local Farm Service Agency office. A considered bid must be for land that has been placed in productive agricultural use for at least two of the last five years and can legally be used for agricultural purposes in future years, or for pasture land that is enrolled in the Water Bank Program or can be planted to trees to serve as a windshield or buffer for a riparian area. If the land is cropland, it must be considered to be highly erodible, a wetland, have significant environmental benefits restored, be located in a Conservation Reserve priority region, surround uncultivated wetlands, or be likely to experience scour erosion. Furthermore, the applicant must have been farming the land for the twelve months prior to the sign-up deadline, unless the applicant acquired the land by deed purchase or inheritance due to the death of the previous owner, the land changed hands in foreclosure procedures, or the Farm Service Agency is relatively certain that the land was not acquired with the purpose of exploiting the program (Farm Service Agency 1997a).

Upon approval for eligibility, the applicant submits a bid that represents the necessary subsidy or lease payment that is required for the applicant to idle his or her land, which for consideration can't exceed a set maximum rental rate. The applicant also includes a description of restoration projects that will be undertaken if the land is approved for funding. If approved plants are established on the land, a cost-share program reimburses 50 percent of the applicant's restoration costs. If the restoration project is to occur on wetlands, up to 75 percent of the restoration costs may be reimbursed (Farm Service Agency 1997a).

Many more applicants apply for funds than the program can accept. Decisions on what lands to protect are determined by a formula called the environmental benefits index (EBI), which assigns points to projects according to six environmental characteristics and the project's cost. The higher the point total, the better the chance that the applicant's land will receive funding. The primary factors are the benefits provided to wildlife (in particular existing or restored habitat cover and the significance of the land for listed species), the quality of water, and soil protection, each having the potential for 100 points.

Management and maintenance plans are awarded up to 50 points based on the probability that the plans will be carried out in the long run. The increased air quality that will result from windbreaks and the resulting decrease in land erosion from wind factors account for a maximum of 35 points. The location of the land is valued at a maximum of 25 points, with the most points awarded to projects in regions deemed the most significant or highest priority for state and national conservation efforts. There is no set maximum point allocation for the cost factor, but more points are earned if no cost-share dollars are needed and if the cost per acre is below the maximum acceptable rental rate, which is determined separately for each county and is based on the soil productivity relative to other counties and the local rental value of dryland (Farm Service Agency 1997a). An applicant's probability of being selected is most influenced by planting the cover mixture that is scored highest, with other significant factors being sensitive lands and bidding for a lower subsidy (Farm Service Agency 1997c).

The second option for lands to be entered into the program is through the continuous sign-up. This option has the same requirements as the periodical sign-up, with the extra requirement that the land has to have a high priority for conservation. To satisfy the high-priority criterion, the land must be suitable as one of the following: "Riparian buffers; Filter strips; Grass waterways; Shelter belts; Field windbreaks; Living snow fences; Contour grass strips; Salt tolerant vegetation; or Shallow water areas for wildlife." The applicant is still able to receive 50-percent cost sharing for restoration and can qualify for additional bonuses of 20 percent and 10 percent of the annual rental rate by providing various lands and land attributes and for location in a designated EPA "wellhead protection area." The duration of contracts for both types of sign-ups is 10 to 15 years (Farm Service Agency 1997b).

A criticism of Conservation Reserve and other conservation leasing programs is that the funds used to lease the land could have been applied to purchasing conservation easements and the land could have been preserved in perpetuity (Wiebe et al. 1996). A response to this critical view is that it is questionable whether one could have secured the same magnitude of land for the cost and that conservation leasing provides the time necessary to obtain funding and evaluate projects and apply the government's limited resources more efficiently. Plus, conservation leasing provides incentives to landowners to provide and improve habitat for endangered species. Some also argue that the compensation that landowners receive might change their attitudes toward species—they now see endangered species as an asset rather than a liability (Environmental Defense Fund 2000).

Pros. Federal and state subsidy programs are usually designed to protect specific attributes of the environment. In general, the process to participate in the program includes an application, conservation plan, and an initial and final inspection. For many subsidy programs, landowners are not paid until the final inspection has been conducted and approved, providing the government agency considerable project discretion and oversight. Government agencies are able to choose the projects that satisfy some predesigned evaluation process and pick those projects that meet the goals of the program at the least cost, examples being the two-stage technical evaluation process employed by the Salmon Recovery Funding Board and the Conservation Reserve Program's environmental benefits index (Farm Service Agency 1997c; SRFB 2000b). Government agencies can oversee those projects and can provide the landowner with cost-reducing technical assistance.

Programs such as Conservation Reserve and Salmon Recovery are designed to generate the maximum amount of benefits per dollar spent, in which the basis for measuring benefits is determined by the program's objectives. A study of the Conservation Reserve Program by Babcock et al. (1996) compares the efficiency of three targeting instruments used to increase the benefits from wind erosion, water quality, soil erosion, and wildlife habitat projects when the regulator is constrained by a limited budget. The targeting instruments are to retire (1) land with lowest costs, (2) land with greatest environmental benefits, and (3) lands with the greatest benefits per dollar spent. The Babcock study finds that using an instrument that retires the land that provides the greatest number of benefits per dollar spent maximizes environmental benefits when summing the benefits from all environmental amenities. When considering each individual environmental amenity, however, they find that the efficient targeting instrument varies.

The regulator should also consider the effect on the landowners' decisions about idle lands prior to establishing and implementing the subsidy policy. Taking land out of production and placing it in conservation may create incentives for the landowner to place idle land into production to try and capture the subsidy. The initial reduction in production may increase the market price of the commodity, or the landowner may face economies of scale that now make land profitable that was not before. In an analysis of the effectiveness of Conservation Reserve in the central United States, Wu (2000) finds that for every 5 acres enrolled in the program, 1 acre of idle land is converted to productive uses, which results in overstatements of benefits by approximately 10 to 15 percent. Wildlife benefits from lands enrolled in the program have been estimated to be approximately $428 million annually (Wu 2000; Wu et al. 2001).

Many programs administered by states and nonprofit organizations are designed to complement federal programs (IDFG 2000), and information that details the different programs and specifies which programs can be used in unison is often provided (see, for instance, the Web pages maintained by the Idaho Fish and Game and Texas Parks and Wildlife departments regarding funding for habitat improvement and wildlife management on private lands). Incentive programs that work with other state and federal incentive programs can reduce the landowner's out-of-pocket expenses and thereby can increase the number of willing participants.

Cons. The primary problem with using a subsidy program as a mechanism for conservation is that it is expensive, requiring the government agencies to fund both the subsidy and the costs of administering the program. As the application and review processes become more extensive, the more costly it is to administer the subsidy, resulting in either a larger budget or less conservation. Every dollar transferred to the landowner to subsidize land conservation actually costs the government more than a dollar because of the idea of opportunity cost, or the cost of forgone alternatives not provided. If the regulator has a set budget, money used for administration is diverted from conservation. The difference between the government's costs to administer and fund the program and the actual subsidy payments is lost to conservation. Economists call this extra cost a deadweight loss (see for instance Laffont 1995; Smith and Shogren 2001, 2002). Estimates of deadweight loss in government programs have been in the range of 10 to 30 percent of every dollar spent (Innes 2000).

The budget required to administer and fund a subsidy program must be appropriated either by imposing new taxes or by taking the funds away from other worthy programs, such as education or health care (Smith and Shogren 2001, 2002). Collecting and distributing taxes further increases the deadweight loss associated with administration and is often opposed by taxpayers. Reallocating existing monies away from other popular programs creates the potential to constitute a loss in total benefits provided to society; society is now getting less overall benefit per dollar spent. The loss in government's provision of total benefits adds to the deadweight loss of the subsidy program.

A regulator who knows with certainty the land use values of each landowner participating in the subsidy program could tailor the subsidy to each landowner and obtain the most net benefits for society. Society achieves its highest benefit level when the subsidy payment to the landowner equals the landowner's cost to conserve the land, and when the costs to the government of both the subsidy and the deadweight loss equal the benefit provided to society from conserving the land (Laffont 1995; Smith and Shogren 2001, 2002).

For example, consider a landowner who receives a subsidy from the government for taking his land out of productive use and placing it in conservation use. We use some illustrative numbers to make our point. The subsidy is equal to the productive value of the land, which is, say, $40 per acre, and is constant across all acres. Suppose the government incurs costs of $1.25 for every $1 paid out in subsidies. Assume the first acre placed in conservation provides society with a conservation value of $99, the second acre $98, the third acre $97, and so on for each additional acre, with the conservation value decreasing by $1 from the previous acre, so that the fiftieth acre provides society with a conservation value of $50. The government retires acres until the per-acre cost of conserving land, $50, equals the incremental benefit received from the last acre conserved. Under these circumstances, 50 acres are set aside for conservation at a payment of $40 per acre. Society receives a benefit equal to the conservation value of $50 for the fiftieth acre, and the government will spend $50 to obtain it, $40 to the landowner and $10 to deadweight loss. Note that if no deadweight loss existed, such that $1 of public money bought $1 of conservation, 60 acres would be conserved at a cost of $40 per acre.

In the first scenario with deadweight loss, society's net benefit equals the sum of conservation values across all 50 acres conserved less the $50 per acre paid in subsidies, which is equal to $1,225. Without deadweight loss, society's net benefit is equal to $1,770, which is the sum across the 60 acres of the conservation value less acquisition costs of $40 per acre. The total deadweight loss of the first situation is $545, and the loss to society increases when the regulator does not know each landowner's private land use information.

It is highly unlikely, however, that the regulator will have full information about landowners' private land use values. If the regulator is limited to setting a uniform subsidy for all types of landowners, she can achieve the desired level of conservation at the price of overpaying some landowner types. For example, suppose the regulator knows that all land parcels are of equal size and each landowner's private use value has an equally likely chance of taking any number within the range of $50 to $100. To conserve half the land, the regulator would set the subsidy at $75. Landowners with private use values of $75 or less enter the subsidy program; those landowners who have private use values greater than $75 will retain their land in productive uses. Landowners with private use values less than $75 earn more by conserving their land than they would earn otherwise; their excess earnings are the information rents we defined earlier, extra rents earned by those with private information about their preferences or skill or both (Smith and Shogren 2002).

Reducing information rents requires that the regulator set a menu of subsidy programs to induce landowners to reveal their private land use values. One way to get the landowner to reveal his or her true private land use value is to correlate a subsidy with the obligation to conserve a specific amount of land, which would provide each landowner with a unique compensation plus land conservation obligation. The regulator sets the compensation and land conservation requirement so that only the type of landowner the subsidy package is designed for accepts that package. Smith and Shogren (2002) show that even with this type of subsidy package, information rents are still earned by low private land use types, but they are less than the information rents paid with a uniform subsidy.

Many subsidies are designed to be cost-share or subsidy payment plus cost-share programs in which landowners pick up a fraction of the conservation expenses. Because landowners are partially compensated for the income lost by taking land out of productive uses or for the costs they incur by restoring their land to its natural state, these subsidy programs appeal to fewer landowners. These programs will attract those landowners who assign a personal value to conserving the land at least as great as the portion of conservation expenses that are not reimbursed. Landowners having a personal conservation value less than the out-of-pocket expense that would be incurred if the landowner were to enroll in the subsidy program are likely to refrain from participating. These nonparticipating landowners may possess land that is ecologically valuable and targeted for protection. A subsidy that does not fully compensate landowners for conservation expenses reduces the number of participants and as a consequence generates fewer conservation acres.

Tradable Development Rights with Zoning

Tradable development rights (TDR) programs specify a predetermined maximum level of development within a specified region and then distribute development rights equal to the permissible total amount of development to landowners within the region. Landowners who keep their development levels below their allotted development rights level can sell their surplus development rights to other landowners, or they can use them to offset development on other properties. To ensure that development rights serve their purpose as an incentive to change development to levels desired by society, total development levels within a given region are limited such that the development rights are seen as a scarce resource that is valuable to developers (Hanley et al. 1997).

TDR programs ensure that development occurs on the properties with the highest development values, but they do not guarantee that the most environmentally sensitive land is left undeveloped (Boyd et al. 1999). This nontargeted result can reduce the net benefits to society when land has a greater habitat value than development value. If this land is still developed under the TDRs, the mechanism has performed poorly. The most common approach to overcome this inefficiency is to combine TDRs with zoning (Mills 1980; Utah CLCC 1997; Miller 1999).

Government agencies responsible for land use planning determine which properties within a specified region should be protected for their valuable environmental characteristics and qualities. They then restrict development of these properties, and landowners are provided with development rights to compensate them for the loss of economic use. These rights can then be sold to developers in the less restricted properties within the region, where development is more desirable. Those properties that are restricted are called sending zones, and development properties are called receiving zones. Once sending and receiving zones are determined, the regulator decides on a formula for transferring the development rights from one zone to the other. A key feature ensures that developers will purchase TDRs from sending zones: the density of development in receiving zones, prior to acquisition of TDRs, is restricted to less than the demanded density (Miller 1999). The price of a TDR is determined through the open market. To facilitate trading and minimize transaction costs, regulators can establish a TDR bank or exchange, which brings together willing buyers and sellers such that each can find mutual gains through trade (Tripp and Dudek 1989).

Tradable development rights can be complex and administratively cumbersome. Establishing this new market involves technical, financial, and legal dimensions that must be addressed prior to the actual trading of development rights. These include: (1) TDR programs should be established with a clear legal authority; one way is authorization of TDR programs by state law to minimize costly legal challenges and delays in program implementation. (2) Ensuring that the program meets its goals requires the employment of expert land planners, lawyers, economists, and scientists to perform biological assessments, determine the total number and distribution of TDRs, establish a method by which development rights are transferred, record such transfers, set the initial zoned development density and maximum allowable density after TDRs are purchased, and monitor and enforce all transactions. (3) The TDR program will have more effective control over land uses if authority rests with one agency and all other methods for obtaining increases in development density are eliminated; the developer has to purchase TDRs to increase his or her development density. (4) The objectives of the land-planning agency should be clear, concise, and rooted in sound scientific knowledge. (5) The demand for development within the region should be significant and impose a significant threat to the region's biodiversity. (6) The regulator should set the supply of TDRs below the demand to ensure that TDRs are seen as a valuable asset. (7) TDRs should be distributed to landowners in a method that is as fair and administratively simple as possible. (8) The regulatory agency should establish a TDR exchange to reduce the friction within the market, which lowers the barriers of bringing together buyers and sellers and increases the efficiency and effectiveness of the program (Tripp and Dudek 1989; Sohn and Cohen 1996).

TDRs have been used by various states for close to three decades to protect historic buildings and landmarks, agricultural and ranch lands, and open spaces and view corridors and to protect riparian areas, forests, and other ecologically sensitive lands. One of the earliest programs was New York City's landmark preservation law. The program was initiated in the 1970s to protect historic landmarks by restricting development of air above historic buildings. The law allows the owner to be compensated for the lost right to develop by transferring the development rights for that air space to surrounding buildings that are allowed to build beyond the zoned height restrictions. New York City also allows development rights to transfer hands via zoning lot mergers between adjacent landowners. These landowners can combine their allowed floor area without joining ownership of the properties, provided the total floor area between the two buildings does not exceed the zoned maximum amount of floor area of the two properties. This system allows a developer to purchase the floor area not in use by an adjacent landowner and exceed the zoning restriction by that amount (Miller 1999; Levinson 1997).

Other TDR programs that have been designed to protect large expanses of environmentally sensitive land from the encroachment of development came into existence in the early 1980s in New Jersey and Maryland. In New Jersey, the Pinelands program encompasses 1.1 million acres of forested expanse, home to several small towns, and more than 1,000 species of plants and animals. The Pinelands have been targeted for preservation by the state, which used a TDR program to limit development. Landowners whose land is restricted from being developed are issued TDRs, the number of which depends on the preservation value of that owner's land. The landowner can then sell the TDRs to other landowners in the Pinelands region where development is allowed. These landowners must possess TDRs to develop their land beyond the predetermined housing density. To reduce the transaction costs associated with buyers and sellers locating each other, New Jersey established a TDR exchange. This exchange serves as the catalyst for transactions between willing buyers and sellers and determines the market price of TDRs (Stewart 1992; Clark and Downes 1996; Benjamin and Weiss 1997).

Other TDR programs have been authorized by state statute in twenty-two states, including six in the west. Kansas and Washington have passed legislation that approves the use of TDRs for the purpose of general zoning. In Idaho, TDRs are used to protect "designated historic properties." Hawaii has approved use of TDRs for the "protection, enhancement, preservation, and use of historic properties and burial sites." Arizona TDRs are used to protect the "public health, safety, and general welfare" of its citizens. Colorado's TDR programs are to be used for the protection of species, species habitat, agricultural and ranching lands, and open spaces (Miller 1999).

Pros. A policy that combines tradable development rights with zoning has three primary benefits. First, as is the case with a zoning policy, the regulator can target specific land attributes and qualities for preservation. The regulator determines the land within the region that is best conserved, based on the land's attributes and qualities, and then specifies it as a sending zone from which TDRs are transferred to developers in receiving zones.

Second, TDRs act as a compensatory tool for the owners of land in the sending zone, who sell their TDRs to developers in the receiving zone. Payment received from the TDR sale compensates the landowner for lost development value. Some landowners in the sending zone who sell their TDRs might not be fully compensated for their lost development value, because the price received for a TDR may be less than the unrestricted land's value. These landowners pay the extra costs of con-

THE NEW JERSEY PINELANDS

Status: The Pinelands was protected as the first national reserve in 1978. It consists of roughly 1.1 million acres of forests, wetlands, farms, and small towns in central New Jersey, which is under constant development threat from the surrounding metropolitan areas of Philadelphia, Trenton, Newark, New York, and Atlantic City. To help protect the Pinelands from increasing developmental pressure, the Pinelands Commission was formed and a comprehensive management plan (CMP) was adopted. The state of New Jersey passed the Pinelands Protection Act in 1979, requiring land use ordinances to comply with the CMP and further designating parts of the Pinelands as a preservation area and a protection area. The preservation area consists of 295,000 acres of forest lands and berry farms and is highly regulated against development. The protection area consists of small towns, existing subdivisions, and farmland and allows greater flexibility for development. As a result, the protection area is more challenging to manage for its environmental amenities. The Pinelands is habitat for numerous federally listed species and plants, including the bald eagle, piping plover, eastern puma, roseate tern, and American chaffseed. It is also home to fifteen pairs of peregrine falcons, which have been delisted (www.pinelandsalliance.org/).

Incentive mechanisms: Tradable development rights, fee simple acquisition

The Pinelands relies on two economic tools to fulfill the objectives of the CMP. First, the government has augmented the original 265,000 publicly owned Pinelands acres with an additional 65,000 acres that were purchased fee simple. Second, the commission, through the CMP, has implemented the Pinelands development credit program. The program designates regions where development is restricted (the preservation area and some agricultural lands in the protection area) and awards development credits to the landowners, who can sell the credits to other landowners in less restricted areas. The purchase of development credits allows landowners to increase development above the zoned level (www.state.nj.us/pinelands/).

servation involuntarily since their choices are limited to selling their TDRs and paying some of the costs of conservation or not selling their TDRs and bearing all the costs of conservation. They are prohibited from developing their land regardless of whether the TDRs are sold or not.

Third, by requiring developers to purchase TDRs to exceed a prespecified density level, the costs of conserving land fall on their shoulders, forcing developers to pay their own way. The regulator can increase the odds that a market will develop by providing that the TDRs are scarce enough to be of value. Flooding the market with permits will reduce the value and hence the effectiveness of any TDR program.

Cons. The mechanism of tradable development rights with zoning has five main shortcomings. First, some have depicted the TDR with zoning as rigid, static, and inflexible, just like a standard zoning policy. Landowners in a sending zone must conserve their land; their only choice is whether they will sell the rights and be compensated. No method has emerged that allows a landowner in a sending zone to change the status of the land to allow development.

Second, a TDR with zoning may be susceptible to political pressure, especially if zoning is the only method to ensure that development does not occur in sending zones. Since zoning is not a permanent feature of land, the zoned uses can change when political power changes. Some TDR programs require that landowners place a conservation easement (discussed in detail later in this chapter) on the title of the land, permanently severing the rights to develop it (Tripp and Dudek 1989). Conservation easements, however, are not a cure-all.

Third, TDRs with zoning do not guarantee that the conservation goal is met at the lowest cost. Four reasons drive this result: (1) Conservation land is selected by the regulator rather than being determined by the market. (2) Even if the market were allowed to allocate resources freely, it would likely do so inefficiently because conservation values differ across land parcels and are often independent of the parcels' developed value. (3) To meet the conservation goal efficiently, the regulator must know the conservation value and the owner's private use value for each parcel of land, information the regulator rarely possesses. (4) Land generates extra benefits when it is combined with other land to create a contiguous habitat (see chapter 7).

In general, a TDR policy is modeled after pollution permit programs for airborne pollutants. The primary benefit of pollution permit programs is that by establishing a set of permits to pollute, allocating those permits to the polluting industries within the region, and then allowing industries to buy and sell permits, government obtains pollution control at the lowest cost. The underlying idea is that firms that incur high costs for pollution reduction will purchase permits from firms with low costs for reducing pollution. The difference between a pollution permit program to control air pollutants and a TDR policy without zoning is the existence of a well-defined measure of quality. Air pollution has an accepted standard of measurement (parts per million), whereas no standard of measurement has been agreed on for biodiversity or habitat loss.

If all land parcels within the region have equal conservation values or if the conservation values correlate perfectly with the development values, such that the land undeveloped happens to be the land with the highest conservation value, the only problem would be determining the number of TDRs that achieve social goals. Unfortunately for TDRs, those scenarios are unlikely. The more likely case is that land good for habitat is the most likely to be developed, which leads to fewer net benefits to society. A TDR policy ensures that development occurs on the land with the highest developed value, but it does not have a component that can target lands and assign them to their best economic use. TDRs should be used in conjunction with other policy tools to accomplish the objective of assigning land to its highest and best use. A common approach for a TDR policy is to use development rights and zoning together (Mills 1980; also see Chapter 7).

Under a TDR with zoning policy, the regulator identifies the land to be preserved, zones that land for nondevelopment or lower density, and then distributes development rights to the restricted landowners, who can then sell them. For this approach to result in conservation at the lowest cost the regulator must again possess the conservation values and private use values for all land parcels and assign each parcel to its highest valued use.

The regulator is also faced with the problem of setting the right quantity of TDRs when information is less than complete. If the regulator knew both the development and conservation value of the land, the regulator would designate development on the lands that had a higher value in development, designate preservation on the lands with a higher conservation value, and then set the number of TDRs accordingly. Since the regulator rarely possesses this information, a problem exists similar to the one discussed for impact fees. The only difference is that for TDRs the regulator chooses quantity and allows the market to determine the price; for impact fees, the regulator chooses price and lets the quantity vary.

Suppose, for example, that the regulator knows the conservation benefits of the land but does not know the development value. If each additional parcel preserved provides society a constant benefit, a TDR policy would perform less effectively. If the regulator overestimates the cost of conservation, then the program will hand out too many TDRs, and too much development occurs. If the costs of conservation are underestimated, too few TDRs are handed out, which leads to too little development. In contrast, if people will pay nearly any price for conservation, the TDR policy performs better. Now if the actual costs differ from the perceived costs, the consequences of setting too few or too many TDRs are minimized. This occurs because, when people want about the same amount of conservation regardless of price, the potential range of TDRs is small. Here TDR policy is preferred to an impact fee policy (Hanley et al. 1997).

Another method to overcome the problems of heterogeneous land values in a TDR policy without zoning has been suggested in theory but not put into practice. Smith and Shogren (2001, 2002) suggest using a subsidy in conjunction with TDRs, in which landowners' who preserve land designated for preservation would receive both a subsidy and the price at which the TDR was sold. This subsidy—an agglomeration bonus—would pay an extra amount for each acre retired that touches another retired acre. Although the TDR-with-subsidy approach still suffers from the regulator's deciding which land receives the subsidy, landowners choose to participate or not, and if the value of the subsidy plus TDR payment exceeds the developed value, voluntary land conservation will occur in designated areas, perhaps at lower monitoring and enforcement costs.

Boyd et al. (1999) suggest another approach, the use of a trading-differential scheme that captures the environmental value associated with a particular parcel and assigns TDRs accordingly. A trading differential allows for land that possesses a higher value in preservation to be traded for a larger amount of development than would a TDR for land with a low preservation value. The regulator would need to set the trading differentials such that landowners with low preservation land values incur greater costs from selling their TDRs than do landowners with high preservation land values. This increases the odds that the costs of conserving land will be minimized through voluntary transactions in which the market determines land uses. The use of trading differentials has its own set of problems that must be addressed. Key issues include establishing an acceptable habitat standard, complications to the market process, increased difficulty in maintaining records, and increased costs to monitor and enforce the development that results from transfer of TDRs.

Fourth, a policy combining TDRs with zoning has significant monitoring and enforcement costs. Land restricted from development must be monitored to ensure that landowners do not undertake prohibited activities; also, developers must be monitored to ensure that the density of development does not exceed their permissible level, zoned plus TDRs. If landowners and developers undertake prohibited activities, the regulator must decide whether and to what degree to enforce the restrictions with the penalties specified by the law.

TDRs with zoning are also open to litigation in court. Developers can challenge the legality of the payment for a TDR on the grounds that they represent unconstitutional exactions, or landowners can question the sending zones by claiming that payment received from the sale of TDRs is not just compensation under the Fifth Amendment (Miller 1999). Although claims that TDRs are unconstitutional exactions seldom occur, recent Supreme Court cases have limited the use of exactions by government. The effect of these limitations on TDR programs will become clearer once lower courts determine how to apply the Supreme Court rulings.

Miller (1999) further states that sending-zone landowners are more likely to claim takings without just compensation, and such claims are subject to broader interpretation. The success of claims that TDRs are unconstitutional takings depends on whether TDRs are viewed as financial or commercial use of the land (the Brennan approach), or if TDRs are a form of just compensation for land use restrictions (the Rehnquist approach). Miller argues for the Rehnquist approach on the basis that it is "more convincing theoretically and will better protect environmental resources, maximize TDR values, and assure fair and equitable treatment of landowners." Miller goes on: "for TDRs to weather the storm of taking jurisprudence, the Supreme Court must revisit the constitutional issues surrounding them . . . using an analysis that is more consistent with the modern constitutional landscape." Programs using TDRs with zoning are susceptible to litigation on constitutional grounds, increasing the costs of monitoring and enforcement.

Fifth, TDRs with zoning are costly to administer because they require experts to establish the program within constitutional constraints, to establish environmental baseline conditions, and to design the institutional framework that assures that TDRs have value and can be traded with minimal transaction costs. The regulator must also monitor the market process, record transfers of development rights, and, if necessary, ascertain that landowners who have relinquished their development rights record a conservation easement on the deed of the land.

Conservation Banking

Developers undertaking a new project are often required to mitigate the adverse effects of their activities, which can be done onsite or the developer can purchase development credits to satisfy the regulation on land use. Development credits can be purchased as needed, or the developer can purchase excess credits and bank them to fulfill mitigation requirements of future projects. Developers purchase these credits from private or publicly owned conservation banks, which determine the prices of the credits based on demand and supply. The developer purchases credits if and only if the cost of mitigation through credit purchase is less than the cost of alternative approaches, such as onsite mitigation or establishment of a separate conservation bank. If profits are to be made by bank owners, other conservation bank owners will be attracted into the market, and market competition lowers the price of the credits.

The amount of credit that a conservation bank, also called a mitigation bank, can sell depends on the quality and type of habitat and the number of a specific endangered species supported on a specific parcel of land. Bank owners can increase the number of credits at their disposal by engaging in land management activities that increase either the quality of habitat or the ability of the land to protect endangered species or both. For example, in Georgia, the Southlands Mitigation Bank, owned by the International Paper Company, is ideal habitat for the red-cockaded woodpecker. These woodpeckers build nests in pine trees at least a hundred years old, and they require stands at least thirty years old for the purpose of foraging, of which International Paper owns 16,000 acres in the Southlands Forest region. In conjunction with the Environmental Defense Fund, International Paper developed a habitat conservation plan covering 5,300 of the available 16,000 acres. The plan established a baseline of two pairs of red-cockaded woodpeckers, and a land management plan was designed to meet a goal of increasing the population to thirty pairs through techniques such as prescribed fire, creating new or restoring existing nesting cavities, and relocating young woodpeckers to the region. As each new pair of woodpeckers is established in the plan area, International Paper obtains a permit to offset an incidental take on its own property, or it can sell the credit to a third party within a specified region and approved by the USFWS (Environmental Defense Fund 1999).

Credits can also be determined according to a particular type and quantity of habitat. The San Vicente Conservation Bank, for example, is a 320-acre parcel in San Diego County, California. The land cover is primarily coastal sage scrub and southern mixed chaparral, and it hosts the California gnatcatcher, listed as a threatened species under the ESA. The habitat is good quality and requires little in the way of management and maintenance. The San Vicente Conservation Bank was approved by the

GIANT GARTER SNAKE
Thamnophis gigas

Status: The giant garter snake was listed as a threatened species under the ESA in October 1993. The species is found in the Central Valley of California.

Habitat: The giant garter snake feeds on frogs and small fish. Its habitat consists of ponds, small lakes, and other wetlands.

Threats: Agricultural practices and development in the Central Valley have reduced the habitat suitable for the giant garter snake to about 6 to 9 percent of its historical range. Some of the remaining ponds and wetlands are not inhabited by the giant garter snake, a condition attributed to fragmentation and predatory fish.

The pressure to develop the Central Valley remains strong and serves to imperil the species further. Under these conditions, conservation banks may be the best incentive mechanism. They create large habitat reserves, reducing the adverse impacts of fragmentation; they protect the habitat in perpetuity; the destroyer of habitat pays for the creation, restoration, and protection of the habitat; new habitat is created and protected prior to the destruction of existing habitat; and because of development pressures it is possible to increase the stock of suitable habitat (*Federal Register* 56, no. 249: 67046–67054).

Incentive mechanisms: Conservation banking

In Citrus Heights, California, the Dolan Ranch Conservation Bank was established by Wildlands, Inc., to protect the giant garter snake. The number of credits available for sale by the Dolan Ranch Conservation Bank is determined by the quality of the vernal pools, their size, the number of listed species, placement within the landscape, and the ability to protect the bank from external risks. Credits can be sold to offset development within the service area, which is determined by the USFWS. Habitat in the Dolan Ranch Conservation Bank is also critical to several other listed species, including the vernal pool tadpole shrimp, Swainson's hawk, and the burrowing owl.

California Department of Fish and Game (CDFG) and the USFWS and was issued 320 credits. These credits can be sold to landowners within San Diego County for multispecies mitigation needs and other endangered and threatened species (Environmental Defense Fund 1999).

The Manchester Avenue Conservation Bank (MACB), another reserve in San Diego County, serves as a corridor for the El Cajon open space. The southern maritime chaparral, a unique habitat, is found here, and because of its rarity, the bank was able to negotiate for 1.8 credits per acre as opposed to the standard 1-to-1 ratio. The bank is owned by a private enterprise that has used many credits to offset its own development and has sold the remainder to other developers in the region (Environmental Defense Fund 1999). Owners of banks can be developers, environmental entrepreneurs, nonprofit organizations, or government agencies (Environmental Defense Fund 1999; Baden and Geddes 1999). Credits can be sold to developers to offset mitigation requirements, used to offset the bank owner's own mitigation requirements, banked for future requirements, and sold to individuals or organizations that wish to retire the credits, thereby reducing development.

Conservation banking with the ESA is a relatively recent development, beginning in the mid-1990s. The banking scheme closely follows the earlier program of wetlands mitigation banking, which has been used since the 1980s. Until 1995, wetland banks were primarily owned by state highway departments and were established to provide credits to mitigate for adverse effects to wetlands as regulated by the Clean Water Act. In 1995 the Environmental Protection Agency and Army Corps of Engineers established guidelines to create and manage wetlands mitigation banks. These wetland banks are designed to provide certainty for private landowners regarding assessing land, earning and selling credits, and defining the present and future obligations and requirements that a bank owner faces. With these guidelines in place, landowners can predict the costs of their present and future regulatory obligations, which decreases the risk to the landowner of investing in a wetlands mitigation bank and results in landowners supplying conservation (Environmental Defense Fund 2000).

In 1995 California used conservation banking to preserve habitat critical to reducing the risks to endangered species. By 1998, forty-three conservation banks were established. Based on their experience, California instituted a plan based on fourteen principles for successful implementation of a conservation bank. These principles are:

- In determining mitigation requirements, priority should be placed on protecting the habitat and species in the long run. This is best accomplished off-site and in conjunction with a conservation bank.
- Banks must be established with a contract or permit that is legal and enforceable.
- A conservation bank can be of any size as long as it is large enough to support an ecosystem approach to conservation. The one exception is when a parcel is one of several parts of a contiguous larger bank that is reasonably certain to be completed.

- Fee title sale or a conservation easement insuring that the land is preserved in perpetuity should be recorded on the title of the land in coordination with the first credit sold.
- Prior to the authorization of a conservation bank, a bank proposal must be approved. For approval the bank proposal must include the assignment of a bank manager, a description of the bank's boundaries and the area for which the credits can be used to offset development, management and maintenance requirements including provisions for how those requirements will be achieved, and the determination of annual reporting responsibilities.
- A plan that details the resources found within the bank, how those resources are to be managed, and how such management is to be funded is required prior to the sale of the first credit.
- An agency should be designated for the long-term management of the bank.
- A plan should detail the steps to be taken in the event of unsatisfactory performance by the bank owner. These steps should ensure the long-term protection of the bank.
- Monitoring and reporting of management activities centered on listed species and their habitats should be provided.
- Agencies responsible for ensuring compliance should be granted an easement for the right of entry to monitor the agreement.
- Bank credits should be determined in accordance with the initial, or baseline, condition. Given the baseline, credits can be earned by preserving the land, enhancing the quality or quantity of a habitat or species on the land, restoring the land to its original condition, or creating habitat suitable for species preservation where such habitat did not exist before.
- The number of bank credits awarded to a bank owner is determined on a case-by-case basis, and negotiations are between the bank owner and the appropriate regulatory agencies.
- A transaction for credits between a bank owner in one region and a developer in another region (out-of-kind mitigation) may be approved on a case-by-case basis.
- Listing of conservation banks with the California Resource Agency is required so as to maintain an inventory of banks throughout the state.

This process serves two primary purposes: to increase the certainty about present and future obligations of the bank owner and to ensure that conservation efforts will meet the goals of the regulatory agency. The process reduces a regulator's monitoring and enforcement costs by requiring the bank to submit both an annual report and a contingency plan for bank failure, and by specifying the regulatory agency's right to enter the property.

Unlike impact fees, conservation banking compensates landowners for the provision of a public good and does so by allowing the market to determine the magnitude of the compensation. Conservation banking differs from TDRs in that TDRs are an ex ante approach, in which the proportion of land to be developed is determined before development. In contrast, conservation banking is an ex post mechanism, in which landowners establish conservation banks in response to developmental pressures. As development increases, the need to purchase credits increases, and hence the supply of credits should increase to meet the higher priced demand. The regulator can determine the quantity of land to be conserved by controlling the ratio of credits the developer must purchase to offset the development at the time of development, which gives the regulator flexibility to meet its conservation goals.

Pros. Before conservation banking, a developer's mitigation efforts were generally undertaken project by project and onsite, which led to a fragmented and inflexible approach to mitigation that usually resulted in ineffective conservation techniques. A good example is a 1991 study by the South Florida Water Management District of more than 100 projects that required mitigation to satisfy land use regulations in Florida. The study provides evidence of the failure associated with onsite mitigation. It found that only 40 of the projects actually attempted to meet mitigation requirements, only 3 had a long-term management plan, and only 8 mitigation sites had been protected from invasive species. Of those with mitigation, about half of the required mitigation was actually performed. An Army Corps of Engineers report from 1989 records a failure rate exceeding 50 percent, with about 40 percent not addressing mitigation requirements at all. A 1998 study conducted in Massachusetts cites a 45-percent failure rate, in which 22 percent didn't undertake the mitigation project. In an assessment of those studies, the Environmental Defense Fund (1999) concludes that regardless of "whether these results should be considered a failure of traditional mitigation or, rather, a failure of the government to monitor and enforce traditional mitigation requirements, the outcome is still the same," mitigation on a project-by-project basis leads to an indeterminate amount of conservation, which may not be completed and if completed may not be effectively managed for the long run.

Such conservation techniques are often ineffective for three reasons. First, landowners' project-by-project mitigation efforts typically lead to smaller preserves, which further fragments an already fragmented habitat area. They treat the area as several subregions rather than as one whole region. Smaller preserves are more susceptible to edge effects, winds, overcrowding of species because of limited habitat, and invasive, exotic species, many of which survive on the edges and then invade the preserve, altering its initial makeup (see the discussion in Parkhurst et al. 2002). Land preserves are typically isolated, inhibiting species movement across the landscape. Connectivity, size and shape of preserves, as well as the preserve's position in the landscape are important elements for successful preserves (Saunders et al. 1991). By combining many developers' mitigation requirements, conservation banking allows mitigation to occur on larger contiguous parcels of land (Environmental Defense Fund 2000), reducing the detrimental effects of fragmentation and increasing the probability of successful mitigation.

Second, if the regulator allows the project-by-project mitigation to occur simultaneously with the development project, the project will be completed long before the success of mitigation efforts can be determined (Environmental Defense Fund 1999). Initially, mitigation preserves may have more species than the area is capable of sustaining, which results in overcrowding, and eventually species will start to die off (Saunders et al. 1991). Some species are threatened by invasive species or require active management of their habitat to survive. For example, the red-cockaded woodpecker requires a mature stand of longleaf pine trees to serve as suitable nesting, foraging, and breeding habitat. As the understory grows and the forest becomes denser, the habitat becomes less suitable for the woodpeckers, which requires the land manager to employ periodically prescribed burning or other methods for thinning the understory to maintain it as suitable habitat. The amount of time necessary to ascertain the effectiveness of each individual mitigation effort may be many years after the development is complete (Environmental Defense Fund 1999).

In contrast, mitigation is assured with conservation banks because a bank is required to have the species and habitat established before credits can be earned or sold. The bank owner must also have a regulator-approved land manager and management plan that will maintain the species habitat, which provides more certainty for long-term conservation than does project-by-project mitigation.

Third, pooling the financial responsibilities for mitigation has allowed conservation banks to capture economies of scale, the reduction of costs per acre that results from conserving a larger parcel of land. A conservation bank has to design and implement only one conservation plan, but mitigation done on a project-by-project basis requires a separate habitat conservation plan for each developer. Designing and implementing conservation plans is an expensive process, and conservation banks can reduce the costs of supplying conservation by combining many developers' mitigation requirements (Environmental Defense Fund 1999). Evidence suggests that costs per acre decline by 31 percent for each 10 percent increase in project size (see Fernandez and Karp 1998; King and Bohlen 1994). Conservation banking increases the probability that mitigation efforts will be successful at lower costs and decreases the regulator's costs of monitoring and enforcing developers' conservation requirements because the number of mitigation projects is reduced significantly (Fernandez and Karp 1998).

Conservation banks induce private involvement in conservation by providing landowners with incentives to conserve their land and, in many cases, to increase the habitat quality of the land. Landowners with land valued for conservation can apply to the regulator for conservation banking status. Once approval is granted and application processes satisfied, the landowner is provided with credits that can be sold to developers to offset mitigation requirements. The value of credits is determined by the market, and if the price is sufficiently high, such that the landowner's highest valued land use is accomplished by preserving the land, the landowner conserves the land.

Banks also provide their owners with incentives to invest in the conservation value of their land by allocating extra credits to the bank owners if they invest resources to improve the quality of the habitat or the species population or both within the bank. A good example is the Southlands Mitigation Bank. This program engages in conservation techniques that increase the quality of habitat and number of individual red-cockaded woodpeckers in the bank, and the bank earns an additional credit for every new pair of woodpeckers it locates to its mitigation bank (Environmental Defense Fund 1999).

In California, credits are typically distributed one per acre for habitat and one per one-tenth of an acre for wetlands (http://ceres.ca.gov/ 1996). If the price of credits is sufficient to induce their investment, landowners could create wetlands or habitat by altering their present land use activities on land that is suitable for hydration or revegetation with indigenous plants. The county of San Diego recognizes this option in its mitigation bank policy and considers areas adjacent to an existing conservation bank or other land permanently preserved as the best for habitat creation (County of San Diego 2000). The revegetation option can be the best strategy for local governments or developers that have long-term development projects or long-term planning horizons.

A landowner might find that establishing a conservation bank and selling the credits may be incentive enough to offset incentives to destroy habitat when facing the possibility of ESA restrictions. Landowners could use conservation banks in conjunction with a safe harbor agreement, which is a voluntary agreement that specifies a level of species protection agreed on by the landowner and the U.S. Fish and Wildlife Service. Landowners entered in the safe harbor program could increase their obligation for protection of species by selling credits to other landowners subject to land restrictions, which may require the landowner and USFWS to enter into a new agreement (Environmental Defense Fund 2000).

Conservation banks target high-quality habitat and low-cost lands for conservation because now conservation is a business, which exists when the bank owner expects to earn an acceptable rate of return on an investment. By employing the land with the largest permit potential per dollar spent, the bank owner has the best opportunity to earn rents. The prospective bank owner voluntarily applies for conservation bank status for the land. Also, since transactions are voluntary, the landowners sell their land to the prospective bank owner without coercion.

Conservation banks can also be used to protect entire ecosystems. Here banks are created with the idea of treating the entire region as a whole unit rather than several small entities. For instance, the state of California passed the Natural Community Conservation Planning Act in 1991 (NCCP 2000). The purpose of the act was to work with state and federal agencies to protect and enhance biological diversity while allowing development and growth to continue. The act separates California into eleven distinct regions, which are further separated into subregions. Each region must prepare a Natural Community Conservation Plan, which has the goal of encouraging cooperation between private landowners and government agencies in the endeavor of protecting the community's natural resources. Each subregion, usually a city or county entity, is required to initiate a subregion plan. This subregion plan specifies the area and boundaries of the plan, the lead government agency, a list of species to protect, permits required to implement the plan, notice to the public that the plan is being prepared, and the public's involvement. Because the CDFG and the USFWS are involved in the planning process from the beginning, subregional plans are usually accepted as habitat conservation plans and incidental take permits are awarded; also an implementing agreement is entered that requires participating parties to verify compliance with the NCCP on a routine basis to the USFWS and CDFG (CDFG 1993).

The subregion plans are called multispecies conservation programs. They address the possible impacts to listed species and their habitat stemming from future development and growth, and they present a plan to mitigate adverse impacts. Multispecies plans further detail the land preservation requirements of the region, including allowable development conservation ratios, or mitigation requirements for specific areas within the region and the use of conservation banking as a mitigation tool (County of San Diego 1998).

Cons. Conservation banking can have significant administrative costs. Both the demand and supply sides of banking credits require regulatory oversight. On the supply side, the regulator has the responsibility to evaluate applications, verify the biological assessment and the base condition, approve the long-term management plan, and then negotiate the quantity of credits the bank can sell. On the demand side, the regulator determines credit demand according to credits the developers must purchase to mitigate their proposed projects. A multispecies plan requires developers to purchase credits as specified in the implementing agreement. Depending on the locations and habitat qualities of both developed land and the conservation bank, credit requirements can range from 0.5 to 3 per acre (County of San Diego 1998).

As with all economic incentive mechanisms, a conservation bank owner has an incentive to try to affect a regulator's decision. If the banker can influence the regulator to limit the credits on the market by slowing entrance of new conservation banks into the market, a credit price and banker rents will be greater. Bank owners collect this extra rent from the developers who pay the price for credits. These developers will increase their lobbying efforts to open up the market to let new banks in to increase supply and lower the price. The lobbying increases the rent-seeking costs of both supplying conservation and developing land, and the costs of lobbying may become large enough that they exceed the price of the credits (Rowley 1988).

Bankable credits have also been criticized for allowing too much development. Developers purchase the right to alter habitat by buying credits that preserve other existing habitat, which guarantees that a net loss of habitat will occur (Environmental Defense Fund 1999). The tradeoff between conservation and development, especially in an area where species are imperiled, may allow for land to be developed that otherwise would not be developed. The argument is that banking just transfers the risk from one location to another. A regulator faces pressure from environmental groups trying to procure favorable legislation, or to persuade the regulator to increase the compensation ratio requiring developers to purchase more credits to mitigate the negative effects of their developments. If the basis for which credits are earned remains constant, a higher compensation ratio leads to a greater amount of land in conservation relative to developed uses. A net loss of habitat still occurs, but the loss is less than it would be absent the environmentalists' efforts.

The amount of habitat and habitat quality determine the amount of credits available for sale by the bank owner. This adds an extra complication for the regulator, who must determine how many credits to supply the market. The regulator seldom knows land preservation information until the landowner actually applies for banking status. Many landowners are hesitant to allow government agents on their land prior to deciding to conserve their land. They fear that the government agent might find an endangered species on their land and subsequently restrict the landowner's choices of land use. Without land preservation information on all parcels of land within the region, the regulator does not have enough information to set with confidence the credits that will provide society the most net benefit.

Even if the regulator did possess information about the initial conservation values across all lands, the incentives for landowners to invest in the conservation value may also make it more difficult for the regulator to set the best supply of credits. In its official policy on mitigation banks, for example, San Diego County recognizes the prospect of investing in the conservation value of the land by establishing its own conservation banks on land that is suitable for or occupied by sensitive and listed plants and animals, or that has "the potential for revegetation of sensitive habitat" (County of San Diego 2000). The county further stipulates that land acquisitions must be voluntary transactions. These conditions are aimed at reducing the level of conflict over species protection, both at the individual level of avoiding fights over eminent domain and at the aggregate level of reducing lobbying.

The regulator needs to know about landowner information on both sides of the equation: landowners' conservation investment costs and land use information. Armed with this information, the regulator can determine the land's best use by comparing the conservation value with the development value. Land parcels where the postinvestment net conservation value is greater than the developed value should be conserved.

Fee Simple Acquisition

Fee simple acquisition is the purchase of land, with all of its inherent property rights. Landowners voluntarily enter into an agreement to sell their land, typically at its fair market value. Local governments often purchase land for public goods such as playgrounds, nature trails, and other park lands (Boyd et al. 1999; Utah CLCC 1997). Sellers are generally private individuals or organizations; land trusts and other nonprofit organizations do purchase land and then sell or transfer the land to government agencies (Land Trust Alliance 1998).

One example of a transfer acquisition is Snake Creek Canyon, on the east side of the Wasatch Mountains in Utah. A local ski resort planned to develop the area. Instead, the ski area sold the land to the Nature Conservancy, acting in the interests of several municipalities, a private industry, citizen groups, and a state agency. This group agreed to reimburse the Nature Conservancy for the initial funds to purchase the land. The land has had its development rights severed. The land trust Utah Open Lands holds the conservation easement; the Utah State Division of Parks has taken on the management of the property. This acquisition demonstrates how agencies and organizations can work together to accomplish land use goals (Utah CLCC 1997).

Another example of cooperation between government agencies and nonprofit organizations is the California Coastal Conservancy (CCC). The CCC offers a wide array of programs to protect the California coastline and the valuable resources that are found there. Since its inception in 1976, the CCC has helped protect nearly 33,000 acres of wetlands, sand dunes, and farmlands by working with nonprofit land conservation organizations through the Nonprofit Organizations Assistance Program. The program provides funding to nonprofit organizations for the purpose of acquiring land or interests in land that satisfies CCC objectives, while the ownership and costs of managing the land fall on the shoulders of the nonprofit organization (CCC 2000).

An example is the cooperative effort of the CCC and the Mendocino Land Trust, which purchased two tracts of land that bordered the ocean. The first tract, a 74-acre beach property in Caspar, California, has a stream that serves as a spawning ground for the endangered coho salmon (CDFG 2000). The second tract is Navarro Point, a 55-acre expanse of coast and open headlands. The purchase price for the two properties was $2.9 million. The long-term management of the Navarro Point property is estimated to cost $300,000; the Caspar Beach property, which allows for public access, has estimated annual maintenance costs of $12,000. The land trust is currently raising money for the management of Navarro Point and working out an agreement to transfer ownership and maintenance of the Caspar property to the California State Parks Department (Land Trust Alliance 2000b).

Land trusts and other nonprofit organizations use fee simple acquisition as a tool to protect land in ecologically sensitive regions, especially focusing on land threatened by urban sprawl. Land trusts originated more than 100 years ago in Massachusetts in 1891. Local citizens sought to protect their landscape from development. Over the last century, land trusts have been used to protect lands ranging from wetlands to ranches, from shorelines to farms, virtually all land valued as open space (Land Trust Alliance 2000c; Gustanski 2000). Land trusts have increased from 53 in 1950 to more than 1,200 today, covering all fifty states (Land Trust Alliance 2000c; Nijhuis 2000a).

Land trusts acquire land by fee simple acquisition, donation of land with all property rights intact, purchased development rights (PDR), and donated easements (Nijhuis 2000b). Purchasing the land or obtaining the land in its entirety through donation gives the land trust more control over land uses. The price of this control is the cost to manage the land, which often requires significant staff and resources. Land trusts try to reduce management costs by serving as a broker or middleman between the landowner and a larger trust or government agency. Land trusts also avoid management costs by acquiring a conservation easement, purchased or donated, which allows the landowner to remain on the land and maintain the land according to the terms of the easement. The land trust is still responsible for monitoring and enforcing the terms of the easement.

Although enforcement costs have been relatively low to date, land trusts expect them to escalate as easement-encumbered land passes from the initial landowner to subsequent landowners. Trusts set aside funds now to enforce easements in the future. More than 90 percent of easement-encumbered land remains with the landowner who signed the contract (Nijhuis 2000a).

Currently in the western United States, about 250 land trusts exist to

KARNER BLUE BUTTERFLY
Lycaeides melissa samuelis

Status: On 14 December 1992 the Karner blue butterfly was listed as an endangered species. These butterflies historically were found along a narrow strip that extends from Minnesota to New Hampshire and existed in eleven states (Minnesota, Wisconsin, Illinois, Indiana, New York, New Hampshire, Ohio, Michigan, Pennsylvania, Massachusetts, and Maine) and Ontario, Canada. They have disappeared from those states except for New York, New Hampshire, Minnesota, Indiana, Wisconsin, and Michigan. It is estimated that 99 percent of the viable populations have disappeared over the last 100 years and 90 percent have been lost in the last 10 years.

Habitat: The wild lupine plant is the Karner blue butterfly's sole source of food during its caterpillar stage and is therefore the only suitable habitat. The wild lupine plant grows in dry soils of open pine and oak savannahs and benefits from periodic fires that create openings in the canopy critical for its survival.

The Karner blue butterfly also requires immigration between populations to increase the species' viability.

Threats: The primary threats to the Karner blue butterfly are habitat loss and fragmentation resulting from development, fire suppression, and butterfly collectors. Fragmentation of habitat destroys the linkages between populations that are critical for maintaining genetically healthy populations (*Federal Register* 57, no. 240 (14 December 1992): 59236–59244).

Incentive mechanisms: Fee simple acquisition

The Wilton Wildlife Preserve and Park, in Wilton, New York, was created in 1996. It provides habitat, in the form of the wild lupine plant, critical to the survival of the Karner blue butterfly. The preserve is a joint effort between the town of Wilton, the New York State Department of Environmental Conservation, and the Nature Conservancy. Roughly 800 acres are protected, and the preserve has a goal of 3,000 acres. Recently the USFWS joined in the effort, presenting the New York State Department of Environmental Conservation with a $321,000 grant that can be used to protect habitat through fee simple acquisition or conservation easements. The funds will be used for fee simple acquisition of 75 acres of quality habitat (http://northeast.fws.gov/karnerls.html).

Table 3.1. Fee Simple Acquisitions in the Western United States

State	People per Acre[a]	Number of Land Trusts	Total Acres	Acres Owned	Under Easement	Transferred to Government
AK	I	4	1,312	395	917	0
AZ	32.3	10	3,339	280	857	2202
CA	190.8	119	536,922	235,571	78,099	283,056
CO	31.8	29	95,593	6,124	79,783	19,791
HI	172.5	4	7	2	5	0
ID	12.2	8	23,042	778	8,315	14,049
KS	30.3	2	219	0	219	0
MT	5.5	9	296,840	261	258,410	38,163
NE	20.5	3	16,846	15,146	1,700	0
NV	10.9	4	4,843	0	118	4,725
NM	12.5	7	28,986	873	28,113	0
ND	9.3	I	4,834	4,154	0	680
OK[b]	45.8	I	0	0	0	0
OR	29.6	13	11,711	386	2,654	8,671
SD	9.2	I	9,062	0	7,760	1,302
TX	64.9	20	11,531	3,244	3,823	4,464
UT	21	4	22,805	19,787	3,000	18
WA	73.1	29	27,230	10,219	11,949	5,062
WY	4.7	2	37,752	1,467	7,585	28,700

Source: State-by-State Summary of the 1998 National Land Trust Census (Land Trust Alliance 1998).
[a] 1990 U.S. Census Bureau, www.census.gov/population/censusdata/90den_stco.txt.
[b] The Ozark Land Trust is a regional land trust also in Missouri and Arkansas.

protect more than a million acres. Land previously held in private ownership is now solely owned by land trusts or owned jointly by private landowners and land trusts (Nijhuis 2000a). Every western state has at least one land trust; the number of trusts in a state correlates with the pressure to develop. For example, in 1998 California had 119 land trusts protecting 536,922 acres, and Texas protected 11,531 acres with 20 land trusts (Gustanski 2000). (Table 3.1 presents data for all the western states.)

A recent trend is the move to more specialization and smaller land trusts. These smaller trusts have clearer ties to the local community and are finding they can best use their resources by working with landowners, by arbitraging the land or by facilitating trades. Smaller land trusts have fewer resources and therefore are less able to acquire easements and monitor and enforce agreements.

Pros. A fee simple acquisition policy has three main benefits. First, fee simple acquisition provides the conservator with ultimate control over land uses, which allows it to restrict the use of the land without incurring the monitoring and enforcement costs that exist with other mechanisms. Also, because the conservator has complete control over land uses, it can more readily incorporate new and better species management technologies as they become available.

Second, landowners enter into fee simple acquisition agreements voluntarily, landowners are fully compensated, and the conservator is able to purchase the land without conflict or threat of future litigation. Fee simple acquisition can be used to purchase lands with varying values in development and differing landowner types, or from landowners with differing attitudes toward conservation. The process is simple, the market already established, all that is required is a transfer of ownership (Boyd et al. 1999; Utah CLCC 1997).

Third, agencies that use fee simple acquisition can target properties that provide the maximum environmental benefits, provided they are willing and able to pay the landowner the market price. If a local government purchases the land, taxpayers who benefit from the local public good pay the cost.

Cons. Fee simple acquisition of land is an expensive approach to land conservation that diverts resources away from other worthy goals like better education. Costs include the acquisition price, land management costs, the lost revenue associated with conservation-compatible land uses, and the possible lost welfare that may result when the goals the money is diverted from would provide society a larger benefit. Also, conservation lands retired by government may not remain in conservation and may be sold or put to other uses if the goals of subsequent administrations differ from the present administration's goals.

When the government purchases the land, the government incurs costs managing the land, and conservation-compatible land uses like ranching and agriculture typically stop (Boyd et al. 1999, p. 4). Compatible land uses are defined as uses that do not "interfere with or detract from the fulfillment of the mission" of the conservation effort (USFWS 2000). Although conservation value remains the same regardless of whether conservation-compatible land uses are employed, the community loses the extra revenues from, say, ranching. The regulator can avoid both costs through the use of PDR and conservation easements. PDR and conservation easements protect the land while leaving the landowner on the land engaged in conservation-compatible uses, and if specified in the easement contract, the landowner remains obligated to maintain the land (Boyd et al. 1999).

Landowners and nonprofit organizations may act strategically and expend valuable resources trying to affect the regulator's land use decisions or to force a sale price higher than fair market value. If a local government plans to acquire land, developers have an incentive to persuade the regulator to buy the land most likely to increase their profits. Locating a public park or habitat reserve adjacent to a property or ensuring that the lands bordering the developer's project will be left as open space will increase the expected profits to the developer. Conservationists also have an incentive to lobby government agencies to push the government's land acquisition decisions toward their objectives. In either case, these private actors engaged in rent-seeking activities are spending time and effort fighting over the distribution of wealth rather than the creation of new wealth (see Rowley 1988).

Landowners also have an incentive to act strategically when the regulator must purchase specific parcels of land for conservation. A landowner who knows that his property must be purchased can increase his asking price above fair market value, without triggering the government's use of eminent domain.

As with any compensation scheme, buying land fee simple can create a deadweight loss as government moves funds from other worthy projects to conservation. In addition, there is no guarantee that the land will remain in conservation in perpetuity. In times of financial downturn or as government agendas change, conservation land may be sold to fund other projects. Conservation efforts can be affected by changes in political fortunes.

Conservation Easement

Ownership of land provides the landowner with certain rights regarding how the land can be used, which include the right to exclude others from using the land, the right to develop the land, the right to produce commodities, and the right to employ other legal rent-seeking activities. A conventional easement is a legal instrument that serves to separate specific rights in the land and transfer those rights from the landowner to another entity. (See, for example, Wiebe et al. 1996; Bick and Haney 2001). A conservation easement serves the same purpose, except that species and habitat protection is the explicit goal.

A conventional easement is generally negotiated between adjacent landowners where both landowners benefit from the agreement. Coase (1960) depicted the concept of an easement in his seminal article, "The Problems of Social Cost." Coase addressed how bargaining rather than government taxation could remove the social cost incurred when a rancher's cattle trample a neighbor's crops on their way to a watering hole. Coase argued that the rancher and the farmer could both increase their well-being (assuming the farmer holds the property rights and transaction costs are low) if the farmer would accept a payment from the rancher in exchange for the right—the easement—for the rancher's cattle to cross the farmer's land.

Conventional easements are typically affirmative and appurtenant. "Affirmative" means that the easement holder is given the right to conduct specified activities, such as a right-of-way. "Appurtenant" means that the benefits provided by the easement belong to and are typically realized only by the easement holder (Wiebe et al. 1996). Such easements have been used to transfer partial interests in land for thousands of years.

Like conventional easements, a conservation easement severs some of the interests in the land and transfers those interests to another party. In contrast to a conventional easement, a conservation easement tends to be negative and in gross. Here "negative" means that rather than allowing the holder of the easement to engage in specified activities, the holder of the easement can restrict the landowner from engaging in specified activities. "In gross" means that the easement holder can be someone other than an adjacent landowner. A conservation easement prohibits the landowner from specified uses on his or her land (Wiebe et al. 1996).

Conservation easements are voluntary contracts between a landowner and the government agency or nonprofit organization. The contracts are negotiated on a property-by-property basis and can be tailored to satisfy individual landowner requirements while maintaining conservation objectives. These contracts typically include a description of the conservation goals for the property, an initial appraisal of the land, acceptable land uses and restrictions on land uses, the landowner's management responsibilities, the conservator's right to access the land, proof of unencumbered ownership, legal requirements in the event of a contract breach, provisions regarding present and future liabilities, and the landowner's requirement of notification when the property is sold (Boyd et al. 1999). Contracts also specify duration of the easement as well as compensation to the landowner.

To illustrate, consider a rancher whose land borders Yellowstone Park in Montana and offers excellent habitat for the grizzly bear, a species listed as threatened by the USFWS (1996). Suppose this rancher is approached by a nonprofit conservation organization (in Montana, only state and federal agencies or nonprofit organizations that are qualified by the Internal Revenue Service are allowed to own a conservation easement), and the terms of a conservation easement are negotiated. A contract between the rancher and the nonprofit organization is created, in which the rancher agrees to refrain from developing any portion of his land and further agrees to limit or discontinue grazing on portions of the land deemed to be valuable and sensitive to grazing. In return, the rancher receives payment for his conservation efforts. The land conserved increases the recovery likelihood and, it is hoped, the eventual delisting of the grizzly bear. The conservation easement provides society benefits from the conservation of the land. Possession of the development rights does not give the holder the right to develop the land; in contrast it gives the holder the right to, and the obligation to, restrict development of the land.

In general, conservation easements are classified into two broad categories: purchased development rights (PDR) and donated easements. The type of sellers, the type of buyers, the mode of compensation, and the duration of the contract characterize the differences between the two easements. A PDR easement is typically entered into by profit-maximizing landowners who require full compensation for their forgone opportunity, the land's development value. The purchaser of a PDR easement is often a government agency, which generally has a larger coffer than most nonprofit organizations and is better able to finance the purchase of the easement. The payment for a PDR easement is typically a one-time lump sum, and PDR easements can be purchased for limited time periods or in perpetuity.

The donated easement is based on a tax incentive, which typically appeals to landowners who value the preservation of land and are therefore willing to be compensated at less than fair market value for the easement. Federal tax law requires that land must be donated to a nonprofit conservation organization and donated in perpetuity to qualify for tax incentives (Small 1998; Wiebe et al. 1996, p. 12). Tax incentives can take the form of a deduction in income taxes, a reduction in the base value for estate or gift taxes, and, if the conservation easement meets certain requirements, an additional reduction in the estate tax base. Consider each type of easement in turn.

PDR Easements

A PDR easement is a conservation mechanism in which the landowner sells the conservation-incompatible uses of the land for a specified period of time for a cash payment, usually at the fair market value of the easement (the difference between the easement-free value and the easement-encumbered value of the property). Determining just compensation is complicated because no easement market exists (i.e., there are no comparables) and the value of the land unencumbered is uncertain and likely to change as the developmental pressure it faces changes (Boyd et al. 1999; Wiebe et al. 1996).

Pros. PDR easements let the government or nonprofit organization restrict development on land without incurring the total expenses of a fee simple acquisition. Easement purchase prices tend to be anywhere from 20 percent to 90 percent of the fair market value of the land (Boyd et al. 1999). As a result, government agencies can spread their limited resources across more conservation projects (Environmental Defense Fund 2000).

Landowners also benefit from PDR easements because they are voluntary transactions. The purchase price of the easement is equal to the opportunity cost of the forgone development. This provides the landowner full compensation that accounts for the expectations concerning future uses, which includes the probability that the land will be developed at a future time multiplied by the stream of returns that would follow.

Since other unknown factors also influence the actual development of the land (e.g., zoning laws and ESA regulations), a PDR easement sale provides the landowner an immediate payment that can be hedged against this uncertainty (Wiebe et al. 1996; Boyd et al. 1999). Voluntary participation is also politically valuable to the regulator; the cooperative properties of PDR easements allow the regulator to avoid the difficulties that result from command-and-control techniques. The PDR reduces the risk of landowner destruction of the land's biota and the risk that landowners will develop land more quickly to escape future land use regulations (Boyd et al. 1999).

The landowner also maintains ownership of the restricted land and is able to pursue profitable land uses that are compatible with conservation and specifically permitted within the contract. Ranching, farming, and some outdoor recreational activities are considered to be compatible with conservation, but compatibility is determined on a case-by-case basis and depends on the affected species. The conservation easement contract may specify obligations for the landowner to manage and maintain the land for its environmental amenities, some of which may increase the quality of the habitat.

PDR easements allow the government to target particular land characteristics and attributes or specific properties for protection. Easements are a useful mechanism to conserve lands where the conservation value of the land exceeds the price of the easement (Utah CLCC 1997). Plus, PDR easements are generally contracted in perpetuity, which means if a landowner sells the land, subsequent landowners are subject to the conditions specified in the easement contract. Easements that encumber the land for the present and all subsequent landowners are said to "run with the land" (Boyd et al. 1999).

Cons. Uncertainty about the value of future alternative uses, the scarcity of buyers, the lack of comparables, and the heterogeneity of property can create inefficiencies in resource allocation for the purchaser of PDR easements. Government regulators who do not know the private conservation value of an easement may overpay landowners for conservation easements. Governments may also lack the internal organizational incentives to ensure that administration costs are minimized or, even more important, to ensure that the land acquired provides a positive net benefit to society (Boyd et al. 1999).

Both the landowner and the conservator, whether a government agency or a nonprofit organization, face costs associated with negotiating the contract for the acquisition of a PDR easement. Contracts are negotiated on a case-by-case basis because of the heterogeneity of land and landowner characteristics. Defining the details necessary to ensure a successful agreement may be a time-consuming and expensive process, and the difficulties increase as contracts become more land- and landowner-specific. To reduce the costs, many agencies have gone to a standardized contract, trading flexibility for greater efficiency.

Monitoring and enforcing PDR easements present their own sets of problems. First, the landowner and the conservator jointly own the land. The landowner has the responsibility to manage the land in a manner that satisfies the conditions set forth in the easement contract. The conservator, to ensure its interests are being fulfilled, must regularly monitor the landowner's actions and enforce the land use restrictions.

Some landowner actions that adversely affect the preservation of the land may be overt and easily detected, but others may be subtle and may continue for years until the accumulated impact becomes noticeable. Monitoring can occur monthly, biannually, or annually, and often the terms of onsite inspections are specified in the easement contract. Monitoring and enforcing the contract must continue for the duration of the easement, which in many cases is forever.

Second, the easement is a permanent attribute of the land. All subsequent owners are subject to the land use restrictions and land maintenance responsibilities specified in the easement contract. The conservator must continue to monitor and enforce the terms of the contract for the new owners. Landowners may not understand fully the restrictions on the land and might believe the easement is too restrictive or might not believe they are bound to the agreement given that they did not sign it (National Research Council 1993). The terms in the easement can be too specific, having been tailored for the initial landowner, and may not account adequately for other contingencies. Alternatively, future landowners may find the terms to be ambiguous and may engage in activities the easement holder had meant to prohibit (Collins 2000). The easement holder may find itself back at the bargaining table or in court pursuing legal remedies, incurring sizable costs that could exceed the initial savings that the easement provided over fee simple acquisition (Environmental Defense Fund 2000; Wiebe et al. 1996).

Nonprofit conservation organizations and government agencies have adapted easement contracts to minimize the probability of these types of future enforcement problems. They have addressed the ambiguity problem by specifying the land uses that can be undertaken by the landowner, rather than trying to restrict all possible uses that are considered conservation unfriendly. Typically, most contracts have clauses that require the landowner to notify the conservator if the land is to be sold and to give the conservator the right of first refusal in that event. Contracts can also require the conservator's approval of future landowners. This provides the conservator the opportunity to meet with new landowners to ensure that the new landowner understands the terms of the easement and to forge a cooperative relationship (Boyd et al. 1999).

Donated Easements

The U.S. Internal Revenue Service (IRS) offers tax incentives to landowners who donate the development interests in their land in perpetuity for conservation purposes to a qualified nonprofit organization or government agency. The IRS requires that the donated easement be for land that provides society with a valued public good, and the recipient must be preapproved by the IRS as tax-exempt and eligible to receive donations used for tax considerations.

Qualifying lands must satisfy one of the following conservation purposes: The conserved land must (1) provide education or outdoor recreation to society; (2) provide protection to species by conserving their natural habitat or ecosystem; (3) provide a scenic vista by preserving open spaces; or (4) provide for the protection of historically significant lands and buildings. Easements must be donated to an organization established for conservation purposes, which can monitor and enforce the terms of the easement, and an easement can be resold or transferred only to a similar agency (IRS 2000; Hunt 1994).

Landowners may receive relief from income tax, gift tax, and estate tax by donating a conservation easement. The deductions provided by a conservation easement to the heirs of an estate are twofold. First, the value of the estate is reduced by the fair market value of the easement. Second, the tax base of the estate may qualify for an additional 40 percent reduction in value up to the exclusion limit, when the land has significant conservation value such that the easement reduces the value of the land by at least 30 percent, and the percentage reduction decreases as the value of the easement decreases in proportion to the total value of the land. The exclusion limit for deaths occurring in the year 2000 is $300,000, increasing to $500,000 for the year 2002 and thereafter. To qualify for the additional tax deduction for high conservation value, the land must satisfy certain ownership requirements and must be within twenty-five miles of a metropolitan statistical area (designated by the Office of Management and Budget) or a federal wilderness area or lie within ten miles of an urban national forest (Tax Payer Relief Act 1998; Small 2000). Of course, the ongoing debate in Congress over tax policy could change these conditions over the next few years.

These two incentives can be the difference between an estate being maintained in one contiguous area or being broken up and sold to meet estate tax liability. Estates that are valued at less than $675,000 have an estate tax liability of zero. For example, suppose an estate is valued at $1,500,000, and a landowner or heir donates a conservation easement valued at $500,000. The estate also benefits from a $400,000 deduction due to the high conservation quality of the land. The estate tax would be levied on an estate valued at $600,000, and the heirs would escape any estate tax liability as a result of the donation (Small 1998; Land Trust Alliance 2000d).

Donated easements may also reduce a landowner's income tax liability. A landowner who donates a conservation easement to a qualified agency can deduct the entire value of the easement from his income tax provided it does not exceed 30 percent of his adjusted gross income. If the easement value exceeds this 30-percent threshold, the landowner can deduct 30 percent of his adjusted gross income for up to six years or until he has exhausted the easement value. The value of the easement is measured as the difference in the land's value with and without the easement (Utah CLCC 1997; IRS 1998).

Pros. Donating an easement in land provides an opportunity for the landowner or the heirs to keep the land intact. Estate taxes can be large enough that the inheritors of the land face the proposition of selling off part of the land to meet the levied tax. Federal estate tax law allows for the landowner or the landowner's heirs to donate the developmental rights in the land, which reduces the tax liability, sometimes eliminating it completely (Land Trust Alliance 2000a). The inheritors of the land can then maintain joint ownership of the land with the easement holder, keeping the land intact and continuing conservation-friendly land practices.

Donated easements typically appeal to landowners or heirs who like the idea of conservation. Donating the easement generally has a net cost to the heirs because the reduced value of the land following the donation of the easement generally exceeds the savings in reduced estate taxes realized by the heirs. The initial tax rate on the estate's tax base is 18 percent and gradually increases to 55 percent for estates with a value of $3 million or greater. An estate may be subject to a lower tax rate when a conservation easement is donated (Johnson and Mikow 1998).

To illustrate, consider the case in which a landowner dies and leaves his heirs an estate valued at $3 million. The land is free of conservation easements and constitutes the whole of the estate. The estate tax would be $1,429,450, which is the $3 million evaluated at the 55-percent estate tax rate ($1,650,000) less the uniform credit of $220,550. Now suppose the land is encumbered with a qualified conservation easement valued at $2,025,000, which reduces the value of the estate to $975,000. The heirs further qualify for the $300,000 exclusion, reducing the value of the estate to $675,000. The estate tax on this amount just equals the uniform credit, making the tax liability zero.

Therefore, the heirs save $1,429,450 in reduced estate taxes by donating the conservation easement, but they lose $2,025,000 in property value, netting them a financial loss of $595,550. To justify this donation, the heirs must have had a sufficiently high conservation value to overcome the financial deficit that results from the donated easement (Boyd et al. 1999). For example, the land may have been in the landowner's family for several generations and the landowner desires to keep the land intact and out of development even after he is dead. He does so by donating the rights to develop the land to a qualified nonprofit conservation organization. If the donor's conservation values are aligned with the community's, the donor's financial net loss acts as a subsidy to the community to ensure that important land attributes are preserved.

Conservators benefit from donated easements by acquiring them with minimal direct costs to the conservator. Their main cost comes from assisting the landowner in understanding and completing the transaction. Nonprofit organizations and government agencies can redirect their limited budgets toward conservation efforts elsewhere.

The conservator could also obtain the easement in the land through a bargain sale, which occurs when part of the conservation easement is donated and part is purchased at fair market value. The donated part of the easement is subject to the same IRS tax benefits and requirements (Land Trust Alliance 2000a). Bargain sales give the acquiring agency more leverage to obtain conservation-targeted lands by appealing to many different types of landowners and tailoring the payment to each individual landowner. The percentage of land acquired by PDR easement is just sufficient to induce the landowner to donate an easement on the remainder of the land, providing the regulator with some flexibility to learn about and adjust for the landowner's conservation value.

Cons. Donated easements are subject to the same monitoring and enforcement costs as PDR easements. They also face the same uncertainty about future landowner actions. Again future landowners of the encumbered land may have a different idea about conserving the land and may take actions that violate the terms of the agreement. The future landowner may overgraze, encroach on boundaries that separate specified land uses, or not completely fulfill maintenance requirements specified in the easement agreement. The easement holder's monitoring and enforcement costs rise as a result.

Although donated easements do not require as much in the form of negotiation costs as PDR easements, given that they are donated and satisfy IRS requirements, they do exhibit several other negative attributes. Donated easements do not fully compensate the landowners for the development forgone and therefore appeal only to landowners who place a nonfinancial value on seeing their land preserved. These landowners are typically willing to pay to ensure that it remains undeveloped (Boyd et al. 1999). Not everyone is so generous. The landowner's payment is in the form of the landowner's lost revenue from not developing the land minus the value of the tax considerations. By targeting the landowner, rather than the land, donated easements cannot guarantee that the land conserved is the land that provides society with the largest net benefit. As long as the land fulfills the requirements of the IRS, the conservator has no incentive to refuse the gift.

Donated easements also leave the regulator uncertain as to the quantity of land conserved. Total conservation efforts are difficult to predict and are usually not known until after the tax year has ended. This raises two problems for the regulator. First, regulators who rely on tax incentives do not know how effective donated easements are at achieving their goals until the landowners have filed their tax returns. As a result, the regulators have lost the flexibility to adjust or employ other mechanisms to ensure that targeted conservation goals are met.

Second, the regulator is uncertain of the expenditures (tax revenue forgone) for conserved parcels until taxes have been filed. If too much land is conserved such that the loss in tax revenues exceeds the projected amount, the budgets of other programs might have to be cut or deficit spending might occur. If the government allocates its resources efficiently across programs such that the last dollar spent on each program's objectives provides society with the same benefit, reallocating funds from one program to another constitutes a net loss to society and decreases the overall benefits to society.

The tax deduction under IRS rules is based on the development value of the land. When a land parcel has a relatively high development value and a low conservation value (i.e., the parcel is surrounded by other developed properties), the tax deduction to the landowner may be greater than the conservation value of the land. The conservator has no incentive to turn down the easement donation. Here society loses the development revenue, plus it overcompensates the landowner for the conservation of the land. Furthermore, given scarce conservation dollars, conserving this parcel, which might be better suited for development, can lead to the development of other parcels that would be better off conserved.

Donated easements are subject to appraisal problems and misrepresentation of the value of the easement by the landowner. IRS regulations stipulate that tax returns with a deduction for a donation of an interest in property that exceeds $5,000 must be accompanied by a qualified appraisal completed by a qualified appraiser. This appraisal is a general description of the land, agreement terms, date of transfer, name of the appraiser, the appraiser's qualifications, and other donation-specific information. The qualified appraiser is someone who must be an active appraiser qualified to appraise restricted land and who must be aware of legal liability (IRS 1998). When the appraised value of the easement exceeds its true value or if the landowner misrepresents the value, the tax relief that results decreases the net benefit to society. Some observers fear that overappraisals and misrepresentation of easement values will be the norm given the lack of recently sold and comparable properties. Valuing the easement-encumbered property requires information on both restricted and unrestricted comparables, information rarely available for species protection.

Concluding Remarks

This review of the economic principles underlying the set of incentive mechanisms highlights some important lessons. First, market instruments, such as TDRs (permits) and impact fees, that have been praised for their ability to control air pollution at minimum costs are not as effective for protecting habitat for two reasons. Because no uniform system of measuring biodiversity exists and land has heterogeneous habitat quality, market systems have to be combined with other regulatory tools like zoning to be effective. In addition, development results in permanent destruction of habitat, giving the regulator only one chance to get it right. Zoning would be effective on its own if political objectives, economic conditions, and environmental preferences never changed, which is highly unlikely.

Second, voluntary mechanisms (such as fee simple purchase, easements, conservation banking, and subsidies) are an effective and flexible method for targeting low cost land with high-quality habitat. Extracting landowners' private information, however, regarding both habitat quality and private use value is expensive and politically charged. The key for all sides is developing a process of informed decision-making. All parties should understand the restrictions and obligations of the mechanism and the consequences of failing to uphold these limits. Such a process includes drafting a plan, implementing it, and evaluating success and failure. A good example of a step-by-step planning process is Bick and Haney's (2001) practical guide for landowners interested in conservation easements. It provides detailed examples of easement contracts for productive agriculture, forests, open spaces, and greenspace.

Third, incentive mechanisms like conservation banking, subsidies, and easements can be designed to induce landowners both to conserve their land and to invest in the conservation value of their land. This is important when habitat needs exceed the quantity of quality habitat and degraded habitat must be restored to meet the ESA objectives, or where habitat fragments can be expanded by creating or restoring a habitat corridor.

Fourth, no one incentive mechanism is best for all cases. Factors such as development pressure (or the lack thereof), funding, the range of land quality, quantity of suitable habitat, the range of land values, and types of landowners should be considered in determining which mechanism or combination of mechanisms would meet the regulator's objectives most efficiently.

Fifth, establishing a method for measuring biodiversity, which takes an ecosystem approach, will aid the cause of spreading minimum conservation dollars across the greatest number of species and habitat acres. By taking an ecosystem approach, rather than a species-by-species approach, society can realize economies of scale, since habitat can protect several species. A measure of biodiversity will bring people together to define and work toward meeting common ESA objectives.

Sixth, conservation approaches (conservation banking and TDRs) can be designed to satisfy both state and federal land use regulations. When all the players are brought to the table (USFWS representing the Endangered Species Act, the Army Corps of Engineers representing the Clean Water Act, state fish and wildlife agencies, and other affected state, local, and federal entities), the regulatory burden on both landowners and affected agencies can be reduced by giving the landowner regulatory certainty and ensuring the regulator's access for monitoring land use restrictions, as well as clear-cut recourse in the event the landowner fails to meet stipulated agreements.

Finally, mechanisms such as donated easements can reduce a regulator's outlays by creating incentives for land trusts and other nonprofit organizations to work together and share the costs of conservation. Cost sharing works in both directions. Land trusts can reduce their costs by purchasing habitat fee simple, placing a conservation easement on the land that they hold, and then donating the land to the government to manage.

References

Altschuler, Alan A., and Jose A. Gomez-Ibanez. 1993. *Regulation for revenue: The political economy of land use exactions.* Washington, D.C.: Brookings Institution.

Babcock, Bruce A., JunJie Wu, P. G. Lakshminarayan, and David Zilberman. 1996. The economics of a public fund for environmental amenities: A study of CRP contracts. *American Journal of Agricultural Economics* 78, no. 4: 961–971.

Baden, John A., and Pete Geddes. 1999. Environmental entrepreneurs: Keys to achieving wilderness conservation goals. *Denver University Law Review* 76, no. 2: 519–534.

Benjamin, Antonio H., and Charles Weiss Jr. 1997. Economic and market incentives as instruments of environmental policy in Brazil and the United States. *Texas International Law Journal* 32:67–95.

Bick, S., and H. Haney Jr. 2001. *The landowner's guide to conservation easements.* Dubuque, Iowa: Kendall/Hunt Publishing.

Boyd, James, Kathryn Caballero, and R. David Simpson. 1999. The law and economics of habitat conservation: Lessons from an analysis of easement acquisitions. Discussion paper 99-32. April. Washington, D.C.: Resources for the Future.

Brown, Gardner Jr., and Jason Shogren. 1998. Economics of the Endangered Species Act. *Journal of Economic Perspectives* 12:3–20.

Brueckner, Jan K. 1997. Infrastructure financing and urban development: The economics of impact fees. *Journal of Public Economics* 66:383–407.

California Coastal Conservancy (CCC). 2000. About the Coastal Conservancy, and Coastal Conservancy programs. www.coastalconservancy.ca.gov [cited August 2000].

California Department of Fish and Game (CDFG). 1993. Southern California coastal sage scrub NCCP conservation guidelines. http://ceres.ca.gov/CRA/ NCCP/ [cited November 1993].

———. 2000. State and federally listed endangered and threatened animals of California. *California Code Of Regulations,* Title 14, Section 670.5. http:// ceres.ca.gov/CRA [cited July 2000].

California Resources Agency (CRA). 2000. Department of Fish and Game, Inland Fisheries Division, Timber Tax Fish (related) incentives for sustainable habitat. www.dfg.ca.gov/timber/ttcp_2.html [cited 7 September 2000].

Clark, Dana, and David Downes. 1996. What price biodiversity? Economic incentives and biodiversity conservation in the United States. *Journal of Environmental Law and Litigation* 11:9–89.

Coase, Ronald. 1960. The problem of social cost. Pp. 109–138 in *Economics of the environment: Selected readings* (3d ed.), edited by Robert Dorfman and Nancy S. Dorfman. New York: W. W. Norton & Co., 1993.

Collins, Dennis G. 2000. Enforcement problems with successor grantors. Pp. 9– 25 in *Protecting the land: Conservation easements past, present, and future,* edited by Julie Ann Gustanski and Roderick H. Squires. Washington, D.C.: Island Press.

County of San Diego (CSD). 1998. Multiple species conservation plan: Implementing agreement. www.co.san-diego.ca.us/cnty [cited March 1998].

————. 2000. Multiple species conservation plan. www.co.san-diego.ca.us/cnty [cited July 2000].

Environmental Defense Fund. 1999. Mitigation banking as an endangered species conservation tool. www.edf.org/ [cited November 1999].

————. 2000. Progress on the back forty: An analysis of three incentive-based approaches to endangered species conservation on private land. www.edf .org/ [cited January 2000].

Epstein, Richard A. 1996. A conceptual approach to zoning: What's wrong with Euclid. *NYU Environmental Law Journal* 5:277–291.

Farm Service Agency. 1997a. Conservation Reserve Program: Fact sheet. U.S. Department of Agriculture. February.

————. 1997b. Conservation Reserve Program: Continuous sign-up for high-priority conservation practices. U.S. Department of Agriculture. February.

————. 1997c. *Online.* Conservation Reserve Program sign-up 16: Environmental benefits index, proposed rule long-term policy. U.S. Department of Agriculture. October.

————. 2000. *Online.* The Conservation Reserve Program. U.S. Department of Agriculture. www.fsa.usda.gov [cited September 2000].

Fernandez, Linda, and Larry Karp. 1998. Restoring wetlands through wetlands mitigation banks. *Environmental and Resource Economics* 12:323–344.

Gustanski, Julie Ann. 2000. Protecting the land: Conservation easements, voluntary actions, and private lands. P. xvii in *Protecting the land: Conservation easements past, present, and future,* edited by Julie Ann Gustanski and Roderick H. Squires. Washington, D.C.: Island Press.

Hanley, Nick, Jason F. Shogren, and Ben White. 1997. Environmental economics. Pp. 58–105 in *Theory and Practice,* New York: Oxford University Press.

Hunt, Dave. 1994. Conservation easements and donations for tax deductions. Habitat Extension Bulletin 14. Wyoming Game and Fish Department.

Idaho Department of Game and Fish (IDFG). 2000. Habitat Improvement Program (HIP): Key to the future for Idaho's game birds. www.state.id.us/ fishgame/hip.html [cited 1 March 2000].

Innes, Robert. 1997. Takings, compensation, and equal treatment for owners of developed and undeveloped land. *Journal of Law and Economics* 40 (October): 403–432.

————. 2000. Takings and compensation for private lands. *Land Economics* 76, no. 2:195–212.

Innes, Robert, Stephan Polasky, and John Tschirhart. 1998. Takings, compensation, and endangered species protection on private lands. *Journal of Economic Perspectives* 12, no. 3:35–52.

Internal Revenue Service (IRS). 1998. Charitable contributions. Publication 526. March.

———. 2000. Determining the value of donated property. Publication 561. February.

Johnson, Barry W., Jacob M. Mikow. 1998. Federal estate tax returns, 1995–1997. Internal Revenue Service. www.irs.gov.

Kayden, Jerold S. 1992. Market-based regulatory approaches: A comparative discussion of environmental and land use techniques in the United States. *B.C. Environmental Affairs Law Review* 19:565–580.

King, D. M., and C. C. Bohlen. 1994. A technical summary of wetland restoration costs in the continental United States. University of Maryland Technical Report UMCEES-CBL-94-048.

Laffont, Jean-Jacques. 1995. Regulation, moral hazard, and insurance of environmental risk. *Journal of Public Economics* 58:319–336.

Land Trust Alliance. 1998. State-by-state summary of the 1998 National Land Trust Census. lta.org/consopt.html.

———. 2000a. Protecting your land. lta.org/consopt.html [cited August 2000].

———. 2000b. Land Trust success stories: Pacific Region. lta.org/s_pacific.html [cited August 2000].

———. 2000c. Land trusts: The front guards of land protection. lta.org/whatlt.html [cited August 2000].

———. 2000d. American Farm and Ranch Protection Act. lta.org/tax97.html [cited August 2000].

Levinson, Arik. 1997. Why oppose TDRs?: Transferable developmental rights can increase overall development. *Regional Science and Urban Economics* 27:283–296.

Mann, C., and M. Plummer. 1995. *Noah's choice: The future of endangered species.* New York: Knopf.

Miller, Andrew J. 1999. Transferable development rights in the constitutional landscape: Has Penn Central failed to weather the storm. *Natural Resources Journal* 39 (summer): 459–516.

Mills, David E. 1980. Transferable development rights markets. *Journal of Urban Economics* 7:63–74.

National Research Council. 1993. *Setting priorities for land conservation.* Washington, D.C.: National Academy Press, pp. ix–261.

Natural Community Conservation Planning (NCCP). 2000. National Community Conservation Planning general process guidelines. http://ceres.ca.gov/CRA/NCCP [cited July 2000].

Nijhuis, Michelle. 2000a. Acre by acre: Can land trusts save the West's disappearing open space? *High Country News,* 28 February.

———. 2000b. A land trust toolbox. *High Country News,* 28 February.

Parkhurst, Gregory, Jason Shogren, Chris Bastian, Paul Kivi, Jennifer Donner, and Rodney Smith. 2002. Agglomeration bonus: An incentive mechanism to reunite fragmented habitat for biodiversity conservation. *Ecological Economics* 41:305–328.

Polasky, Stephen, Holly Doremus, and Bruce Rettig. 1997. Endangered species conservation on private land. *Contemporary Economic Policy* 15:66–76.

Rowley, Charles K. 1988. Rent seeking versus directly unproductive profit-seeking activities. Pp.15–26 in *The political economy of rent seeking,* edited by Charles K. Rowley, Robert D. Tollison, and Gordon Tullock. Boston: Kluwer Academic.

Salmon Recovery Funding Board (SRFB). 2000a. Second round 2000 salmon grant application forms, report 18a, June.

———. 2000b. Policies and project selection grants manual, second round, 2000 cycle, report 18, July.

Saunders, Denis A., Richard J. Hobbs, and Chris A. Margules. 1991. Biological consequences of ecosystem fragmentation: A review. *Conservation Biology* 5, no. 1:18–32.

Settle, Chad, Terrance Hurley, and Jason Shogren. 2001. Citizen suits. Pp. 217–248 in *The law and economics of the environment,* edited by A. Heyes. Cheltenham, UK: Edward Elgar.

Skidmore, Mark, and Michael Peddle. 1998. Do development impact fees reduce the rate of residential development. *Growth and Change* 29 (fall): 383–400.

Small, Stephen J. 1998. *Preserving family lands: Book 1, Essential tax strategies for the landowner.* Boston: Landowner Planning Center.

———. 2000. An obscure tax code provision takes private land protection into the twenty-first century. Pp. 55–66 in *Protecting the land: Conservation easements past, present, and future,* edited by Julie Ann Gustanski and Roderick H. Squires. Washington, D.C.: Island Press.

Smith, Rodney B., and Jason F. Shogren. 2001. Protecting species on private land. Pp. 326–342 in *Protecting endangered species in the United States: Biological needs, political realities, economic choices,* edited by J. Shogren and J. Tschirhart. New York: Cambridge University Press.

———. 2002. Voluntary incentive design for endangered species protection. *Journal of Environmental Economics and Management* 43:169–187.

Sohn, David, and Madeline Cohen. 1996. From smokestacks to species: Extending the tradable permit approach from air pollution to habitat conservation. *Stanford Environmental Law Journal* 15:405–451.

Stewart, Richard B. 1992. Models for environmental regulation: Central planning versus market-based approaches. *Boston College Environmental Affairs Law Review* 19:547–562.

Tax Payer Relief Act. 1998. Public Law 105-34. *The 1997 Tax Payer Relief Act,* amended by *The Internal Revenue Service Reform Act* of 1998. Cited at http://ltg.org/taxlaw.html.

Tripp, James T. B., and Daniel J. Dudek. 1989. Institutional guidelines for developing transferable rights programs. *Yale Journal on Regulation* 6: 369–391.

U.S. Fish and Wildlife Service (USFWS). 1996. Report to Congress on the recovery program for threatened and endangered species. Washington, D.C.

———. 2000. Land acquisition planning, 341 FW 2. P. 11 in *Fish and Wildlife Service manual.* www.fws.gov/directives [cited 10 May].

Utah Critical Land Conservation Committee. 1997. Land conservation in Utah: Tools, techniques, and initiatives. www.governor.state.ut.us/. January.

Wiebe, Keith, Abebayehu Tegene, and Betsey Kuhn. 1996. Partial interests in land: Policy tools for resource use and conservation. Economic Research Service, USDA, AER-744, November.

Wilcove, D., M. Bean, R. Binnie, and M. McMillan. 1996. *Rebuilding the Ark.* New York: Environmental Defense Fund.

Wu, JunJie. 2000. Slippage effects of the Conservation Reserve Program. *American Journal of Agricultural Economics* 82, no. 4:979–992.

Wu, JunJie, David Zilberman, and Bruce A. Babcock. 2001. Environmental and distributional impacts of conservation targeting strategies. *Journal of Environmental Economics and Management* 41:333–350.

PART II

CHALLENGES TO USING ECONOMIC INCENTIVES FOR SPECIES PROTECTION

CHAPTER 4

Endangered Species Protection and Ways of Life: Beyond Economy and Ecology

FRIEDA KNOBLOCH AND R. MCGREGGOR CAWLEY

Ethics are possibly a kind of community instinct in-the-making.
ALDO LEOPOLD (1949, P. 239)

Any group that sees its way of life at stake in a dispute will, obviously, be reluctant to compromise.
ROBERT DAHL (1967, P. 272)

The possibility of offering financial incentives to encourage landowners to protect endangered species on private property raises questions about how economic and ecological well-being can be connected in environmental policy. These questions are not new. Roughly 70 years ago, Aldo Leopold set down his ideas on this matter in "A Conservation Ethic" (an early version of his more famous "Land Ethic" essay). Using the wildlife conservation movement as an example, Leopold suggested, "At the inception of the movement fifty years ago, its underlying thesis was to save species from extermination. The means to this end were a series of restrictive enactments. . . . The whole structure was negative and prohibitory." Leopold went on to argue that a new "positive and affirmatory ideology" was developing in the 1930s, "the thesis of which is to prevent the deterioration of the environment" through "ecological research" and the "same tools and skills already used in agriculture and forestry" (1933, p. 641).

But Leopold contended that knowledge and ability had to be accompanied by a willingness to use them: "A rare bird or flower need remain no rarer than the people willing to venture their skill in *building it a habitat*" (his emphasis). It is the question of how to create this willingness that Leopold explores in his subsequent essay, "Land Ethic" (1949). The essence of a land ethic was the belief that a "thing is right if it tends to preserve the integrity, stability, and beauty of the biotic community. It is wrong when it tends otherwise" (p. 262). This belief required changing "the role of *Homo sapiens* from conqueror of the land-community to plain member and citizen of it. It implies respect for his fellow-members, and also respect for the community as such" (p. 240).

Roughly twenty years after Leopold's death, President Richard Nixon delivered a special message to Congress in which he declared that an "environmental awakening" had led to a "new maturity of American public life. It is working a revolution in values, as commitment to responsible partnership with nature replaces cavalier assumptions that we can play God with our surroundings and survive" (Nixon 1974, p. 174). The task ahead, Nixon continued, was to "crystallize" this awakening "into permanent patterns of thought and action" that created a "new and higher environmental way of life." As a step toward accomplishing this task, he called on Congress to enlarge and strengthen federal policy in regard to endangered species. Congress responded a year later with the Endangered Species Act of 1973 (ESA).

In the early 1970s, there was certainly reason to believe that the basic components of Leopold's land ethic were taking shape in the United States. Though still incomplete, the knowledge and skills needed for ecological management were far more developed than in the 1930s, and the apparent widespread political support for environmental protection efforts seemed to indicate that a willingness was also developing. Now, roughly thirty years later, the national political climate is more difficult to read.

Opinion polls continue to show relatively strong public support for environmental protection efforts. In fact, some of these polls contain rather surprising results. For instance, in one recent national survey, 55 percent of the respondents disagreed with the statement "Plants and animals exist primarily for human use," and 88 percent agreed with the statement, "Humans have an ethical obligation to protect plant and animal species" (Steele and Lovrich 1997, p. 10). In another survey, 59 percent of the respondents agreed with the statement "Protecting the environment should be given priority, even at the risk of slowing down economic growth" (p. 13). At the same time, opposition to environmental protection efforts has also grown, resulting in a natural resource policy arena that is mired in acrimony and gridlock. Particularly troublesome in this regard is the failure of Congress to reauthorize the ESA since 1992.

There are a variety of factors that help explain the current controversy over the ESA. The one of primary importance to this project, however, was triggered by the recent U.S. Supreme Court ruling that extended the ESA to private property. It seems likely that the task of extending species protection to private property would be problematical at any time, but it is even more difficult in our current political climate. Opponents of environmental regulations challenge the extent to which governmental policy may violate constitutionally guaranteed protection of private property rights.

On the face of it, the approach proposed in this project would seem to provide an appropriate response. The use of incentives recognizes the potential clash between species protection and private property rights. More important, offering compensation for endangered species protection may be an expedient in ensuring some measure of compliance with the law. In theory, it affords a way to create an economic value for endangered species and thereby alters the decisional calculus so that the benefits of compliance with the ESA outweigh the benefits of opposition to it. The argument we want to advance in this essay, however, is that the controversies over the ESA, and environmental protection in general, remind us that financial loss or gain is not the only measure of economic well-being.

Consider, for example, environmental historian Samuel Hays's assessment of opposition to environmental protection efforts in the year after World War II (Hays 1985). Noting that this opposition was "persistent, often uncompromising, and many times successful," Hays suggests, "At the root of these controversies was not just 'interest' in the conventional sense of an economic stake but values. The economic interest of producers undergirded their opposition. But at a deeper level of human response was the degree to which producers' values were offended. They could not accept the notion that what environmentalists thought was useful and valuable was, in fact, so" (pp. 529–530). Building on this assessment, we want to argue that much more is at stake in both species protection and land use than the financial value attached to each. We believe it is not merely financial well-being that many private property owners seek to protect but a way of life, for which no financial incentive or compensation may be adequate.

In pursuing this argument, we will sketch out the reasons why we believe that environmental controversies are best understood in terms of ways of life. We then offer some tentative suggestions, drawing on the historical roots of concepts like economy, ecology, and property, on how it might be possible to add extra texture to the discourse of the incentive approach by making it more attentive to the cultural factors shaping the values that connect people to the land and each other.

Ways of Life

According to *Henderson's Dictionary of Biological Terms,* "biota" refers to the "fauna and flora of a region" and "biotic community" is "a community of plants and animals as a whole" (Holmes 1979). These concepts define the essential concepts of species preservation. Protecting a species requires attention to preserving the community on which it depends. There is a sense, then, in which the fundamental goal of the ESA can be defined as an attempt to preserve the way of life of endangered and threatened species. This interpretation is consistent, at least in part, with the etymological root of the word "biota."

"Biota" is the Latin form of the Greek word *biotē,* which means way of life. But the root of *biotē* is the word *bios,* which, though frequently defined as simply life, originally meant "not animal life, but mode of *life* . . . *manner of living.*" It was also used to indicate *"livelihood, means of living . . .* to make one's *living* off, to *live* by a thing" (Liddell and Scott 1925, p. 316). It is abundantly clear that a human way of life organized around the tenets of capitalism and industrialism creates disruptions that threaten the ability of other species to pursue their way of life. A mainstay of American environmentalism has been a call for a series of changes, ranging from moderate to radical, in our industrial way of life to make it less disruptive of the nonhuman environment. Although the logic of this argument is more or less accurate, we believe that it tends to misunderstand and devalue the importance of way of life in human community. In doing so, it also adds extra layers of controversy to conversations about species protection efforts.

In human terms, a way of life is a holistic concept that constitutes a "dominating interest or occupation" that "governs all one's actions." It includes the "habits (of an individual or a community) with regard to food, habitation, intercourse, etc." (OED 1971). In this regard, it closely mirrors the concept of culture as traditionally understood by anthropologists: "the total way of life of a people" (Kluckhohn, in Geertz 1973, p. 4). It is important that both culture and ways of life are social—that is, public, and shared. They are not disembodied systems, with component parts (financial, religious, filial, etc.) governed by discernible laws, but "webs of significance" in which people's lives are experienced as meaningful (Geertz 1973, p. 5).

Viewed in this context, we can begin to appreciate why arguments over environmental protection provoke what Hays called "a deeper level of human response." No single component of a way of life can be altered without affecting an entire range of cultural identity, knowledge, and experience. Changes in ways of life always contain potential threats to the way people understand themselves both individually and as communities.

It is safe to say, of course, that much of American history revolves around the tension between different communities' ways of life, their mutually incompatible values, or their incompatibility with the founding democratic principles of the nation. Not every way of life has an enduring place in American society (slave-based plantation agriculture, for example). But because a way of life encompasses the everyday values, knowledge, experiences and interactions of people and communities that make people's lives meaningful, one is ill-advised to ignore signs that an action (like protection of endangered species on private property) threatens someone's way of life. Failure to acknowledge and respect such claims could create a reservoir of cynicism and mistrust that would only deform efforts to secure environmental protections. Two admittedly extreme cases of the place of ways of life in the resource-use debate suggest how high the stakes are when such issues are ignored.

In the redwood forests of northern California in the early 1990s, the environmental protection agenda of Earth First activists faced intense hostility from both logging companies and loggers themselves. The conflict between loggers and activists revolved around the loggers' perception that environmental protection would come only at the expense of their livelihood *and* an encompassing way of life. Lifelong logger Ernie Pardini told Earth Firster Judi Bari that his priority in logging was "earning a living to feed the babies," whereas "Earth First! stands for Earth first." Pardini's rationale identifies the source of environmental protection, not in activists or environmental regulation, but within the household (a point we return to later): "[the babies] are here on this Earth, and they're the ones that are going to be taking care of the Earth." Activist response to overlogging created "mixed emotions" for Pardini because, he said, "logging was my life," not just a livelihood. At the same time, Pardini identifies the real environmental threat, not as logging per se, but as the commercial value of logging to large corporations.

"Most of the loggers that I know are going to do as good a job environmentally as they can with what they have to work with. But if L-P [Louisiana Pacific] says, okay, this is a clearcut . . . you're going to go in there and cut every tree. . . . [S]tart fingering L-P themselves, and stop picking on the little logger guys" (Bari 1992, pp. 253–261).

Similarly, Raymond Rogers, former Nova Scotia fisherman, identifies the commercial value of fish to corporations as the real culprit in the 1980s fisheries collapse, not the primary work of fishermen. Conservation efforts and environmental regulation are captive to "the economic and technological forces which destroy nature," forces that dominate "people who live in Atlantic coastal communities" and denigrate "the way Atlantic coastal communities . . . see the world and talk about it." What was lost in the collapse of the fisheries was not merely fish but the fishers' knowledge and communities. "All the edges you fished along, all the little humps you know, the sense of being a part of a world on the ocean, and what's underneath it, all of the knowledge that was passed down to you by older fishermen will be lost." Direct knowledge of the earth and its forms of life is "located knowledge that comes from inhabiting a place over a long period of time and knowing the comings and goings of the beings that live there with you" (Rogers 1998, pp. 182–184).

These examples also help identify some of the larger factors at play in these controversies, especially among people engaged immediately in resource extraction. Critiques of "modern farming, logging, fishing, ranching and industry" identify work as "the enemy of nature," according to historian Richard White (1996, p. 180), because environmental effects are seen to be the result only of those activities themselves. This view tends to misread the situation in several important ways. First, as White notes (p. 172), working the land has been an important source of knowledge and understanding of nature.

> Work that has changed nature has simultaneously produced much of our knowledge of nature. Humans have known nature by digging in the earth, planting seeds, and harvesting plants. . . . They have known nature by shaping wood and stone, by living with animals, nurturing them, and killing them. . . . They have pulled, tugged, carried, and walked, or they have harnessed the energy of animals, water, and wind to do these things for them. They have achieved a bodily knowledge of the natural world.

White's comment here is clearly reinforced by the comments from Rogers.

Second, this view tends to make individual landowners directly responsible for the effects of an entire society's commodity consumption, of which they are only a part, closest to nature. In reality, all Americans' livelihoods—and ways of life—depend on the primary extractive work many landowners perform. Once again, as White (1996, p. 185) notes: "There are few articles or letters denouncing university professors or computer programmers or accountants or lawyers for sullying the environment, although it is my guess that a single lawyer or accountant could, on a good day, put the efforts of Paul Bunyan to shame." To lay the burden of environmental protection on private landowners, without acknowledging the full cast of players (consumers, corporate interests, etc.) who shape our ways of life and consequent environmental demands, neglects an important relationship between land use and more attenuated threats to native biodiversity. Put simply, if there were no meat eaters and meat packers in the United States, or wooden houses to build from cuts made on corporate land, there would be no conflict over range cattle or timber production endangering now rare species.

Finally, many (but not all) of those who benefit from resource production and own the land are the same people who work it. Not all landowners are necessarily longtime farmers or ranchers concerned about shared knowledge, community stability, and an enduring way of life. Those who are not, like the corporate interests identified by Pardini and Rogers, may view disruptions simply as part of the normal flow of business. Some landowners, however, may already feel that their way of life is threatened by government regulation as well as market forces beyond their control and react with resistance and resentment. For them, government regulations and market forces often fail to recognize the value of ways of life, including land-based knowledge and community life, and the larger system in which land-based commodities become financially valuable (and increasingly inexpensive).

A recent editorial by University of Nevada historian Hal Rothman helps tie these various points together and frame our thinking as to why financial incentives may not be as effective an approach as they may otherwise seem. "I always cringe," Rothman (2000, p. 17) complains, "when people from the rural West tell the rest of us how to live. There's an arrogance to their pronouncements, a foolhardy pretension that they are the real world and that the 95 percent of us who live in Western cities somehow don't matter." Asserting that the "rural West has become a playground, a colony the rest of us visit when we want to relax or indulge our fantasies," Rothman poses the question "Why should the rest of us subsidize their condescending culture and custom arguments? The rural West sure doesn't pay the bills—look at tax revenues in any state and you'll see that clearly enough." As a possible solution, Rothman suggests, "Go to ranchers and farmers and tell them that we'll give them their best year plus annual cost of living raises to match inflation. . . . They can pretend to ranch and farm . . . and they won't even have to worry about inevitable fluctuations in crop and animal prices."

To be sure, Rothman intended his editorial to be read as a caricature. Moreover, the subject of Rothman's editorial was water, not endangered species. Nevertheless, his comments bring into sharp relief the point we are trying to make here. Viewing farming and ranching as simply activities pursued for financial gain makes a compensation approach appear both practical and feasible. Viewing them as parts of a way of life that defines community leads to quite a different assessment. The potential loss of community and way of life is as threatening as all other major losses and cannot be addressed with compensatory programs.

Returning to the fisheries example, the Canadian government established a program that included retraining and compensation. The failure of this program, according to Rogers (1998, pp. 183–184), was in part a failure to honor coastal communities:

> How do you explain the importance of living in a community and wanting to stay in a community to someone who has never lived in one? . . . The fishery collapses, and . . . you have to go up to Ontario to take your retraining course. Your family is back here. . . . The teacher made you feel like dirt. Your buddies don't like it either, but you can't comfort each other because you've told all the fishing stories three times over, and it only depresses everyone to talk about it anyway. [The Canadian Department of Fisheries and Oceans] has tried to talk you out of [the knowledge the community shared] by claiming that science and management know better . . . that resource management regulation is the way to go. [But what really happens is that corporate] interests come in and make their money by overexploiting the resources of the area, leaving local communities dependent on handouts, if there are any. So this is the situation you share with communities like your own . . . you start to spend more time worrying about qualifying for

handouts than you do being a fisherman. [Retraining and compensation are part of a] program for those who are newly stupid.

A Land Ethic

"Political conflict," Deborah Stone (1997, pp. 33–34) observes, "is
never simply about material conditions and choices, but over what is legitimate." What makes political conflict in a democratic society intriguing (or troublesome) is that often there are competing, and equally valid,
definitions for "legitimate." As Stone (p. 1) notes, "Paradoxes are nothing but trouble . . . and political life is full of them."

As a case in point, saving endangered species is certainly legitimate.
So too is preserving ways of life that create meaning and community
even if they threaten species. As long as we separate these pursuits, there
is no paradox. However, the extension of the ESA to private property
forces a recognition that these pursuits cannot be separated and, therefore, presents a situation with apparently paradoxical overtones. Offering financial incentives is certainly one way to finesse this problem, but
as we have tried to argue here, it is an incomplete approach. Incentives connect landowner income to species protection but without addressing the potential disruptions to ways of life that define cultures and
communities.

Leopold's land ethic offers another way to finesse the problem. At the
heart of Leopold's argument is a recognition that the disjuncture between human and nonhuman ways of life is the root problem. By developing a land ethic that was based on an "understanding of ecology" and
rejected the "belief that economics determines *all* land-use" (Leopold
1949, pp. 262–263), it would be possible to make human and nonhuman ways of life more compatible. Yet, in our view, Leopold's approach
is also incomplete. As we have seen, often the people and communities
directly engaged in resource extraction activities understand that the
"bulk of all land relations hinges on investments of time, forethought,
skill, and faith rather than on investments of cash" (p. 263). However,
their ability and desire to pursue a way of life organized around a land
ethic is threatened by the intrusions of corporate interests on the one
hand and the misperceptions of environmentalists on the other hand.

What we want to suggest is that both of these approaches presuppose
that economy and ecology represent opposing ways of thinking. Such is

certainly a familiar and pervasive theme in the contemporary environmental discourse, but in a historical sense, this was not the case. Indeed, the historical meanings of economy and ecology, as well as property, point to a repository of cultural values in which landowners' work, consumers' goods, environmental protection, and ways of both human and nonhuman life can be viewed as intimately connected and reconcilable. By reacquainting ourselves with these older meanings, we believe it is possible to enhance the discussion of an incentive approach with a more complete interpretation of the species protection problem.

Although it is widely known that "economy" and "ecology" share the same etymological root, there are implications of this connection that warrant consideration. Both words are derived from the Greek root *oikos,* meaning household. Economy, in its broadest sense, is the management (*nomos*) of a household. Ecology is the science (*logos*) of the household. In current usage, the household of concern to economy is human centered, and the household of concern to ecology is nature. Historically, however, the two concepts were closely related. As Donald Worster (1994, p. x) explains, "the *idea* of ecology is much older than the name. Its modern history begins in the eighteenth century, when it emerged as a more comprehensive way of looking at earth's fabric of life: a point of view that sought to describe all of the living organisms of the earth as an interacting whole, often referred to as the 'economy of nature.'"

The need to distinguish between economy and ecology resulted, at least in part, from a narrowing of the meaning of economy. The earliest recorded meaning (c. 1530) of "economy" in English was household management including household expenses. By the seventeenth century, "economy" described the "administration of the concerns of any community or establishment with a view to orderly conduct and productiveness," and by the eighteenth century, it referred especially to the management of money. It was in the eighteenth century that the phrase "political economy" came into being, which meant "managing the resources of a nation so as to increase its material prosperity" (OED 1971). Adam Smith (1776, p. 397) in his book *The Wealth of Nations,* clearly established the purpose of modern political economy: "to provide a plentiful revenue or subsistence for the people . . . and . . . to supply the state . . . with a revenue sufficient for the publick services."

In common usage, then, the meaning of economy shifted from managing households to managing financial resources. This shift made a great deal of sense against a backdrop of emerging capitalism and the expanding use of money in which the economy of nations and households was increasingly understood in financial terms, and nature became a resource to be aggressively used or transformed (Merchant 1980, 1989). Yet the same European and American cultures that optimized financial gain through natural resource use—the economy—also produced the amateur naturalists and trained scientists who described nature as a complex, and increasingly vulnerable, system of relationships (Worster 1994). Hence the need, by the mid-nineteenth century, for a concept (ecology) capable of expressing the broader kinds of relationships that economy had formerly embraced.

We can trace a similar trajectory in the changing meaning of property. John Locke is widely recognized as the patriarch of private property in the modern European and American tradition; however, his meaning of property was considerably broader than our current usage. On the one hand, he defined property as the "general name" that included people's "lives, liberties, and estates" (Locke 1689, p.66). His use of "estates" was clearly intended in the broader sense and, therefore, suggests a direct connection with the notion of household in the earlier meaning of economy. On the other hand, Locke's basic premise that property is created through labor also implied that a person's labor was a form of property. It was Locke's formulation that Adam Smith (1776, pp. 121–122) invoked when he asserted, "The property which every man has in his own labor, as it is the foundation of all other property, so it is the most sacred and inviolable."

Perhaps a more important connection here is a 1792 essay entitled "Property," written by James Madison. Madison drafted the original version of the Bill of Rights, including the passage in the Fifth Amendment that states, "nor shall private property be taken for public use, without just compensation." In the essay, Madison argued that the concept of property had both a specific "application" and a "larger and juster meaning." As examples of the specific application, Madison offered "land, or merchandize, or money," and among the examples of the larger meaning, Madison listed "the free use of his faculties and a free choice of the objects on which to employ them" (p. 101). "Faculties" in this phrase refers to the skills and abilities used to pursue an occupation and is, therefore, a variation of labor as property, a point Madison confirmed later in the essay when he asserted, "That is not a just government, nor is property secure under it, where arbitrary restrictions, exemptions, and monopolies deny to part of its citizens the free use of their faculties, and free choice of their occupations, which not only constitute their property in the general sense of the word; but are the means of acquiring property strictly so called" (p. 102).

Working with these older meanings, we believe it is possible to reframe the contemporary discourse in ways that are conceptually useful in anticipating opposition to the incentive approach. Resources are managed within households, among people who know and are accountable to one another, and it is within households—including the ecological household of the environment at large—that people most immediately live. Though *oikos* was pressed into service to describe other forms of community, the values implied by household management and membership are not necessarily those that emerged in growing nations in the eighteenth century. A household is a dwelling furnished with goods and occupied by an organized family, and may include other residents; it is associated with what is familiar and intimate (OED 1971). When resource users refer to ways of life, and refer as Ernie Pardini and Raymond Rogers do to knowledge and experience shared by families and communities, they are identifying values literally born into households and maintained through filial relationships within households, and communities of similar households. Household management demands negotiating a financial living, but that does not describe the household's full identity. What lies inside a household is a set of relationships: responsibility and dependency between members, generational memory that connects the present to the past, and ideally affection and esteem among members that sustain rather than undermine the fullest social and cultural as well as financial stability of the whole. It is important that household members know and communicate with one another, even if they do not always understand or like one another. These intimate, everyday habits of households were captured more accurately in the meaning of ecology than in the abstract and financially dominated understandings of economy that we have inherited.

The idea of a household of nature connects people and their work to nature in intriguing ways. First of all, nature does not name or describe itself—people do. Naming nature through ecological description applies an intimately known social experience to the world at large, one too often regarded as merely metaphorical. Second, by naming the environment as a household, rather than a set of resources, we imply intimate knowledge and memory of, and interaction with and esteem for, materials and beings among whom we live. A house is, after all, "a building for human habitation" (OED 1971) and can meaningfully describe the earth itself, as well as suggest an ethic of memory and care that would prevent, one might say, the house from burning down. Economy as household management (extended here to mean ecological management) could be seen to do just that: prevent the ecological house from burning down. But taking the metaphor seriously, more is at stake in household management than management; the household itself is central in defining people's identities, moral sensibilities, and knowledge of the world.

Leopold believed that true environmental well-being would be the result of extending the "boundaries of the [social] community to include soils, waters, plants, and animals, or collectively: the land" (Leopold 1949, p. 239). He understood this process in evolutionary terms, a fundamental change in how people lived with the land. But whereas Leopold relied on the concept of community as the model for environmental dwelling and stewardship, the household embedded in both economy and ecology provides a model less abstract and closer to hand. As long as nature is out there, apart from our households and livelihoods, it is merely a resource to be exploited or a vulnerable entity in need of protection from human work and living. If it is instead our household, where we live and work as human beings, our experience of family and household living provides at least some longstanding cultural background for creating a land ethic.

Finally, by reclaiming the notion of occupation as property, it would be possible to finesse the kind of cynicism and resentment that too frequently characterize the political discourse. For instance, invoking Madison, we might respond to Rothman's question, "Why should the rest of us subsidize their condescending culture and custom arguments?"—because a "just government" seeks to protect for "its citizens the free use of their faculties, and free choice of their occupations." More important, this broader conceptualization of property connects directly with the kind of communities and household experiences within them that Pardini and Rogers view as central in recovering both damaged environments and human lives. In doing so, it offers hope of adding species protection to the list of "obligations above self-interest," which Leopold (1949, p. 245) argued were "taken for granted in such rural community enterprises as the betterment of roads, schools, churches, and baseball teams."

Financial incentives or compensation for endangered species protection may be expedient. They may satisfy some landowners' need for compensation for lost income, but such an approach does not and cannot by itself address the very large field of financial relationships and conflicting obligations within which landowners make their living and their ways of life. Financial reward for species protection is part and parcel of the systems of belief and action that endanger ecosystems in the first place; they can encourage only further enlightened self-interest without meaningfully laying the cultural groundwork for a genuinely effective land ethic. Values and activities that could accompany such an ethic can be found literally close to home and already in some measure available to us. Endangered species protection in the end has to involve people's knowledge, memory, affection, and experience in addition to their financial interest to reconnect people's livelihoods and ways of life fully to environmental health and stability.

References

Bari, Judi. 1994. *Timber wars*. Monroe, Maine: Common Courage Press.
Dahl, Robert. 1967. *Pluralist democracy in the United States: Conflict and consent*. Chicago: Rand McNally.
Geertz, Clifford. 1973. *The interpretation of cultures: Selected essays*. New York: Basic Books.
Hays, Samuel P. 1987. *Beauty, health, and permanence: Environmental politics in the United States, 1955–1985*. Cambridge: Cambridge University Press.
Holmes, Sandra, ed. 1979. *Henderson's dictionary of biological terms*. 9th ed. New York: Van Nostrand Reinhold.
Leopold, Aldo. 1933. A conservation ethic. *Journal of Forestry* 31:634–643.
———. 1949. *A Sand County almanac*. Reprint 1966, New York: Sierra Club. [Originally published in 1949 by Ballantine Books.]
Liddell, Henry George, and Scott, Robert. 1925. *A Greek-English lexicon*. Oxford: Clarendon Press.
Locke, John. 1689. *Second treatise of government*. Reprint 1980, edited by C. B. Macpherson. Indianapolis: Hackett Publishing.
Madison, James. 1792. Property. Reprinted 1906 in *The writings of James Madison 6*, edited by Gallard Hunt. New York: G. P. Putnam's Sons.
Merchant, Carolyn. 1980. *The death of nature: Women, ecology, and the scientific revolution*. San Francisco: Harper & Row.
———. 1989. *Ecological revolutions: Nature, gender, and science in New England*. Chapel Hill: University of North Carolina Press.
Nixon, Richard M. 1974. A special message to Congress outlining the 1972 environmental program. In *Public papers of the presidents of the United States: Richard M. Nixon*. Washington, D.C.: Government Printing Office.
OED. 1971. *Compact edition of the Oxford English Dictionary*. Oxford: Oxford University Press.
Rogers, Raymond. 1998. *Solving history: The challenge of environmental activism*. Montreal: Black Rose Books.
Rothman, Hal. 2000. Do we really need the rural West. *High Country News*, 24 April.

Smith, Adam. 1776. *An inquiry into the nature and causes of the wealth of nations*. Reprint 1937, edited by Edwin Cannon. New York: Modern Library.

Steel, Brent S., and Nicholas P. Lovrich. 1997. An introduction to natural resource policy and the environment: Changing paradigms and values. In *Public lands management in the West: Citizens, interest groups, and values*, edited by Brent S. Steel. Westport, Conn.: Praeger.

Stone, Deborah. 1997. *Policy paradox: The art of political decision making*. New York: W. W. Norton & Co.

White, Richard. 1996. Are you an environmentalist or do you work for a living? In *Uncommon ground: Rethinking the human place in nature*, edited by William Cronon. New York: Norton.

Worster, Donald. 1994. *Nature's economy: A history of ecological ideas*. 2nd ed. New York: Cambridge University Press.

CHAPTER 5

A Critical Examination of Economic Incentives to Promote Conservation

DEBRA DONAHUE

The ESA undoubtedly can be made more effective in achieving its conservation and recovery goals, and the use of incentives would assuredly encourage greater and more willing landowner efforts to that end. However, many observers, including this author, do not believe that an incentives-based approach would solve all of our habitat ills. An imperiled species conservation program should be multifaceted, and a strategy that depends too heavily on monetary incentives has at least four shortcomings:

- Finite funds (in both government and private coffers), and a seemingly infinite array of good causes on which to spend them, will always limit the program.
- Incentives are often piecemeal efforts, involving no systematic planning as to what kind of conservation tactics might yield the greatest benefits, or where or when action should be undertaken. Compensation or exemptions occur on a case-by-case basis, with development proceeding on individual tracts at the whim of individual owners. As a result, protection of ecosystems and landscapes can never be assured, nor can cumulative impacts be measured, much less controlled.
- In the long run (if not sooner), incentives will fail unless backed up by regulations with teeth.
- Paying for every incremental benefit to threatened species on private land (or forgone opportunities to develop those lands) thwarts the inculcation of a land ethic among landowners and citizens.

The first shortcoming is an obvious one. The second is important, but beyond the scope of this chapter. In the remainder of this chapter I explore the final two considerations, along with the role of learning in conservation.

Although it may be "theoretically possible" to achieve conservation goals "solely by providing landowners with incentives to manage their land" appropriately, empirical research and practitioner experience support the conclusion that "landowners generally will not engage in higher levels of species protection in a completely deregulated land use regime" (Farrier 1995, pp. 307–309). Aldo Leopold reached this unhappy conclusion a half-century ago. A modern scholar and practitioner has concluded, "The likely consequence of completely eliminating the ESA's land use restrictions for listed animal species would be to drive more animal species into extinction" (Ruhl 1998, pp. 40–53). Carrots like those suggested in Chapter 3 should be seen as efficacious supplements to, not substitutes for, regulatory sticks, whether embodied in the current ESA or some alternate regime.[1]

Command-and-control regulations can coerce compliance with government programs, such as endangered species conservation. Financial and other incentives can help to "entice or purchase support" for the same programs. In addition, an ESA program should contain a third component: "persuasion" (Reading and Kellert 1993, p. 578).[2] People, especially property owners, need to be persuaded that the government's chosen conservation program is worth supporting, or at least capable of improvement to the point that it is supportable. More fundamentally, some people need to be persuaded that imperiled species and habitats are worth preserving. If people can be persuaded, or educated, to recognize values in land other than financial, the need for coercive or prohibitory conservation regulations is thereby reduced.

Scientists Richard Reading and Stephen Kellert concluded that "decreasing opposition and developing a supportive public are clearly desirable objectives" of efforts to reintroduce endangered species to former habitats. The same can be said of accomplishing ESA goals generally. Traditional public education methods, however, are often inadequate to achieve these objectives, because merely providing "additional information and knowledge about a species" is "rarely effective in changing attitudes and values, especially if they are strongly held." This is particularly true for people who "perceive themselves as having knowledge of an issue, . . . especially if their knowledge is derived from personal experience." For these people, "effective public relations programs require more than simply education" (Reading and Kellert 1993, p. 578).

Private landowners, particularly longtime owners of rural land, commonly believe they know their land better than anyone does. (Some probably do; many, of course, do not.) Add to that perceived knowledge the typical American attitudes toward property rights, and you have a formula for trouble under any governmental scheme that depends on restricting property owners' use of their land or subjecting them to liability for the consequences of that use.

If government and other advocates of current ESA programs are to be effective in persuading more property owners to support, or at least not actively oppose, conservation efforts on their land, they must reexamine their message, their methods, and the roles assigned to educators and audience. The "strength, salience, clarity and source of the message" are all important, as are the manner and setting in which the message is presented, and the number and kinds of independent sources of information. "Using people with similar cultural and socioeconomic characteristics to convey the message can often help." The appropriate method will vary with the audience; a one-size-fits-all approach is doomed to fail. Species recovery efforts "will rarely succeed," Reading and Kellert concluded, "if they do not actively consider and incorporate those views that are the basis for local support" (1993, pp. 578–579).

Ecologist Tim Clark's recommendations for enhancing species recovery also focus on people not biology; in his view, people are both the source of the problem and the solution. He too emphasizes the importance of education, though from the broader perspective of learning rather than teaching. He "reframe[s] the work of endangered species recovery as a policy process problem," the solutions to which will depend significantly on continual learning by all those involved in the process. He describes the policy process as "the interaction of people as they try to solve problems, find meaning, and forge a workable society for themselves." Citing the "widespread recognition that scientific, legal, and regulatory tinkering will not result in more successful programs" for recovering endangered species, he writes that we must focus instead on the "human envelope." [3] As Clark puts it: "We need to devise a more functional understanding of the very *process* of people and organizations interacting in the recovery task." A public policy process-oriented approach "rests directly on the inclusive model of policy process and problem solving." This "functional view suggests that the human system of individuals, organizations, and policies that make up the species restoration process has *intrinsic* behavioral properties that largely determine if a recovery effort will be successful or not." These intrinsic properties will vary to a certain extent among sites and projects, depending on the individuals and institutions involved. In contrast, the "conventional view holds that *extrinsic* factors," for example, funding shortfalls, deficiencies in scientific knowledge, less interference by outsiders or the media, "are the major causes of programmatic failures" of conservation schemes (Clark 1997, pp. 164–168).

In part 2 of his book *Averting Extinction,* Clark encapsulates his ESA "reconstruction" proposals in the "single precept that . . . we must learn" (pp. 225–227). He calls for a "new commitment to" and improvement on learning by conservation professionals (scientists and managers), bureaucracies, organizations, and citizens. "As citizen participants in the public policy debates over biodiversity," he writes, "we must accept, first, that restoring endangered species is fundamentally an effort in public policy making. . . . At heart it is not a biological task [but] a social process." Second, "we must accept the irrationality of the political process." Finally:

> We must learn the knowledge and skills of competent and responsible civic participation, of not surrendering to inadequate government solutions or to narrow experts with all the biases of technical rationality. The American people must help build new relationships with government through which they can share in decision and policy making for better conservation of biodiversity.[4]

Successful implementation of the ESA (or any conservation strategy) at any site will depend in large part on unique, site-specific circumstances, but Clark (p. 166) asserts that "there are useful ways of understanding the human envelope that promise improved performance in all cases." He offers three tools (among several available) for improving policy processes by "improving participants' knowledge of decision and social processes and their ability to participate effectively." These tools, he says, have had success in a few endangered species cases as well as in other contexts. A full discussion is not possible here; briefly, however, the three tools are: (1) Regular, independent appraisals of the program and the policy process. Evaluations of individual projects or parts of the program should be aggregated, and the net results should be widely circulated and made public. (2) Decision seminars. This is a policy decision-making technique, based on integrating and focusing the efforts of specialists representing relevant disciplines and decision makers working on a particular problem. "It uses the policy sciences' problem orientation, contextual mapping, and multiple methods to gain insight into community problems, clarify community goals, and generate alternative policies." Government and nongovernment interests are represented, but the participants are few in number, must have similar understandings of the problem, and must remain committed for months or years as necessary. (3) Prototypes. These are "small-scale project[s] designed to implement a trial change in a social or policy system, such as changing people's assumptions about how they should interact or who should share what kinds of power." Prototypes by definition are "provisional, improvising, [and] exploratory." Inherently learning-based, this approach operates "through self-observation, insight, and understanding to devise better strategic and tactical programs" (pp. 177–184).[5] Prototyping was used successfully in the recovery program for the endangered Australian eastern barred bandicoot.

A policy-oriented view of conservation, Clark says, is "adaptive and promotes open-ended learning on individual, organizational, and political scales" (p. 2). His work, like that of Reading and Kellert, suggests that adaptive-management principles could enhance public education and public relations efforts, as well as on-the-ground conservation efforts. Devising innovative, more effective conservation education tools will require continual examination of what we've learned about what does and doesn't promote communication. As Reading and Kellert's work suggests, this learning and reevaluation process must encompass both our methods for enlisting public support for conservation and, more fundamentally, our message.[6]

In this author's view, stewardship should be a crucial element of that message. Instilling and cultivating in citizens, especially property owners, a sense of land stewardship will be essential to preserving this country's—indeed, this planet's—biological diversity. Embracing a stewardship ethic will necessitate basic attitudinal changes on the part of some, perhaps many, and a redefining of property expectations concerning land.

Lawyer John Kunich wrote that public support for endangered species conservation "would be much easier to garner if, to put it crassly, there were something in it for them." By "something," the author was referring to "positive incentives," for example, tax breaks for owners of endangered species habitat; direct payments for raising endangered species; "just compensation" for restrictions on property use; "allowances" based on the presence of threatened or endangered animals or plants, which could be sold, exchanged for tax credits, or traded for exemptions from other regulatory requirements; and private ownership of imperiled species, which would give the owners a "direct incentive" to care for these resources (Kunich 1994, pp. 575–577).

But the methods employed in conservation can subvert the message. Poorly designed or executed economic incentive systems run the risk of commodifying endangered species and undermining efforts to inculcate a sense of stewardship among landowners and others. Carried to its logical extreme, Kunich's approach implies that property owners have (or at least should have) the right to rid their property of any unwanted organisms, and that only by compensating them for forgoing that right can society hope to conserve the natural heritage of this and future generations. To illustrate: He commends the environmental organization Defenders of Wildlife for paying ranchers for documented livestock losses to wolves, because it "shift[s] the economic burden of wolf preservation away from the ranchers and to the people who want to support wolves" (Kunich 1994, p. 576). In his view, the government should encourage, if not subsidize, such efforts. Apart from its questionable, implicit premise that ranchers have some right to be free of wolves (or perhaps of all predators, or all inconvenient native species?), this statement is, in itself, an example of the need for better education and public relations. Neither wolves nor any other species has value only for those people who want them. On the contrary, every approach to valuing species recognizes that biodiversity has value to society as a whole and to future generations. According to environmental policy professor Bryan Norton, "the breadth of consensus favoring the protection of biological resources [includes] serious scholars from every relevant discipline, and embrac[es] virtually the entire intellectual landscape" (Norton 1998, p. 253).[7]

An unwisely designed incentives program can convey a message to participants as well as to the general public that biodiversity has no value unless it can somehow be reduced to monetary terms. It may even communicate that species have value only to those humans who find value in them. Under this view, if a property owner does not value a given animal or plant, she should be free to alter its habitat despite the consequences for the organism. Alternatively, she should be paid to forgo her right to develop. (See generally Sunstein 1996 and Farrier 1995, p. 400.) In other words, incentive programs, like conservation itself, have ethical implications. Relying too heavily on poorly designed financial incentives can deter stewardship, by teaching citizens that they have no individual obligation to care for the land and its nonhuman inhabitants, and communicating to all that society has no right to expect such care without paying for it. Incentive-based conservation systems can legitimize habitat impairment or destruction, just as air or water pollution trading programs may "legitimize pollution," so long as it occurs within the rules of the trading "game" (Salzman and Ruhl 2000, p. 622).[8]

Adoption of a statutory duty of care to the environment, supplemented by "motivational incentives" (Young et al. 1996), would help avoid this pitfall. Such a measure is not without precedent. The Australia Industry Commission recently (1998) proposed a strategy for ecologically sustainable development of natural resources, which would "ensure that resource owners and managers take into account the environmental impacts of their decisions" and "encourage conservation on private land." To achieve these aims, the commission endorses a legal duty of care to the environment, enacted by statute in each state and territory, implemented chiefly by "voluntary standards and codes of practice," and reinforced by mandated standards only as a "last resort." An individual stewardship obligation is also consistent with a provision of the draft International Covenant on Environment and Development, released by the International Union for the Conservation of Nature's Commission on Environmental Law in 1995. In particular, article 12 of the draft covenant, which addresses the rights and obligations of persons (rather than of states), provides that "all persons have a duty to protect and preserve the environment."[9]

Economic incentives that lack an explicit stewardship component can have the effect of legitimizing habitat destruction. The source of the legitimization, arguably, is the term "economics" itself. *Webster's Third New International Dictionary* defines economics as "a social science that studies the production, distribution, and consumption of commodities." "Commodity" in turn means "an economic good; esp. a product of agriculture, mining, or sometimes manufacture as distinguished from services." A traditional view of economics either excludes from its purview noncommodities, such as plant or animal species (other than agricultural products) and ecosystem services, or requires commodification of these things if they are to be afforded value and considered in social and political decision making. This is not to say that economics does not provide a useful perspective for valuing and allocating resources, but rather that economics is simply ill-designed to account for ecological or ethical values. (See Salzman and Ruhl 2000, p. 633, n. 64.)

Neither this author nor the Congress that passed the Endangered Species Act subscribes to the commodity view of species or habitats. Many writers, most notably Aldo Leopold, have explored the existence and

nature of stewardship, or a "land ethic," as well as the need for education concerning it. Recently Professor James Karp wrote, "Although a
legally recognized landowner has extensive rights to use, to exclude and
to convey the land to others, those rights should be limited by a duty of
land stewardship." Karp finds significant support for such a duty in the
common law duty to prevent waste and in the concept of nuisance,
which has been recognized by the U.S. Supreme Court as a limit on
property rights. Karp concludes that using land in ways that "[threaten]
natural systems or community survival substantially and unreasonably
interferes with the rights of other members of the community" (Karp
1993, pp. 748–749; see also Freyfogle 1990). The law defines nuisance
as a substantial and unreasonable interference with another's use or en-
joyment of land. Considered thus, the duty of stewardship is seen as "an
intrinsic and essential part of the prevention of nuisance" (*Lucas v.
South Carolina Coastal Council* 1992).

Law professor Joseph Sax (1993, p. 1441) agrees that traditional
nuisance law was "wide-ranging," though he cautions that "it did not
characterize property as having inherent public attributes which always trump the landowner's rights." Still, the principle that landowners
"should be able to expect some beneficial use of the land . . . does not
necessarily mean, in all cases, the right to develop the land for economic
purposes" (Karp 1993, pp. 756–757). The "economic benefit," to which
property owners are apparently entitled under U.S. Supreme Court
doctrine, "may be confined to continuing the current, non-nuisance-
creating use of the land" (Sax 1993, pp. 1437–1442). What constitutes
a reasonable, beneficial use of the land depends in part on "the community's environmental interest in the land" (Karp 1993, p. 757).

Landowners must be disabused of the notion that they are somehow
entitled to compensation for restrictions on use of their land. (Many in
government also need to learn this lesson.) Property rights are not, and
never have been, absolute. They are cultural, legal creations, not im-
mutable rules. The limit placed on individual rights in land by "the
rights of society as a whole" is "one of the [law's] oldest concepts"
(Karp 1993, p. 751). Landowners have "never had a legally supported
expectation" that they could use their property in any way they chose,
nor for its most beneficial economic use (McElfish et al. 1996, p. 27). In
1972, in *Just v. Marinette County,* the Wisconsin Supreme Court held
that a landowner "has no absolute and unlimited right to change the
essential natural character of his land so as to use it for a purpose for
which it was unsuited in its natural state and which injures the rights of

others. . . . [It] is not an unreasonable exercise of [the police] power to prevent harm to public rights by limiting the use of private property to its natural uses" (Sax 1993, pp. 1438–1439).

The U.S. Supreme Court has not gone so far. In fact, according to Sax, *Lucas v. South Carolina Coastal Council* may be viewed as the U.S. Supreme Court's long-delayed answer to, and repudiation of, *Just*. Nevertheless, Sax writes, "public claim[s] or servitude[s], both limiting full privatization and demanding that any private benefits be compatible with public goals, [are] not uncommon." In other words, "privatization was never as complete as is often assumed today." [10]

Shifting endangered species conservation policy too abruptly and too heavily in favor of an incentives-based approach could send property law evolution in exactly the wrong direction. "Property law has always been functional," Sax has written, "encouraging behavior compatible with contemporary goals of the economy. Indeed it would be difficult to identify a time when a given community's property law encouraged behavior at odds with its social values." The peremptory abolition of landowners' riparian rights "because they were unsuited to the physical conditions" of the arid West is one of many examples, he says, of "property law's adaptations to social changes." (It might be more accurate to relate this change in the law to physical geography and environmental conditions.) Arguably, it would be no more draconian to terminate development rights in barrier beaches or wetlands, types of land that Sax asserts, "by today's standards, should never have been subject to private ownership at all." Today, all owners of "fragile lands . . . are, in a sense, victims of a changing world." But "innocent loss in the face of unexpected change did not generate a right of compensation" under property law norms in the past, Sax points out (Sax 1993, pp. 1441–1448, citing *Yunker v. Nichols*). There is no reason for it to do so today.

Sax spurns the *Lucas* court's view of property as "outdated" and "not satisfactory in an age of ecological awareness." He suggests a newly configured system of property rights, "designed to accommodate both transformational needs and the needs of nature's economy." Among this system's minimum features are: "Less focus on individual dominion," "More focus on public decisions, because [land] use would be determined ecosystemically," "Increased ecological planning," and "Affirmative obligations by owners to protect ecological services, with owners functioning as custodians, as well as self-benefitting entrepreneurs" (Sax 1993, p. 1451).

Sax recognizes that reforming property law as he proposes would

have "considerable . . . negative implications for many traditional pro-
prietary opportunities." He advises that "some enhanced judicial willingness to protect against arbitrary regulation, and to assure propor-
tionality between ecosystem needs and imposition on private uses, is
needed to achieve an acceptable balance between the demand of the
transformational economy and those of the economy of nature." But
"as the services of the economy of nature are increasingly recognized,"
he asserts, "consensus[es] can be expected to develop as to which [natu-
ral] functions are important enough to demand maintenance" and "the
range of acceptable burdens on landowners" (Sax 1993, pp. 1452–
1455). These consensuses will be the products of *learning*. They will
reflect not only what scientists and conservation biologists (and subsequently all of us) have learned about species' needs and the services provided by intact, healthy ecosystems but also what we continue to learn
from each other about how humans affect the environment and how the
environment affects the quality of our lives.[11]

At least until *Lucas,* the dimensions of property rights had changed
as the world changed, and those changes seldom gave rise to a right of
compensation for property owners. Consistent with the legal history,
Sax's proposed reforms presuppose that landowners would not be compensated for the adjustments they would have to make. An endangered
species conservation program that required payment for every restriction on land use would be overwhelmed by problems. Compensation
funds would undoubtedly be limited, and the costs (in time and money)
of assessing the impact of regulation on property values, to determine
the appropriate compensation, could easily swamp the program. Only
those who were compensated and those who possess an inherent sense
of stewardship would conserve. That would lead to inequities (between
paid and unpaid landowners), incomplete geographic coverage, and
temporal inconsistency (as lands changed hands or as funds for incentives ran out). It would offer no assurance of management of habitats to
promote species recovery, only the discontinuation of land uses considered harmful. Finally, payment for land use restrictions related to endangered species would likely lead those subject to other environmental
statutes (the Clean Water Act, the Clean Air Act, etc.) to clamor for
compensation.

As a compromise, any new land use regulations, whether under the
ESA or a new regime, probably should distinguish between existing land
uses and proposed or speculative ones. It will be more difficult and less
fair to disrupt existing uses, and the result is more likely to be an un-

lawful taking if compensation is not paid. (As discussed elsewhere in this volume, restriction of new uses or development will constitute a taking only in rare circumstances.) Even where existing activities are restricted, Australian law professor David Farrier cautions, it is "important to pay careful attention to the question of quantum. There is a strong argument that, in determining the amount of compensation, the private benefit forgone, in terms of loss of the existing use, should be discounted to take into account the public costs that have been avoided by termination"— for example, loss of biodiversity (Farrier 1995, pp. 398–399).

The foregoing criticisms are not meant to discount the utility and wisdom of incorporating incentives into a species conservation program, nor is advocacy of certain incentives inconsistent with opposition to compensating landowners for land use restrictions. Incentives should be used to encourage socially responsible behavior and to adjust the burdens of effectuating an important social program, not to extort landowner compliance with statutes and regulations. As Leopold asked pointedly nearly sixty years ago, "If we are going to spend large sums of public money anyhow, why not use it to subsidize desirable combinations in land use, instead of to cure, by purchase, prohibition, or repair, the headache arising from bad ones?" (Flader and Caldicott 1991, p. 200). More recently, Farrier couched the "real issue" with respect to incentives as whether the "payment should be delivered in a form different from compensation." He points out:

> By offering to pay compensation, we put landowners in a better position by reducing the element of individual risk frequently associated with investment in development, particularly agricultural activities. We also allow landowners to externalize the problem and *deny that they have any responsibility for the conservation of biodiversity.* Compensation is backward-looking and has nothing to say about the future management of land.

Farrier concludes that compensation systems allow landowners to "wash their hands" of biodiversity conservation because they send the message that government bears the entire burden of conserving species (Farrier 1995, p. 397; emphasis added). Any conservation strategy that allows or promotes this result should be assiduously avoided. If conservation is to succeed, it must be the job of all, not merely of government.

The determination to conserve biodiversity and the ecosystems on which it depends is a social choice. Society should bear the costs of this choice because society ultimately will be the beneficiary of successful conservation efforts. That reasoning, however, neither invites nor justifies the rationalization that individuals have no conservation duty, affirmative or negative, unless compensated for their labors or forbearance. Overplaying the incentives card could send that message—and set back the cause of conservation immeasurably.

Drawing on one of Leopold's proposals, Farrier (1995, pp. 400–401) suggests that owners of lands subject to conservation restrictions be *paid* to manage their lands to promote the program's objectives. "Unlike compensation, stewardship payments are forward-looking." They are more equitable than compensation (which may be based on "chance factors" such as location or development plans), and, more important, they "encourage landowners to perceive elements of biodiversity, such as endangered species, as assets." Consistent with the chief argument in this chapter, Farrier states:

> Stewardship payments are also congruent with . . . developing a sense of personal responsibility to the community. Instead of telling landowners that they are being compensated to keep their destructive hands off the land, the message is that they have a vital role to play, a role that the community regards as sufficiently important that it is prepared to pay for it. The symbolism inherent in the language is crucial.

He further asserts:

> By making the conservation of biodiversity viable as an alternative, economically beneficial use of the land, we specifically address the scenario contemplated by the *Lucas* decision. A market for land that attracts stewardship payments will inevitably develop, and frustrated developers will be able to sell to those seeking an alternative lifestyle, albeit at a price that . . . is likely to be heavily discounted.

A stewardship program could help small ranchers and farmers to stay on the land, which would confer additional political and social benefits. Stewardship payments might be funded in part by a "habitat maintenance and restoration trust fund." Such an account could be funded by "savings from eliminating harmful subsidies, and/or from taxes and fees on waste and resource depletion." This fund "could be the source of matching funds for state and private conservation projects" and for "a real 'safety net' under the HCP program, to provide a ready source of money to fund corrective actions when failures occur" (Parenteau 1998, p. 306). Stewardship program funds might come from a variety of other sources as well: general agency appropriations (nearly all observers agree that the recovery budgets for the federal services should be enhanced), Land and Water Conservation Fund monies, foundation gifts, private donations, a tax on all real estate transactions, impact fees, to list a few.

Control of stewardship-oriented conservation programs "must be both decentralized and based on existing local conditions and institutions," argues Farrier (1995, p. 404). This tactical recommendation, which comes from the literature on biodiversity conservation in developing countries, is equally applicable, he says, to "conservation outside park boundaries in developed countries." It suggests both that local knowledge and opinions should be taken into account in designing and implementing programs and that "management payments should be delivered by government through locally based bodies." This advice is reminiscent of Reading and Kellert's message (1993, pp. 578–579) that successful species recovery will be responsive "to the needs, desires, and opinions of the local public." Although local knowledge and input are crucial, the knowledge and concerns of others must not be discounted or excluded. The making and implementation of social policy should be inclusive processes. (See Clark 1997; Cortner and Moote 1999.) James Karp (1993, p. 759) called for "full public participation in the process of developing criteria [for land stewardship] that are as specific as possible to guide owners and others in the market."

One of the biggest challenges in endangered species conservation is to involve all interested persons in developing policy. As an initial matter, this will include persuading all citizens, whether landowners or not, that they have a stake in conservation and a reason to participate in policymaking and implementation. The nature of policy is aggregative: it reflects the views of those involved in formulating the policy. As Clark warns, this "means that there are no guarantees that policy will meet the needs of society as a whole" (1997, p. 169). Accordingly, the more inclusive policy-setting is, the more likely that the policies devised will serve society as a whole.

All those involved in making conservation policy, but perhaps especially politicians and other official policymakers, should examine their attitudes toward landowners and ownership. It is extremely likely that nearly all policymakers in this country are themselves owners of real property. Land ownership can be a source of either bias or insight on matters of social and environmental policy. Private (individual) property rights must be protected (courts serve as a check on the legislative branch in this regard), but safeguarding the collective public interest should be the foremost concern of legislatures and regulatory agencies.

A common theme in modern political discourse is that property owners are increasingly burdened, especially by federal regulations. This view is particularly prevalent among certain economic sectors, notably farmers and ranchers; in certain forums, including state legislatures; and in certain regions, chiefly the West. Perceived burdens probably exceed actual burdens, however, and even the perception that regulations are increasingly onerous may not be as widely held as news accounts and commentary would lead us to believe. For example, even though measures designed to protect property rights (often called takings bills) had been introduced in 31 states as of 1996, only 5 states enacted compensation statutes. Two states, Florida and Texas, have comprehensive compensation statutes; Louisiana and Mississippi have more limited laws, applicable only to agricultural or forestry lands. Perhaps even more telling, voters in Washington and Arizona passed referenda *rescinding* takings statutes passed by their legislatures. (Juergensmeyer and Roberts 1998, p. 453; Wright and Gitelman 1997, p. 489–491; Donahue 1998, pp. 276–277.)

Landowners should be seen not as a beleaguered class but as a privileged one. Although the right to acquire and possess property is a privilege of citizenship, not all are sufficiently affluent to own land (and some suffer under discriminatory lending policies). Even among landowners, not all have the good fortune (yes, *good* fortune) to own healthy land capable of supporting endangered species or of contributing directly to a species' recovery. It surely is possible to distribute the financial burdens of endangered species conservation more fairly than we do now, but a fair allocation of responsibilities should analyze both the costs and the benefits. In other words, the analysis should give at least some consideration to the intangible benefits of hosting imperiled species on one's property—the simple rewards of knowing animals or plants are present, occasionally seeing or hearing them, and feeling satisfaction at helping to ensure their survival.[12] Federal regulations allow these "existence" or "option" values to be taken into account in determining liability for natural resource damages under the Oil Pollution Act and Superfund,[13] but they remain unrecognized and unaccounted for in incentive-based habitat conservation strategies.

Readers may be inclined to scoff at that last suggestion. Many landowners, it seems, consider the presence of endangered species or suitable habitat on their property a liability. On the other hand, most recent opinion polls show decided majorities of Americans believe that legal protections for endangered species should be retained or strengthened, not relaxed. Before discounting the notion that imperiled species can be an asset, readers should reconsider the importance of learning, discussed earlier. Convincing landowners that there *is* something in land conservation for them, and for the human community, something more fundamental and lasting than financial gain, should be the number-one objective of educational and public relations efforts (Kunich 1994, p. 575). These efforts should be founded on the assumption "that a healthy biosphere is in the common interest of humanity," an assumption that is subscribed to by the "vast majority of biological scientists" (Clark 1997, pp. 224–225).[14] If government also believes this (and there is substantial evidence that the Congress that passed the ESA did), its laws must embody that conviction and convey it to its citizens. No expenditure of public money, no matter how large or how long continued, will accomplish the "job of intergenerational conservation." That task is "too big, too complex, and too dispersed to be left to governments," Karp exhorts (1993, pp. 749–750). "It must emanate from a conservation ethic among private landowners, and be facilitated and backed up by the imposition of a legal duty of stewardship where someone falters."

Until landowners adopt the cause of species and habitat conservation as their own, paying them not to use their lands in ecologically destructive ways (rather than rewarding them for implementing effective conservation practices) will run the risk of defeating the learning most crucial to the cause of conservation. Once they are convinced of the importance of the task and their individual role in helping to accomplish it, however, the personal satisfaction derived from contributing to species recovery will become part of the incentive.

Extinction, the saying goes, is forever. Given that so much is at stake, Clark has written, nothing less than "our best efforts in conserving the nation's biological wealth" should be acceptable (Clark 1997, p. 237). What should our best efforts consist of? Farrier summarizes (and criticizes) the literature as suggesting that "if we utilize the full range of policy instruments available, something should work" (Farrier 1995, p. 323). This suggestion is too facile, certainly, but it holds a kernel of truth. Until fundamental changes in both attitudes and legislation can be accomplished, our best efforts will consist of making the most of all available tools: the laws on the books, appropriated funds and private donations, private and nongovernmental-organization efforts. Eventually, though, policy reforms will be required. Most reform will be incremental, and all parties should be at the table participating in the process. No option should be foreclosed or off-limits. Reform options could include legislative repeal of certain provisions of the ESA; amendment of the act to require proactive ecosystem conservation, supported by stewardship incentives; retraction of certain ill-advised regulations and policies; and promulgation of new policies more suited to the tasks of conservation and recovery.

Most scholars and commentators agree that implementing section 9 of the Endangered Species Act will not suffice to recover species. Farrier (1995, p. 326), for example, concludes that private land conservation efforts "must go beyond ensuring that destructive or damaging activities are prevented." Law professor Patrick Parenteau (1998, pp. 293–295) concurs. He urges, for instance, that private property owners be required to *promote* recovery to obtain an incidental take permit, not merely to convince the service that their proposed conservation plan would "not appreciably reduce the likelihood of [the species'] survival and recovery." Widespread adoption of a stewardship ethic would undoubtedly facilitate this reform; a legislated stewardship mandate might help. One risk of such reform, of course, is that landowners will decide not to apply for incidental take permits, opting instead to pursue a particular land use, hoping either that their activities will not result in a take or that any take will not be discovered and prosecuted. That possibility simply argues (as has this chapter) for teeth to back up any incentives provisions. (See Endangered Species Act, section 10.)

Certain features of the current ESA and the implementing regulations actually frustrate the kind of solid conservation that can be built only on an individual sense of land stewardship. Perhaps most inconsistent with a stewardship duty is the current no-surprises policy. This policy is founded on obligations that come, not from the relation between land and owner, but from a contract between owner and government regulator. Once the landowner meets her contractual commitments, she has satisfied her duty to the species, even if unforeseen circumstances later put the species at renewed or increased risk. Although the government or third parties may undertake further actions at that juncture, the government may not require the landowner to restrict further her use of the property. This approach to conservation is illogical and shortsighted. It is fair and sensible to compensate a landowner for taking additional or extraordinary measures on behalf of a threatened species, but flatly precluding future, additional land use restrictions may tie society's hands in ways deleterious to conservation goals. Discontinuing the current land use on one or more tracts of land may be the only means of counteracting the effects of habitat loss (e.g., by a fire or hurricane) on other parcels or other risk factors, such as disease. The assurances afforded by the no-surprises policy eviscerate the meaning of stewardship and undermine society's ability to recover imperiled species. This policy sends two unambiguous messages: that private preferences regarding land uses outweigh conservation objectives and that only governments (or society as a whole), not landowners, have affirmative conservation responsibilities.[15]

No Surprises and the other new federal policies for implementing the Endangered Species Act are touted as examples of regulatory flexibility. But as Farrier (1995, pp. 364–388) points out, "regulatory flexibility" may simply be an opportunity, if not an attempt, to disguise regulatory failure. This potential exists with any mitigation program. For instance, law professors James Salzman and J. B. Ruhl claim that "project-by-project compensatory mitigation" in the wetlands context, governed by the Clean Water Act, section 404, is "widely regarded as having failed miserably in terms of environmental protection" (Salzman and Ruhl 2000, p. 653, n. 122). Many would no doubt agree that the record under section 10 of the ESA has been no better. Providing mitigation off-site, whether by habitat banking, contribution to a fund, or other methods, or after impacts occur, is especially risky.

Many proponents of ESA reform, including this author, advocate combining sticks and carrots. As Farrier warns, however, neither development controls nor incentives should be "delivered on an ad hoc basis." Instead, "interventions should be targeted through careful forward planning that takes a precautionary approach" (Farrier 1995, p. 391). This advice involves two crucial elements: that conservation efforts should be both precautionary and coordinated.

With the term "precautionary," Farrier refers specifically to precaution in listing decisions. In "a situation of potential irreversible loss," he wrote, we should "presume listing is required when faced with scientific uncertainty." Instead, Farrier argues, the listing process, as it is currently conducted, "risks potentially irreversible mistakes" by requiring too much scientific proof of biological status and risks. As a result, the act is "preordained" to fail. Proof of endangered status, or of the impacts of a proposed land development, clearly is not possible for species for which information is inadequate or nonexistent, an unfortunately common state of affairs. A precautionary approach, Farrier suggests, would be preferable (Farrier 1995, pp. 382–389).[16] This is the preferred tactic of conservation biologists and, indeed, of any true steward of the land. Err conservatively with respect to impacts; choose not to alter land use if the ecological impacts are uncertain or unknown and the risks are significant.

Employing a precautionary approach may involve reversing the burdens of proof; that is, a "lack of evidence about a species' conservation status would be regarded as evidence of endangerment until proven otherwise" (Farrier 1995, p. 388). In other words, the precautionary principle would shift the burden "to those who propose a use or development to show that the proposed action is harmless, rather than requiring those who oppose the use to show it would be harmful" (Kuhlman 1996, p. 197). The 1992 Convention on Biological Diversity elaborates on the precautionary principle by noting in its preamble that "where there is a threat of significant reduction or loss of biological diversity, lack of full scientific certainty should not be used as a reason for postponing measures to avoid or minimize such a threat." (See also Barton 1998.)

The precautionary principle recognizes what scientists term a Type II error. Put most simply, a Type II error involves a prediction that a proposed action will have no effect when in fact it would. A Type I error, in contrast, predicts an impact that in fact would not occur if the action were implemented. Plainly, the consequences of a Type II error are more significant for species. For this reason, an axiom of the precautionary principle is that Type II errors should be avoided to the extent possible (Noss and Cooperrider 1994, p. 258). They cannot be wholly evaded, of course, but their potential consequences for species may be mitigated by, for instance, forgoing or altering proposed actions when the uncertainty or the magnitude of the potential consequences reaches some predetermined level. A drawback of this approach is that the more restrictive land use regulations are, the less opportunity landowners have for adaptive behavior, which current ESA policies encourage and which can promote the desirable goal of learning. Given the uncertainty surrounding the status and biology of many species, this may seem an undesirable outcome. One option may be to use the prototype approach to test new conservation strategies (Clark 1997, pp. 182–184).

Farrier's second basic recommendation is to coordinate conservation undertakings. One way to achieve coordination would be through recovery plans. Indeed, the services must develop recovery plans for all species if conservation efforts are to have any chance of averting their course toward extinction. Recovery plans could and should serve as frameworks for coordinating individual private landowners' stewardship plans. Some such framework will be necessary to avoid cumulative harm, secure cumulative benefits, and facilitate conservation at the appropriate level of ecosystem, landscape, or region. Government incentives, like market incentives, can "produce distortions in the management of ecosystems" by promoting conservation efforts that benefit certain species or ecosystems at the expense of others. The consequence can be diminished, rather than enhanced, biodiversity. This undesirable outcome could be ameliorated or avoided by coordinated recovery planning (Farrier 1995, pp. 391, 396).

Finally, coordination would also be advanced if governments stopped sending mixed policy signals to citizens and the regulated public. Farrier, among many others, has noted the United States' outlandishly contrived agricultural price support schemes, which discourage crop rotation, promote overproduction, and disrupt wildlife habitat (Farrier 1995, pp. 401–402; Bowles et al. 1998, pp. 238–243). Others cite tax policies that act as disincentives for achieving conservation goals. According to Parenteau (1998, p. 254, citing Repetto et al. 1992),

> It is axiomatic that you get less of whatever you tax. Thus a rational tax policy should seek to tax those things that are "bad" and avoid taxing things that are "good." Our tax policy, by and large, does the opposite. Instead of taxing waste we tax income. Instead of encouraging resource conservation, we reward depletion with tax benefits. Instead of creating incentives to keep large holdings intact, we force divestiture with steep investment taxes.

Efforts to eliminate these "perverse incentives" have met with some success (Bowles et al. 1998, pp. 238–240). For instance, in 1982 Congress passed the Coastal Barrier Resources Act, which ended the eligibility of developments on barrier islands for federal flood insurance, and in 1996 it suspended the emergency livestock feed program, which had been widely criticized for encouraging overstocking on western ranges. Some reforms, however, have been short-lived or are limited in scope. Drought conditions in the West in 1998, for example, led stockgrowers to pressure Congress successfully for aid to replace the suspended emergency feed payments (Holechek and Hess 1995, pp. 133–134). Certain land use restrictions on lands held under Conservation Reserve Program leases can be lifted during emergency conditions, such as drought, when arguably the lands most need protection. To avoid the unintended legislative subversion of public conservation policies, legislators must continue to test proposed measures for consistency with established policies and to avoid special interest pressures for exceptions. More and better voter education about the interrelations of government policies would also serve conservation interests.

Conclusion

"To live in real harmony" with the land, Aldo Leopold observed, "seems to require either a degree of public regulation we will not tolerate, or a degree of private enlightenment we do not possess." He became convinced, by a lifetime of observing land use issues and contemplating the need for conservation, that enlightenment is essential but regulation will also be required, at least until a "code of decency for man-to-land conduct" can evolve. Leopold hypothesized that this evolution might require nineteen centuries, the time it has taken to "define decent man-to-man conduct," a process that is only "half done" (Flader and Caldicott 1991, p. 179). Plainly, we haven't the time. Current species extinction rates are thousands of times greater than natural background rates. Harvard entomologist E. O. Wilson, one of the most widely respected conservation biologists, estimated that one-fifth of all species on Earth would become extinct within twenty years. He offered this prediction more than ten years ago.

As regulation, the Endangered Species Act paradigm for imperiled species conservation falls short of both our society's expectations and the species' needs. Most would agree it is neither effective nor fair. Even if it were perfect regulation, as laws go, it could not ensure long-term conservation. Government cannot achieve conservation goals merely by prescribing or prohibiting conduct or by lavishing public money on problems. Unless government policy is not only consistent with but also reinforced by an individual stewardship ethic, conservation efforts will fail. To hasten the development of a functional "ecological conscience," Leopold advocated according "decent land-use . . . social rewards proportionate to its social importance" (Flader and Caldicott 1991, p. 345). No one has made a more passionate, persuasive case for this approach than he. "I plead, in short," he wrote in 1935, "for positive and substantial public encouragement, *economic and moral,* for the landowner who conserves the public values—economic or esthetic—of which he is the custodian" (Flader and Caldicott 1991, p. 216; emphasis added).

As part of such public encouragement, the ESA should be amended to incorporate incentives that promote and reward stewardship. In the meantime, ESA and other federal and state policies (e.g., relating to taxation, agriculture, or land development) and their implementation should be amended in ways that are consistent with and cultivate an individual duty of stewardship. A widely held stewardship ethic would ensure that conservation is an implicit consideration of land use decisions, rather than an after-the-fact remedy for problems related to land use. Scholars and critics invariably agree that proactive, preventive measures are more sensible and more efficacious than the emergency-room or deathbed conservation strategies embodied in the ESA.

Successful reform of our conservation policies will depend on adaptive learning. There is no guarantee that we can learn enough, or fast enough, to save what we want to save. But the more widely held the stewardship ethic, the better our chances. In the long run, it may be our only hope for a diverse and healthy planet.

Notes

1. Recognizing that the "experience of the United States suggests that exclusive reliance on either land use regulation or voluntary cooperation is inadequate," Farrier's ultimate recommendation combines command-and-control regulation with "payment for stewardship" (pp. 327, 392–408). Ruhl (1998) cites his own experience in private legal practice and research findings by Rachlinski (1997, 1998). Regarding Leopold's views, see generally Flader and Caldicott (1991).

2. Reading and Kellert identified three methods for accomplishing public relations goals: "pressure, purchase, and persuasion."

3. The "human envelope" expression originates with R. Westrum (1994). Clark notes that according to the USFWS, endangerment of the grizzly bear is "largely a result of social belief systems in the American West" (p. 186, citing the agency's 1993 recovery plan).

4. Compare Doremus (1997, p. 1152), who asserts that "better science . . . does not always produce better policy decisions."

5. Clark quotes Lasswell and McDougal (1992, p. 895), regarding prototyping, and cites numerous other sources.

6. In Part 2 of his book Clark critically examines the policy and policy-process literature and concludes that it provides considerable guidance and case studies.

7. Norton summarizes four distinct approaches to valuing biological resources: (1) economic/utilitarian, (2) intergenerational equity/stewardship/sustainability, (3) biocentric, and (4) ecocentric. Ecosystems (including their component species) provide immense benefits in terms of the ecological health of the

planet. See, e.g., Costanza et al. (1997), calculating a value of $33 trillion annually for seventeen ecosystem services, such as water purification and soil generation. But Salzman and Ruhl (2000, pp. 634–635, nn. 68–69) note the impracticality of attempting to determine monetary values of ecosystem services, and they cite other sources.

8. Salzman and Ruhl cite Steven Kelman (1981).

9. The draft covenant was prepared in response to recommendations of the 1992 U.N. Conference on Environment and Development in Rio de Janeiro.

10. In *Lucas* a divided (5–4) Supreme Court ruled that a South Carolina law, which prohibited the plaintiff from constructing houses on his barrier island property, had taken his property, thus entitling him to compensation. The majority gave scant attention to the evidence of such coastal lands' vulnerability to hurricanes or to the contribution of beachfront construction to erosion and other ecological damage. Law professor Eric Freyfogle (1996, p. 20) wrote that South Carolina lost the case because not enough Supreme Court justices "were able to understand the ecosystem disruptions that come from building on ecologically sensitive lands." Sax (1993, pp. 1438–1439) adds that the Wisconsin court may itself have retreated "from the most extreme implications" (of *Just*), and on privatization he cites several examples from Revolutionary and frontier America.

11. With "transformational economy," Sax refers to the "conventional" view of private property, one that "builds on the image of property as a discrete entity that can be made one's own by working it and transforming it into a human artifact." In contrast, the term "economy of nature," which Sax says is "emerging as a prominent viewpoint" (p. 1446), describes an ecological view of property, in which land "is not a passive entity waiting to be transformed" by its owner, but interconnected "systems defined by their function, . . . performing important services in its unaltered state" (p. 1442). The conventional view has a technological base and presupposes that tracts are separate, subject to the dominion of individual owners, and transformable by individual will into anything. The ecological view holds that land is "in service" (not waiting to be put to use by man), governed by ecological needs, and part of a community. "Use rights are determined by physical nature," not by owner predilections. This emerging ecological view generates "a different attitude toward land and the nature of land ownership" and "greatly affects conceptions of owner entitlement" (pp. 1445–1446). On the other hand, Sax asserts that his approach is consistent with the Supreme Court's decision in *Penn Central Transportation Co. v. New York City*, noting that the custodial obligation upheld in *Penn Central* and historic preservation cases generally can be analogized to an ecological stewardship duty.

12. As Leopold (1949, p. 249) wrote, "If the private owner were ecologically minded, he would be proud to be the custodian of a reasonable proportion of such areas [e.g., "marshes, bogs, dunes and 'deserts'"], which add diversity and beauty to his farm and community."

13. The methods for determining existence, option, and other nonuse values are referred to as contingent valuation (see Donahue 1998, pp. 65–66).

14. An open letter to Congress, signed by academic scientists and environ-

mental activists, stated that the "vast majority of biological scientists agrees fundamentally about the importance of conserving the diversity of life on Earth." See "On Reauthorization of the Endangered Species Act," p. 1.

15. Parenteau (1998, pp. 295–300) argues that the policy is illegal and advocates replacing it with a "permit shield" provision that "provides appropriate protection from enforcement for permittees who are in compliance with their permit." Models can be found, he notes, in the Clean Water and Clean Air acts.

16. Section 10 incidental takings permits, Farrier asserts, are the functional equivalent of "shut[ting] the stable door after the horse has already bolted" (p. 388).

References

Australia Industry Commission. 1998. *A full repairing lease: Inquiry into ecologically sustainable land management.* Report 60. 27 January.

Barton, Charmian. 1998. The status of the precautionary principle in Australia: Its emergence in legislation and as a common law doctrine. *Harvard Environmental Law Review* 22:509–558.

Bowles, Ian, David Downes, Dana Clark, and Marianne Guerin-McManus. 1998. Economic incentives and legal tools for private sector conservation. *Duke Environmental Law and Policy Forum* 8:209–243.

Clark, Tim W. 1997. *Averting extinction: Reconstructing endangered species recovery.* New Haven, Conn.: Yale University Press.

Convention on Biological Diversity. 1992. Montreal, Quebec: United Nations Environmental Program.

Cortner, Hanna J., and Margaret A. Moote. 1999. *The politics of ecosystem management.* Washington, D.C.: Island Press, 1999.

Costanza, R., R. d'Arge, R. de Groot, S. Farber, M. Grasso, B. Hannan, K. Limburg, S. Naeem, R. O'Neill, J. Parudo, R. Raskin, P. Suttan, and M. van den Belt. 1997. The value of the world's ecosystem services and natural capital. *Nature* 387:253–260.

Donahue, Debra L. 1998. *Conservation and the law: A dictionary.* Santa Barbara, Calif.: ABC-CLIO.

Doremus, Holly. 1997. Listing decisions under the Endangered Species Act: Why better science isn't always better policy. *Washington University Law Quarterly* 75:1029–1153.

Endangered Species Act. 1996. Section 10. *U.S. Code,* vol. 16, sec. 1539(a)(2)(B)(iv).

Farrier, D. 1995. Conserving biodiversity on private land: Incentives for management or compensation for lost expectations? *Harvard Environmental Law Review* 19:303–408.

Flader, Susan L., and J. Baird Caldicott. 1991. *The river of the mother of God and other essays by Aldo Leopold.* Madison: University of Wisconsin Press.

Freyfogle, Eric T. 1990. The land ethic and Pilgrim Leopold. *University of Colorado Law Review* 61:217–253.

———. 1996. Owning and belonging: The private landowner as ecosystem member. *Sustain* 1:16–23.

Holechek, Jerry L., and Karl Hess Jr. 1995. The emergency feed program. *Rangelands* 17:133–136.

Juergensmeyer, Julian Conrad, and Thomas E. Roberts. 1998. *Land use planning and control law.* St. Paul, Minn.: West Group Publishing.

Just v. Marinette County, 201 N.W. 2d 761 (Wisc. 1972).

Karp, James P. 1993. A private property duty of stewardship: Changing our land ethic. *Environmental Law* 23:735–761.

Kelman, Steven. 1981. *What price incentives? Economists and the environment.* Boston: Auburn House.

Kuhlman, Walter. 1996. Wildlife's burden. Pp. 189–201 in *Biodiversity and the law,* edited by William J. Snape III. Washington, D.C.: Island Press.

Kunich, John Charles. 1994. The fallacy of deathbed conservation under the Endangered Species Act. *Environmental Law* 24:501–579.

Lasswell, H. D., and M. S. McDougal. 1992. *Jurisprudence for a free society: Studies in law, science, and policy.* 2 vols. New Haven: New Haven Press.

Leopold, A. 1949. *A Sand County almanac, and sketches here and there.* New York: Oxford University Press.

Lucas v. South Carolina Coastal Council, 112 S. Ct. 2886 (1992).

McElfish, James M. Jr., Philip Warburg, and John Pendergrass. 1996. Property: Past, present, future. *Environmental Forum* (Sept.–Oct.): 20–35.

Norton, Bryan G. 1998. Biological resources and endangered species: History, values, and policy. Pp. 247–264 in *Protection of global biodiversity: Converging strategies,* edited by Lakshman D. Guruswamy and Jeffrey A. McNeely. Durham, N.C.: Duke University Press.

Noss, Reed F., and Allen Y. Cooperrider. 1994. *Saving nature's legacy.* Washington, D.C.: Island Press.

Oil Pollution Act. 1990. 15 C.F.R. sec. 990 & appendix (Oil Pollution Act regulations).

On Reauthorization of the Endangered Species Act. 1994. *Conservation Biology* 8:1.

Parenteau, Patrick. 1998. Rearranging the deck chairs: Endangered Species Act reforms in an era of mass extinctions. *William and Mary Environmental Law and Policy Review* 22:227–311.

Penn Central Transportation Co. v. New York City, 438 U.S. 104, 124 (1978).

Rachlinski, Jeffrey J. 1997. Noah by the numbers: An empirical evaluation of the Endangered Species Act. *Cornell Law Review* 82:356–389.

———. 1998. Protecting endangered species without regulating private landowners: The case of endangered plants. *Cornell Journal of Law and Public Policy* 8:1–36.

Reading, Richard P., and Stephen R. Kellert. 1993. Attitudes toward a proposed reintroduction of black-footed ferrets (*Mustela nigripes*). *Conservation Biology* 7:569–580.

Repetto, Robert, Roger Dower, Robin Jenkins, and Jacqueline Geoghegan. 1992. *Green fees: How a tax shift can work for the environment and the economy.* Washington, D.C.: World Resources Institute.

Ruhl, J. B. 1998. The Endangered Species Act and private property: A matter of timing and location. *Cornell Journal of Law and Public Policy* 8:37–53.

Salzman, James, and J. B. Ruhl. 2000. Currencies and the commodification of environmental law. *Stanford Law Review* 52:607–694.

Sax, Joseph L. 1993. Property rights and the economy of nature: Understanding *Lucas v. South Carolina Coastal Council*. *Stanford Law Review* 45:1433–1455.

Sunstein, Cass R. 1996. On the expressive function of law. *University of Pennsylvania Law Review* 144:2021.

Superfund. 1980. 50 C.F.R. sec. 11, *Comprehensive Environmental Response, Compensation, and Liability Act* (CERCLA).

Westrum, R. 1994. An organizational perspective: Designing recovery teams from the inside out. Pp. 327–349 in *Endangered species recovery: Finding the lessons, improving the process,* edited by T. W. Clark. Washington, D.C.: Island Press.

Wilson, Edward O. 1992. *The diversity of life.* Cambridge, Mass.: Harvard University Press.

Wright, Robert R., and Morton Gitelman. 1997. *Cases and materials on land use.* 5th ed. St. Paul, Minn.: West Publishing Group.

Young, M. D., N. Gunningham, J. Elix, J. Lambert, B. Howard, P. Grabosky, and E. McCrone. 1996. Reimbursing the future: An evaluation of motivational, voluntary, price-based, property-right, and regulatory incentives for the conservation of biodiversity. Biodiversity Series paper 9: A report to the [Australia] Department of the Environment, Sport, and Territories. January.

Yunker v. Nichols, 1 Colo. 551 (1872), 1449–1450.

CHAPTER 6

Appraising the Conservation Value
of Private Lands

STEVEN W. BUSKIRK AND SAMANTHA M. WISELY

The conservation of scarce biological resources on private lands commonly involves the biological and market valuation of the resources in ways that identify targets for conservation and facilitate negotiations between property owners and potential buyers. For our purposes, a buyer can include any individual or institution with an interest in conservation, the "conservator" of Parkhurst and Shogren (chapter 3). The problem of estimating the values of biological resources and the benefits of conserving them are complex and cross disciplinary boundaries between science, policy, and economics. Our goal is to help create markets for the conservation values of species and habitats in limited supply. In this chapter we identify some key issues in valuing biological resources and describe the bioappraisal, a process and document that determine and describe the biological resources on private property so that conservation can be facilitated via informed and willing transactions between buyers and sellers. In this chapter we are primarily concerned with determining and documenting the conservation value of resources; setting an economic or market value is treated separately.

Most of the publicly owned conservation reserve system in the United States has been chosen for attributes other than biodiversity and its protection. For example, most of the land area of our National Parks System has been selected on the basis of its scenic, cultural, historical, and recreational values, particularly unique features of national interest. Grand Canyon, Yosemite, and Gates of the Arctic national parks might not be logical choices for areas to protect the maximum number of species. Similar patterns are seen for our national forests, national wildlife refuges, and wilderness areas; they were selected to conserve particular biological resources of special interest or concern, but not to maximize the conservation of biodiversity per se. Of course, some of these nature reserves provide some of the strongest conservation protection possible in this country. Few of our public nature reserves, however, provide the highest level of protection, Category I (scientific reserve, strict nature reserve) protection, under the criteria of IUCN (1984). To achieve Category I status, a nature reserve cannot allow extractive uses (e.g., fishing, hunting, berry collecting) or develop sites for recreation, common uses of public nature reserves in the United States. Another salient pattern in the historical selection and establishment of nature reserves in the United States is the avoidance of competing, higher priority uses of the land, particularly agriculture. Especially during the settlement phase of our nation's history, we gave human livelihoods precedence over nature conservation, so that most of the acreage in our nature reserves is in relatively unproductive habitats, passed over by settlers, and with low biodiversity. We have yet to develop a public system for the effective conservation of representative ecosystems or areas of high diversity or high endemicity. An increased involvement of the private sector in conservation of endangered species has the potential to correct partially that historical shortcoming in the selection of our nature reserve system.

The bioappraisal is a process whereby the factors that affect the conservation value, and hence the market value to a conservator, of land or water are described and documented through a formal contract between the appraiser and a client. For simplicity, we assume that the biological resources are of value to pursuing a conservation goal, although amenity and negative values associated with the resource are difficult to isolate in a market setting. For example, if a rare wetland amphibian tended to occupy habitats that produced mosquitoes, and if the land were valued for conservation as well as for recreation, the conservation value of the wetland habitat and the nuisance value of the mosquitoes might influence market price in confounded ways. We use "conservation value" to convey the importance of the resources to the pursuit of a conservation goal: the conservation value of a resource depends on the conservation goal. If conservation of an endangered species is the goal, then a description of the species' population, habitat, competitors, predators, prey, and diseases on a piece of land, placed in the context of its distribution, abundance, and trends globally, will characterize its conservation value. Conservation value therefore includes the abundance and fitness of the organisms of interest on the property. Additionally, conservation value may describe or predict the potential abundance and fitness of resources under alternative management regimes or under alternative regional contexts. For example, conservation value might predict the population size and productivity of an endangered species if oil development were to increase or grazing were to decrease, or compare the conservation value of the area appraised to that of a comparator property that holds the same species.

The bioappraisal is intended to facilitate transactions informed by shared knowledge of conditions. The transaction for which the bioappraisal is conducted could take various forms, described by Parkhurst and Shogren in chapter 3. For each of these kinds of transactions, the abundance of the resource on the property and its scarcity in general determine the conservation value of the resources on the property. For the purposes of this chapter, the diverse entities such as government agencies, private land trusts, and nonprofit conservation organizations that might enter into these various kinds of transactions with property owners are called "buyers." As with standard real estate appraisals, we expect that bioappraisals will be initiated at the request of and become the property of the owner, although some sharing of information is implicit in its effective use. We assume that the bioappraisal is conducted under a contract and that the property has conservation value related to the conservation goals of some entity other than the owner, particularly a private organization or individual.

What Determines Conservation Value?

Typically, wildlife biologists have identified habitat as the necessary, sufficient, and overriding factor in the conservation of animal species (Frankel and Soulé 1981). It is almost a truism that to have wildlife, we must have habitat, and if we have habitat, we will have wildlife. Here, we recognize a more complex relationship between the biota and the factors needed to sustain it. First, plants and vegetation communities may be said to require some habitat features and to compose others. The factors that affect the distribution and abundance of flora are reviewed by Grubb (1977) and include such habitat factors as climate, elevation, soil attributes, and landform (e.g., slope and aspect). Also, the distribution and abundance of flora are influenced by levels of herbivory, disturbance regimes, and, for some species, the availability of animal seed dispersers.

For animals, we recognize two broad phenomena that affect distribution, abundance, and conservation value: habitat and community interactions. We define animal habitats as the more or less permanent, yet seasonally fluctuating features of landform, limnological attributes, snow, and vegetation that affect life needs of species or guilds. Typically, habitat for terrestrial animals is described in terms of elevation, slope, aspect, climate, snow characteristics, plant species dominants, structural features, successional stage, plant biomass, or landscape attributes. For aquatic organisms, in addition to some of the above attributes, biologists use water depth, stream velocity, water temperature, water chemistry, substrate attributes, and attributes of ice in winter. Habitat defined in this way, however, does not explain a large part of the variation in the distribution and abundance of animals. Community interactions are those with all other nonhabitat biota on the site, interactions that may not be permanent or seasonally predictable: competitors, predators, prey, and disease-causing organisms. These factors tend not to be regarded as elements of habitat because they tend to fluctuate too widely and unpredictably to be sampled or analyzed in the same way as vegetation and landform. It would be possible to produce a habitat map for bighorn sheep (*Ovis canadensis*) showing vegetation and slope, which had utility over a period of decades in predicting the distribution of bighorns, but a sudden epizootic of pneumonia might eradicate a bighorn population on high-quality habitat, rendering the habitat map an academic instrument. Similarly, prey populations fluctuate widely and unpredictably, so that a predator that had specific habitat needs might still fluctuate in abundance in ways that habitat could not predict or account for. That is not to say that distributions of potential predators, competitors, and disease organisms cannot be mapped, but they tend to fluctuate in distribution and abundance more than does vegetation, and to be highly labile relative to landform and elevation. So, we consider conservation value in terms of the more or less stable features of habitat and the less predictable features of community interactions. Examples of how these two kinds of attributes can be appraised are given below.

The Real Estate Appraisal as a Model

Estimation of conservation value requires information about resources on the property of interest, information provided by the bioappraisal. The clearest justification for bioappraisals is to help seller and buyer agree on a price by presenting reliable, quantitative information about the biological resources on the property and the context for them. The closest analogy to the bioappraisal is that of the real estate appraisal, a key tool in the real estate industry. A real estate appraisal is an estimation of value, usually a written opinion of the value of an adequately described property on a specific date, with supporting data (Lusht 1997). A bioappraisal is not intended as a substitute for a standard real estate appraisal, although both kinds of appraisal will provide some redundant information. A bioappraisal does not estimate market value, but it will provide the basis for considering conservation value in setting a price. It should accompany a real estate appraisal in cases where biological resources and conservation goals are expected to affect the price of a property strongly.

The key elements of a bioappraisal, and their points of similarity and contrast to a real estate appraisal, are presented here in the order in which an appraiser is likely to confront them.

Description of Property and Resources of Interest

In order for an appraisal to describe the biota on a property accurately, it must first identify the size and boundaries of the property offered for sale (Land Trust Alliance 1999), although in this case a sale could mean any number of kinds of transactions in addition to fee simple acquisition (Parkhurst and Shogren, this volume). Additionally, contractual or other constraints on the use of the property, including but not limited to subsurface rights, water rights, and existing easements, which may enhance or detract from the conservation value of the land, must be identified. The property owner is responsible for conveying this information to the appraiser as part of the contract covering the bioappraisal; the appraiser proceeds under the assumption that all relevant information has been provided, and the appraiser is not responsible for inaccuracies in the appraisal arising from a lack of disclosure by the property owner. Of course, the surest method of identifying easements or contractual constraints on the property is via a licensed title company.

No appraisal can list all of the kinds of organisms living on a piece of property, let alone their distributions, abundances, habitats, competitors, predators, and diseases, so the resources of interest must be delimited in negotiations between the property owner and the appraiser. The owner may limit the kinds of surveys conducted, not wishing to generate or possess knowledge about certain species or habitats. Alternatively, the owner may contract with the appraiser to exercise professional judgment in searching for taxa of conservation concern. The appraiser will have an interest in minimizing the cost of conducting the appraisal by limiting the scope of surveys but may serendipitously identify resources on the land that are of keen interest to the conservation community. In its extreme form, this could include discovering and describing taxa not previously known to science and apparently very rare or highly restricted in distribution. Clear communication between the property owner and the appraiser, reflected in language in the contract, is essential to avoid problems arising from such contingencies. The resource of interest might be a single species (e.g., mountain plover, *Charadrius montanus*), a higher-level taxonomic group (e.g., birds, fish, invertebrates), a specified subset of a taxonomic group (e.g., rare vascular plants), or a statutory or regulatory group (e.g., listed or candidate species under the Endangered Species Act), or a rare or threatened community type (e.g., vernal pool, bog). The more comprehensive the list of resources of interest, the more costly will be the bioappraisal.

Description of Spatial Context

Knowing how the biological resources on the property relate to those surrounding the property is central to understanding the value of the former. Are the populations and habitats on the property contiguous with larger ones, or are they isolated? If they are isolated, then to have conservation value they must function as a viable population or undergo exchanges with other populations. If they are connected to other important populations or habitats, knowing about dispersal corridors that connect populations on the property with others is central to understanding the viability and value of the resources on the property (Wilcove et al. 1986). This aspect of the bioappraisal is closely analogous to the real estate appraisal: the neighborhood bears centrally on a property's value (Appraisal Institute 1996). As an example of the importance of context in a bioappraisal, assume that a property holds a subpopulation of endangered animals that traditionally have migrated seasonally across other private land (a migration corridor) to a large area of public land. This seasonal migration is critical to population persistence; without it, the private land will lose its population. If the private land containing the migration corridor is undergoing human-caused changes that will interfere with migration, it can be expected that the animal species of interest will not persist on the property of interest. This bears on the conservation value of the property and must be reflected in the appraisal.

Description of Potential Species and Habitats

This information can be derived from secondary and tertiary sources, without on-site data collection, and resembles the characterization that a real estate appraiser can make based on quantitative data (lot size, square footage, number of bedrooms), without inspecting the property. For some purposes, a description of potential conservation value may suffice, in which case the bioappraisal would end here. The appraiser for biodiversity surveys the literature or records of government agencies or of private institutions for information about the species of interest in the region of interest. Of particular utility here is the national system of natural diversity databases, the Biological and Conservation Data System, founded by the Nature Conservancy but now organized on a state-by-state basis and administered through state agencies or universities. These programs specifically emphasize rare taxa and therefore are of particular relevance in conservation-related appraisals. Another important secondary data source is the Gap Analysis Project reports for various states (Scott et al. 1993). This program, implemented by the Biological Resources Division of the U.S. Geological Survey, provides spatially explicit information on a fairly coarse scale. It is available on Web sites for many states (summarized at www.gap.uidaho.edu/). Another potential data source is published distribution maps (e.g., Hultén 1968, Hall 1981); however, these maps suffer from several problems. They sometimes extrapolate distributions from only a few points so that inferences about the property of interest may be incorrect, and they cannot reflect distributional changes since their publication, a particular problem for older accounts or highly dynamic species. On the other hand, were they to show an individual record for the property of interest along with a museum reference, the data would be considered primary and would have considerable weight in placing the species on the property.

Description of Actual Species and Habitats

On-site inventories will provide primary data; the appraiser will detect the species or vegetation type on the property and describe that observation in the appraisal report. Analogous to the site visit by a real estate appraiser, this is the most costly aspect of the bioappraisal. It may produce several kinds of data, listed here in order of increasing specificity and cost:

Diversity (species list). The appraisal can identify presence or apparent absence of species or vegetation types on the property, using survey methods appropriate to the taxa of interest. Of course, absence cannot be proven, especially for low-density or cryptic species, so the appraisal will only be able to identify the number of detections given a specified level of effort. Clear reporting of effort expended in presence-absence surveys is critical for comparing appraisals among properties. Survey methods are highly taxon-specific; the methods used to determine broad vegetation types (remote sensing) will differ sharply from those used to survey for aquatic insects (drift nets), fish (electro-fishing), breeding birds (visual and auditory surveys), small mammals (baited traps), bats (mist nets), and carnivores (baited track plates, remote cameras, or hair snares followed by DNA analysis). The greater the diversity of taxa to be surveyed, the more diverse the survey methods needed, the higher the equipment capitalization for the appraiser, and the higher the cost of the appraisal. Such presence-absence surveys are in many cases more technical and costly, but they are also much more powerful than their counterparts of 25 years ago in their ability to detect a species that is present. For taxa that have been listed under the ESA, a specific survey protocol likely will have been developed, and this should be used by the appraiser and described in the bioappraisal. Such a protocol may provide for minimal amounts of search effort needed to clear an area for a particular species, one of the few ways that an appraiser could certify that a species is absent from a property.

Distribution. The appraisal can, at the request of the owner, report the estimated distributions of community types or species on the property. In its coarsest form, this would involve maps of broad cover types (forest, rangeland, riparian zones) on the property, but such maps could provide distributions for individual species if they are habitat-specific (e.g., aquatic species or forest obligates) or have low mobility (e.g., plants, dispersal-sensitive mammals). Few tracts of private lands are large enough to allow mapping of species that are habitat generalists or have high mobility (e.g., coyotes, ravens, flying insects). Mapping of distributions will require determinations of presence versus absence over the entire property of interest.

Abundance. Abundance, either relative or absolute, is the most challenging and, for animals, temporally variable attribute that a bioappraisal can report, yet this characteristic may be of high interest to sellers and buyers. If a species or community type is rare outside the property, the population size or area of that species or community on the property must bear centrally on conservation value. For different biological resources, abundance will be expressed in different currencies. For community types, size or extent (area or volume for land or lakes, length for cliffs or streams) will be familiar currencies. A property, for example, might be characterized by 13 kilometers of second-order streams, 25 kilometers of first-order streams, a 7-hectare lake, and 36 hectares of prairie dog colonies. These measures will derive from maps, remote sensing, and site visits.

For individual species, the metric of interest likely will be population size (N), or an index thereof. N can be estimated as a direct count of all members of the species on the property, especially if they are sessile, called a census. For animals, biologists more commonly estimate N by various methods that involve sampling (measurements taken on a subset of the population that are extrapolated under a set of assumptions to generate estimates of N). An example of a sample-based estimate of N would be a mark-reobservation procedure: a part of a population is detected and identified as having been detected, then a subsequent second sample is detected, and the proportion that is previously detected animals is used to estimate N. Traditionally, these methods have involved applying marks or tags to captured animals, but modern molecular methods provide the means to use the animal's own DNA as its mark and the hairs shed by the animal as the means of capture. An index of N is less costly to estimate than N itself and may be adequate to identify variation in N across areas and over time. A substantial part of animal ecology (Seber 1982), but only a small part of plant ecology (Hickman 1979), has been devoted to the estimation of N, and the problems of doing so are complex and highly taxon-specific. Several problems are of particular interest here.

For some species, particularly animals, detection may be difficult and costly. Factors that predispose animals to low detectability include low densities (e.g., predators), fossorial living (e.g., the tiger salamander, *Ambystoma tigrinum*, and pocket gophers, Geomyidae), and inactivity during daytime. For the most cryptic species, special methods are available that infer presence based on sign, DNA, or photographs (Cutler and Swann 1999). Those who conduct bioappraisals, therefore, may expend effort and charge amounts that vary strongly with detectability of the target organism, and these variations may not seem warranted to the property owner. This large variation in effort and cost emphasizes the need for explicitness and clarity in the contract governing the bioappraisal.

A description of the uncertainty associated with sampling is a key element of the description of abundance. Where species can be censused by direct and complete counts, no sampling error is incurred or reported. For example, in prairie habitats with few trees, the number of tree-nesting raptors might be counted directly, and no error estimates will accompany the estimate. For many species, however, N will be estimated from samples, and such estimates have associated sampling errors that also can be estimated from sample data, under certain assumptions. Where sampled, information about sampling error should be included with the estimate; this information will be expressed in forms such as confidence intervals, standard deviations, or standard errors.

One special kind of question regarding abundance deals with population viability, specifically the probability that $N = 0$ (the population goes extinct) by some specified future date. Population viability, a central concept of conservation biology, considers not only population size but also density dependence, demographic variation, temporal variation, individual variation, and genetic variation (Soulé 1987). Formal population viability analyses are commonly undertaken for high-profile populations at risk and are plausible as a subtask within the bioappraisal; however, such analyses require parameterization of models of population persistence that few agencies, let alone private landowners, will be able to afford. In most cases, analysis of population viability will be impractical and cost-prohibitive.

Carrying capacity and nonhabitat factors. Another attribute of interest is carrying capacity (K), the maximum number of organisms that can be supported by a piece of land or water at a specified time. Carrying capacity varies temporally, so a population that is within carrying capacity $(N < K)$ at one time, for example summer, might exceed it at another, for example winter. When that occurs, N tends to decline, sometimes abruptly, to less than K. Although carrying capacity is commonly thought of as an attribute of habitat alone ("carrying capacity of the habitat" is a common phrase), carrying capacity reflects forces that are generally considered beyond habitat, although habitat may mediate their influence. These include predators, competitors, and disease. So, as used here, carrying capacity is the sum of all the factors that affect the distribution and abundance of the biota, including the habitat, predators (herbivores in the case of plants), prey, competitors, and disease-causing organisms.

For animals that are killed and eaten by others (virtually all animal species), predators are not considered a component of habitat but are potentially important at the population level. For example, lynx and coyotes are not considered a component of habitat for snowshoe hares, but predators are important in determining the abundance of snowshoe hares in the North (Krebs et al. 1995). This means that an appraisal of snowshoe hare populations should mention the possible effect of predators (a nonhabitat factor) on observed densities of snowshoe hares. Habitat might mediate the hare-predator interaction; for example, physical structure near the ground affects vulnerability of hares to ambush. So, habitat influences the relationships between predators and prey, but it should be described separately. Likewise, populations of predators can respond strongly to populations of prey; the carrying capacity of habitat for cougars, for example, is hard to imagine except through the carrying capacity of the habitat for the prey of cougars. Characterizing the carrying capacity of an area for cougars will largely involve describing populations and habitats of ungulates or other prey.

Competition likewise can be an important limiting factor for plants and animals of conservation concern (Goodrich and Buskirk 1995), especially fish (Zaret and Rand 1971), but competitors are not usually considered a component of animal habitats. Potential competitors with a species of interest should be described, and they may need to be estimated to understand the biological context of the species of interest. For example, kit foxes (*Vulpes macrotis*) are highly susceptible to killing by coyotes (*Canis latrans*), so any land being considered for conserving kit foxes should be characterized in terms of its coyote populations. For fish, the line between competition and predation is blurred because so many kinds of fish eat smaller fish that use the same resources. Regardless of how they are labeled, these trophic or competitive interactions are overwhelmingly important in structuring fish populations (Zaret and Rand 1971).

The last of the nonhabitat factors that can be strongly limiting to animal populations is disease. Diseases, particularly those introduced by humans, are increasingly recognized as limiting the distribution and abundance of animals, especially species of conservation concern (Thorne and Williams 1988). The black-footed ferret (*Mustela nigripes*) is a classic example: it became extinct in the wild when the few remaining ferrets were taken into captivity in 1985, in the face of outbreaks of plague (*Yersinia pestis*) and canine distemper in the wild ferret population and its prairie dog prey. Efforts to reintroduce ferrets to the wild have met with mixed success, in part because of the geographic distribution of plague, which extends from the West Coast to approximately the 104th meridian. Eastward, in the midwestern states, plague is absent, and ferrets have enjoyed their highest reintroduction successes in such plague-free areas. Clearly, the evaluation of potential ferret reintroduction sites must consider habitat (prairie vegetation), prey (prairie dogs), potential competitors (e.g., coyotes), and disease (e.g., plague).

Seen as a complex of habitat and nonhabitat factors, the concept of carrying capacity has utility to property owners and appraisers. Land use practices can affect K, so that it is plausible that an appraiser might identify some inequality between N and K. For example, an appraiser might provide a statement that N for prairie dogs was estimated at 360 with a 90 percent confidence interval of 310–410, but that reduced predation by coyotes, reduced harassment by free-ranging domestic dogs, and exclusion of cattle from the area could result in a higher N for prairie dogs. In other words, the current N is less than K under assumed modified conditions. In this case, an appraised value based on the conservation value added by alternative management might be conceivable. The opposite case would occur when a population of interest is held at artificially high levels on the property of interest through the provision of supplemental food or other life needs. Under such circumstances it might be possible and useful for the bioappraisal to state that N exceeds what K would be, lacking such artificial supplementation of resources.

Although estimating K is more difficult than estimating N, estimating habitat quality is a common practice in wildlife biology. Various approaches have been used, including habitat capability models and habitat evaluation procedures, the latter developed initially by the U.S. Fish and Wildlife Service (Schamberger et al. 1982) but now adapted and modified by many state and provincial agencies (e.g., California, http://ice.ucdavis.edu/Toads/Cwhrbref5.html). Habitat evaluation procedures use habitat suitability index (HSI) models. These are based on knowledge of the habitat needs of a species, require on-site measurements of from one to several attributes of importance to the species of interest, make assumptions about how the habitat attributes interact to affect the species of interest, and generate an index (HSI) between 0 (no value) and 1 (optimal value). Habitats tend to be regarded as good if they produce high densities of the species of interest; however, some species violate this pattern by exhibiting high densities of nonbreeding subadults in suboptimal habitats (Van Horne 1983). HSI modeling could be an important component of bioappraisal if used comparatively. Determining that a property has 600 hectares of habitat with an HSI of 0.5 for a species of interest may not be highly informative by itself, but if comparing two potential purchases of similar size, knowing that one has an HSI of 0.5 and the other an HSI of 0.9 could be decisive.

Description of Temporal Constraints

Real estate appraisals are specific to a point in time, but bioappraisals may, depending on circumstances, have to consider seasonal or inter-annual variation in distribution and abundance of resources. If a property owner wishes to have migratory birds appraised in December, only the coarsest data on distribution might be available at that season; site-specific surveys would have to wait until summer, when migratory birds are present. Likewise, some flowering plants may need to be surveyed during the flowering season to assure identification to species. For some rare carnivores, surveys may need to be conducted during mid-winter, when tracks accumulate on the snow surface. By contrast, vegetation mapping from existing databases during December might be fully feasible. Aside from these issues of seasonal variation, nature exhibits striking temporal variation, so that what is optimal habitat or a high population one year may not be so the next. The bioappraisal must be specific as to the time to which it applies: a particular date or month, a multi-season period, or a multiyear period.

A Written Report

The bioappraisal report should be organized along the lines identified in this chapter, with supporting descriptions of resources, appendices, and maps. A highly simplified report prepared for an appraisal of a conservation easement is described by the Land Trust Alliance (1999). In contrast to a real estate appraisal, a description of scope, level of search effort, temporal constraints, and methods will figure prominently. As a general outline for the written report, we propose the following:

I. Name and address of property owner
II. Name and address of appraiser
III. Legal description of property
IV. Easements, rights-of-way, subsurface rights, and other statutory or contractual constraints on uses or conservation value of the property
V. Biological scope: a list of taxa or ecological entities (e.g., community types) covered by the appraisal

186 Steve W. Buskirk and Samantha M. Wisely

VI. Methods
    A. General description of data collected
    B. Survey methods used for each taxon or kind of organism
    C. Levels of search effort or survey effort for each taxon or community type
    D. Dates of field visits
    E. Dates of remote sensing images used
    F. Operational definitions (terms defined for the purposes of the appraisal, e.g., "stand," "colony," "cliff," "pool")
    G. References to publications, reports or database sources used

VII. Results
    A. Description of spatial context (neighborhood)
    B. Taxa or community types potentially present, from secondary or tertiary sources
    C. Taxa or community types actually present, from surveys of the site
    D. Relative or absolute abundance of taxa of interest
    E. Habitat suitability indices for taxa of interest
    F. Distribution or location of community types of interest

VIII. Conclusions
    A. Factors that affect interpretation or limit the utility of the data, including survey effort and estimated levels of uncertainty and temporal constraints on interpretation
    B. Factors that create inequalities between population size and carrying capacity
    C. Factors that influence the conservation value of the property
    D. Comparisons of conservation value with that for comparator properties that hold the taxon of interest or its habitat

Qualifications and Certification

The development of a successful national system of bioappraisal will require the training and certification of appraisers. Such a program should be specific to a taxonomic subject; the field of biology is highly specialized and compartmented, and few or no individual biologists can, for example, claim competence in identifying rare plants and estimating amphibian populations. Likewise, appraisers qualified to collect and identify insects may not be qualified to conduct searches for large carnivores or to estimate carrying capacity for bison. The same is true, although perhaps to a lesser extent, for real estate appraisal; someone qualified to appraise residential property may not be qualified to estimate the value of agricultural land, conservation easements, or potential industrial sites. A successful system will require the more or less simultaneous evolution of programs and teaching materials, private-sector professional organizations and standards, and governmental certification of appraisers and regulation of some aspects of the appraisals. Of course, the evolution of a body of common law regarding contracts covering appraisals will create the body of precedent that will give the field its legitimacy. Again, this follows closely the real estate model: training courses and materials (e.g., *Appraisal Journal*) are available; a professional society (e.g., Appraisal Institute, www.appraisalinstitute.org/) creates standards and provides print, Internet, and other forums for exchange of information; and state and local governments certify appraisers as qualified to practice in particular jurisdictions.

Conclusions

The bioappraisal, although newly named here, is not a new concept; implementation of the ESA, the National Forest Management Act, and other biodiversity mandates relies on the evaluation of conservation value through surveys of literature or site visits to identify populations and habitats of taxa of conservation concern. However, the standardization of the information contained in a bioappraisal is critical to the comparative nature of the bioappraisal. For different properties to be compared, standardized methods must be used, and results must be expressed in standardized terms. The development of contractual language covering issues of privacy should increase the value of the bioappraisal to all those involved in the conservation of biotas on private lands. A clear need is for the certification of appraisers, which should be conducted along lines of taxonomic subject. Only through an evolutionary process that includes at least some government regulation will it be possible to develop a comprehensive set of certification criteria and procedures that will lead to the establishment of the business of bioappraisal as a profession, with commensurate standards of objectivity and peer review.

Acknowledgments

M. Sunderman provided helpful reviews on an early draft.

References

Appraisal Institute. 1996. *The appraisal of real estate.* 11th ed. Chicago: Appraisal Institute.

Cutler, T. L., and D. E. Swann. 1999. Using remote photography in wildlife ecology: A review. *Wildlife Society Bulletin* 27, no. 3:571–581.

Frankel, O. H., and M. E. Soulé. 1981. *Conservation and evolution.* New York: Cambridge University Press.

Goodrich, J. M., and S. W. Buskirk. 1995. Control of abundant native vertebrates for conservation of endangered species. *Conservation Biology* 9: 1357–1364.

Grubb, P. 1977. The maintenance of species richness in plant communities: The importance of the regeneration niche. *Biological Review* 52:107–145.

Hall, E. R. 1981. *The mammals of North America.* New York: John Wiley & Sons.

Hickman, J. C. 1979. The basic biology of plant numbers. Pp. 232–263 in *Topics in plant population biology,* edited by O. T. Solbrig, S. Jain, G. B. Johnson, and P. H. Raven. New York: Columbia University Press.

Hultén, E. 1968. *Flora of Alaska and neighboring territories.* Stanford, Calif.: Stanford University Press.

IUCN. 1984. Categories and criteria for protected areas. Pages 47–53 in *National parks, conservation, and development: The role of protected areas in sustaining society,* edited by J. A. McNeely and K. R. Miller. Washington, D.C.: Smithsonian Institution Press.

Krebs, C. J., S. Boutin, R. Boonstra, A. R. E. Sinclair, J. N. M. Smith, M. R. T. Dale, K. Martin, and R. Turkington. 1995. Impact of food and predation on the snowshoe hare cycle. *Science* 269:1112–1115.

Land Trust Alliance and the National Trust for Historic Preservation. 1999. *Appraising easements.* 3rd ed. Washington, D.C.: National Trust for Historic Preservation in the United States.

Lusht, K. 1997. *Real estate valuation: Principles and applications.* Homewood, Ill.: Irwin.

Schamberger, M., A. H. Farmer, and J. W. Terrell. 1982. *Habitat suitability index models: Introduction.* USDI Fish and Wildlife Service, FWS/OBS-82/10.

Scott, J. M., F. Davis, B. Csuti, R. Noss, B. Butterfield, C. Groves, H. Anderson, S. Caicco, F. D'Ercha, T. C. Edwards Jr., J. Ulliman, and R. G. Wright. 1993. Gap analysis: A geographical approach to protection of biological diversity. *Wildlife Monographs* 123:1–41.

Seber, G. A. F. 1982. *The estimation of animal abundance and related parameters.* New York: Macmillan.

Soulé, M. E., ed. 1987. *Viable populations for conservation.* Cambridge: Cambridge University Press.

Thorne, E. T., and E. S. Williams. 1988. Disease and endangered species: The black-footed ferret as a recent example. *Conservation Biology* 2:66–74.

Van Horne, B. 1983. Density as a misleading indicator of habitat quality. *Journal of Wildlife Management* 47:893–901.

Wilcove, D. S., C. H. McLellen, and A. P. Dobson. 1986. Habitat fragmentation in the temperate zone. Pp. 237–256 in *Conservation biology: The science of scarcity and diversity,* edited by M. E. Soulé. Sunderland, Mass.: Sinauer Associates.

Zaret, T. M., and S. Rand. 1971. Competition in tropical stream fishes: Support for the competitive exclusion principle. *Ecology* 52:336–342.

CHAPTER 7

Markets for Conserving Biodiversity Habitat: Principles and Practice

THOMAS D. CROCKER

As residential, commercial, and industrial developments continue to erode the integrity of natural areas, public interest in interactions between ecological and economic systems has intensified. This interest registers in frequently contentious debates about the validity of goals to preserve natural areas and the efficiency and the equity properties of the means to do so. Arguably this same public has denied the goals of environmental protection more frequently than necessary because regulatory authorities have used unnecessarily costly means of implementation.[1]

The devices used to implement the goals of the Endangered Species Act (ESA) seem a prime example of those means of implementation. Only the most insensitive, strictly urban beings would dare assert in polite company that it is not good in principle to protect the earth's nonurban life-forms and the habitats in which they live. Witness the consistently high standing in polls that the public gives the generic concept of environmental protection, including habitat conservation. The rub appears to be in how to implement the ESA and whether its goals are always feasible, have been made too costly by perverse bureaucratic rigidities and complexities, or are simply feel-good expressions.

Much of the land to which the ESA is meant to apply is privately owned. Some threatened or endangered species currently exist only on private land held in multiple ownerships. Suggestions and actual attempts to make implementation of the ESA more flexible and more predictable and less costly for private owners than can be achieved by simply issuing management injunctions to them from on high have not been lacking. Incidental take permits in which development is allowed if a landowner can show that it will not lead to species extinction are granted by the ESA authority. Safe harbor plans in which federal authorities and landowners negotiate no-fault contracts, where owners are not liable for harm to a species if they manage their land in accordance with contract terms, are now sometimes used by federal authorities (Turner and Rylander 1998). Economists and those who now and then listen to economists have proposed variants of tradable effluent permit allocation instruments (Crocker 1966; D. Montgomery 1972), such as tradable habitat preservation credits (Merrifield 1995) and tradable development rights (Stavins 1989). The flexibility and predictability these devices purportedly offer owners have, however, been met with skepticism by occasional commentators, including even some economists. Frey et al. (1996) worry that marketlike instruments will reduce the demand for and crowd out environmental virtue (morality). But virtuous attitudes and the social norms that manifest them can breed disrespect when they ask for more than people can accomplish.

Boyd et al. (1999) center their criticisms on the costs of designing site-specific contracts, claims, or rights, owner by owner. Granted, the complexity of designing an ecologically and economically sound system of permits, claims, or rights to develop sites can be daunting. This is an inadequate reason, however, to dismiss out of hand such systems when the only recognized alternative to them is a command-and-control system of questionable virtue in which middle-level bureaucrats and biological technicians are given free rein to designate restricted development sites and to redistribute wealth while using little more than biological criteria to do so. Given that society values natural habitats and the varied organisms that enjoy them, economic efficiency decrees that private landowners be held accountable for the effects their activities have on the socially valued dimensions of these habitats. Nevertheless, accountability must be achieved at the least cost to landowners and to the rest of society if the public is to ungrudgingly accept the ESA.

The next section argues that substantial scope exists for the use of tradable permits or credits in habitat conservation efforts. It also compares the economic efficiency and the wealth distribution features of tradable credit schemes to command-and-control schemes. A third section forms the core of the essay. It argues (and, for stylized conditions, formally demonstrates in an appendix) that neither tradable credit systems alone nor wealth redistributing command-and-control systems alone are capable of providing the flexibility and predictability that a socially least-cost design for habitat protection requires. Least-cost designs will initially involve private landowners in a tradable habitat credit system and, subsequently, in a transfer payment, command-and-control exercise operated by a central authority. Contrary to the standard perception that tradable permits or credits and environmental use taxes or subsidies are substitute policy instruments, this chapter suggests that they can be complements. They can reinforce each other's strengths while sidestepping their weaknesses. The fourth section comments on the practical issues likely to be involved in implementing such a hybrid scheme of economic incentives and regulation, with particular attention to the relevance to outcomes of the accuracy of information about habitat attributes and its division between landowners and the regulating authority. In conclusion, I argue that the hybrid scheme is worthy of serious consideration. Circumstances are likely to be plentiful on multiple-ownership private lands where the scheme can achieve public habitat conservation goals in a flexible, predictable, efficient, and equitable fashion.

Habitat Conservation Instruments

The Biological Scope for Private Owner Discretion

Whether the focus is a single species or preservation of a coherent landscape, most ESA schemes for implementing habitat conservation start with some conception of biosphere zones (Swallow 1996; UNESCO 1996) in which land is arranged in concentric zones with the least developed portion in a core area defined on biological criteria alone. This core area is buffered by one or more biologically defined zones of progressively fewer restrictions on types and magnitude of development. The zones prioritize the preservation of point and linear features and of keystone species thought to help maintain ecosystem functions. Because a variety of population dynamics models of species and their interactions with landscapes exist (Erickson 1996; Taylor 1995), each frequently having different implications for the temporal and the spatial forms of conservation strategy, the appropriate dimensions for any particular conservation reserve can, on solely biological grounds, be subject to considerable debate. Even when nonbiological issues are set aside, the choice of parcels for protection is a complex exercise in dealing with ambiguity.
 The significance of this ambiguity has been tempered considerably, however, by recent work that suggests that for a conservation problem in a given locale there will often be a substantial number of spatial configurations of a finite number of different sites consistent with conserva-

tion objectives (Arthur et al. 1997; Csuti et al. 1997). Ando et al. (1998) point out that if, for example, biological criteria require the set-aside of only 3 of 10 equally sized parcels in a proposed conservation reserve area, there are 120 possible combinations of the required 3. There are 5.6 billion ways to choose 12 of 40 parcels, and 30 trillion ways to combine 30 of 100 parcels. This is not to suggest that each of this plethora of combinations will service biological objectives equally well or even service them at all, but it seems highly unlikely that biological systems are so rigid and unyielding that there won't be at least a few of the 5.6 billion or the 30 trillion parcel combinations that will do pretty well. The key implication is that when private land ownership prevails, there can and will likely be some parcel combinations that maintain or produce landscapes capable of approximating habitat conservation goals. The point is intuitive, given that important features of natural habitat conditions in a locale are often highly correlated. Consider weather, for example. Flexibility in reserve designation and design is feasible. It follows that there exists scope for allowing the set of parcel owners some discretion as to how they will sort parcels to meet a conservation goal the ESA authority sets.

Private Owner Discretion and Tradable Habitat Credits

In organized markets, discretion is accorded individuals by having a legitimated authority grant them and enforce rights to, claims over, or permits for use of designated assets. Use includes exchange with other individuals. Perhaps the major result of more than two centuries of economic theory and application is that conditions exist for which the relative market prices induced by the production, exchange, and consumption of these assets will provide all the information and incentives necessary to cause disparate individuals to coordinate their activities such that the sum of the individuals' well-beings, as gauged only by the individuals themselves, is maximized (i.e., is economically efficient). Simply put, relative market prices ensure that production involves only those who can generate gains for society as well as for themselves, and that consumption is undertaken only by those who most highly value the asset. No central guiding hand is necessary to plan how individuals are to behave because the market removes all slack (gains from trade) from the system. The role of a central authority is restricted to being a rights creator and enforcer. Economic efficiency is independent of who owns what.

The practical applicability of this deservedly famous "invisible hand" result depends on simultaneously meeting four conditions. Absence of any one causes the result to break down, raising the possibility (though not the guarantee) that a degree of centralized coordination will enhance economic efficiency. First, and most obvious, rights for any scarce asset must have been defined and socially legitimated in the eyes of those to whom they are to apply. Second, asset rights must be defensible, such that he who holds them can at low cost exclude nonholders from using the asset in question. Third, assets and the rights tied to them must be rival, such that no two persons can use an asset as cheaply as one person can use it. Finally, asset rights must be transparent, such that all interested parties can predict what the right entails in terms of the consequences for them of its use. Included in the transparency condition are low transaction costs (low costs of the act of exchange), which ensure that any attempt by an asset holder to shift society's gains from his use of the asset to himself will be successfully challenged by someone willing to take less of these gains.

As is well known, one or more of these four conditions for markets to be organized and to be efficient are often lacking in environmental settings. Species, habitat, and ecosystem protection issues can embody all four failures. Landowners may have clear title to the obvious commercial uses the embodiments of an organism present on their sites, but the title to the genetic reservoir the body units represent may be muddy or nonexistent. Even when title to the genetics is not muddy, many organisms or entities that can harm them are mobile, making it costly to defend one's claims. An organism present on one owner's parcel may enhance the noncommercial but socially valued, unclaimed dimensions of habitats on other owners' parcels. Species population dynamics and ecosystem behaviors are not well understood, making the habitat consequences of the use of claims less than transparent. The ESA can therefore be interpreted as an attempt by a legitimate control authority to express and to bring to bear on landowner decisions societal values about species, habitats, and ecosystems that markets fail to capture.

Unfortunately, the devices ESA authority employs to implement societal claims on nonmarketed land uses often conflict with landowner private interests, including marketed commodity interests.[2] The public inclusiveness the authority tries to foster conflicts with the landowner's private exclusiveness because inclusiveness has been interpreted as requiring coercive restrictions on the landowner's efforts to exclude anything that does not service his private interests. Devices that complement rather than conflict with private interests could do much to moderate opposition to the goals and the implementation of the ESA.

Because the restrictions that current implementation of the ESA imposes on landowner discretion are held to be duties, trade separable from the land among landowners in the land uses being restricted is not possible. The dimensionality of the validated claims that landowners possess is reduced, or the owners' putative or presumptive claims are threatened. Owner time horizons are shortened, incentives for investments in land are reduced, and the ability to collateralize tenure is squeezed. These landowners cannot soften their private losses in tenure security by reassigning these duties to others better able and more willing to bear them. Those who pay for the provision of habitat cannot be separated from those who supply habitat.

In the last thirty years, tradable development permits and credits that unbundle claims to an environmental asset so that claim holders can trade separate elements of the bundle have become a favored allocation instrument for commentators with a feel for economic analysis (see, for instance, Bayon 2002; Bellandi and Hennigan 1977; Danner 1997; Johnston and Madison 1997; Levinson 1997; Panayotou 1994; Potts 1999; Pruetz 1997; Thorsnes and Simons 1999). They recommend these credits as a device to make private landowners and lovers of habitat accountable for the consequences their activities have for the broader public. Policymakers in some environmental arenas such as air pollution, water pollution, ocean fisheries management, and climate change have been listening; the ESA authority has so far been a less enthusiastic audience (Stavins 1989).

Habitat conservation could, however, be brought within the orbit of market processes such that private landowners would perceive they have a substantial stake in it. That is, habitat conservation would be made a financially plausible alternative to developed uses of land if the ESA authority defined desirable habitat within an appropriate locale, specified its scarcity, and then granted to landowners tradable credits for providing habitat that helps to meet the targeted scarcity. Anyone wishing to alter habitat on his land would have to sacrifice that number of secure, collateralizable preservation credits consistent with whatever degree and type of development he desired. If his inventory of credits is insufficient to accomplish his wishes, he would have to purchase additional credits from other landowners in the locale. These other landowners would sell a credit if and only if the would-be developer's willingness to pay for the credit exceeded what they expect to receive from developing their own lands. A market price for the scarce credits would be established that compensated the sellers of credits for the trouble their losses of development opportunities cause them. All landowners would end up holding that number of credits at which their individual marginal gains from development equal the market price of a credit. The motivation for trade in preservation credits is simply that the value of development varies across landowners. In addition, landowners may have different levels of risk aversion, implying different demands for risk-buffering tradable credits. If owners can observe the habitats present on each other's parcels, they can buy and sell preservation credits among themselves and reduce the losses they suffer by not being able to develop at will.

Any credits used for development would deplete the stock of such credits, since development on a particular parcel is more or less irreversible in terms of its habitat impacts. Whether a used credit is originally owned or obtained by trade, the market price of credits not yet used would then increase. The depletable stock of permits introduces rivalry among landowners just as economic efficiency requires. Holders of preservation credits not yet used would then have an incentive to account for the impact of all current local development on future local collective habitat in their decisions to continue to hold or to sell or use these credits. If the fulfillment of habitat conservation objectives is moderately insensitive to the spatial configuration of undeveloped parcels, or if biological knowledge is sufficient to say what a credit unit on one parcel means to conservation objectives when transferred to another parcel, the tradable credit device has undeniable appeal. Alternatively, if objectives are fairly sensitive to the spatial configuration of land uses, the device gives each holder of tradable credits the incentive to search out and cooperate with other owners holding credits who can contribute to the desired configuration. By cooperating with other owners, the single owner has to forgo fewer valuable tradable credits to make his contribution to a given conservation goal. In general, the tradable credit scheme arguably services the goal of habitat conservation by making it worthwhile for private landowners to help achieve the goal: it seems efficient and it appears fair. Landowners are free to use their land as they see fit as long as the habitat conservation goal within a general locale is met. They are able to appropriate a positive share of the rents generated by the provision of habitat and to share the cost of provision among themselves. If nonowners are allowed to buy credits as well, the potential for cost sharing is increased, implying that the cost share for landowners is reduced. Landowners for whom the cost of contributing to the conservation goal is excessive can shed their costs to those for whom the cost of meeting the goal is low. Within the locale, then, the cost of habitat conservation relative to the cost of habitat alteration is less than under a command-and-control procedure where the owner of each parcel is allotted on biological grounds alone a habitat conservation quota that he cannot shed. The flexibility that tradable credits offer owners lowers their costs without increasing their risks.

Additional plausible advantages of a tradable credit system for habitat conservation efforts are readily cited. Command-and-control implicitly presumes that all worthy information about the structures and behaviors of habitats resides with the ESA authorities and those who work for them, but much knowledge of this sort is possessed by the individuals who actually live in the locale. Though this indigenous knowledge may be idiosyncratic and nonsystematic, it has been accumulated by living with the land. Tradable credits for preserving local habitat provide landowners with opportunities, albeit limited by conservation goals, to use their private information to find low-cost ways to fulfill these goals. Unless, implausibly, command-and-control approaches are constructed under perfect information and can be perfectly enforced, these approaches will fail to incorporate many low-cost conservation measures that may voluntarily be undertaken by landowners.

A system of tradable habitat preservation credits can also relieve the control authority of the considerable responsibility it has under a command-and-control system to define details of site-specific land use practices. With tradable credits this responsibility falls on the landowner and any technical consultants he hires. With a tradable credit system the control authority requires fewer technical staff with expertise in habitat conservation design. Control authority resources otherwise used for site-specific habitat design can now be dedicated to monitoring and enforcing the conditions specified in the credits. Transparency is enhanced because all landowners would know the responsibilities and privileges any particular credit entails. One-on-one, landowner-by-landowner dealings with the central authority, as under the currently favored command-and-control system, could be set aside.

A tradable credit system in habitat preservation can also reduce monitoring demands on the central authority relative to those of a command-and-control system. This is because of increasing returns to the spatial scope of an area on which habitat conservation is practiced. The costs to each parcel owner of making a contribution to the habitat goal fall as the number of parcels contributing increases, and the most self-satisfying action for each owner to undertake depends on what other owners are doing. These increasing returns from spatial scope economies mean that owners have an incentive to form agreements among themselves about the habitat conservation measures each will undertake: each owner now gains valuable credits not only from his own conservation contribution but from those of other participating owners as well. Any supplemental gain from joint conservation effort gives the individual owner an incentive to watch his peers' activities to see that they do not increase his costs of contributing to the overall habitat conservation goal. Peer monitoring substitutes for central authority monitoring. This peer monitoring can lead to the formation of enforceable side agreements about these behaviors. For less wealthy owners, tradable credits represent an opportunity to shuffle assets to minimize losses from tenure insecurity and to minimize risk exposure. For wealthier owners, tradable credits open a new dimension in which to accumulate yet more wealth.

Unfortunately, in spite of the preceding recitation of the advantages of a tradable credit regime, the allocation of credits likely to occur in the presence of spatial scope economies with multiple ownerships is unlikely to be fully efficient in economic terms. A dilemma exists. The efficiency of a tradable credit regime fundamentally depends on having multiple owners and others who participate in trade; the presence of spatial scope economies involving multiple owners undermines the ability of the tradable credit scheme to generate fully efficient outcomes. The next section explains intuitively why this is so. It also suggests a combination of tradable credits and command-and-control transfer payments that has the potential to overcome the efficiency failings of the stand-alone tradable credit scheme or of the freestanding command-and-control approach. An appendix presents a formal, stylized version of the argument in the text.

Trading with Subsequent Redistribution

If land is privately held, ownerships are multiple, and habitat conservation involves economies of spatial scope, then we are talking about an impure public good (Cornes and Sandler 1986). Habitat preservation on any parcel generates an opportunity cost in forgone commodity production for the owner of the parcel but a positive spillover (externality) for other owners, who do not have to spend as much effort on habitat preservation on their parcels when another owner protects his or her own habitat. Any single owner's habitat preservation activities are partly but not wholly nonrival with respect to habitat preservation on other owners' parcels. This combination of partial nonexcludability and of partial nonrivalry also gives the individual owner an incentive to free-ride (i.e., to let his fellow owners contribute to the collective habitat goal while he devotes himself to his strictly private endeavors). When all owners behave as free-riders, no habitat preservation is attempted in spite of the central authority's specification of the habitat conservation goal. Even if an owner sees some benefit from habitat provision on his land (so as perhaps to establish a degree of credibility with a central ESA authority, who will then redirect its scarce monitoring and enforcement resources at other owners), habitat will still be underprovided since the owner has no incentive to take into account the benefits his habitat provision provides other owners. The individual owner ignores the benefits that accrue to other owners when he decides how much habitat to provide. Owners whose fortunes are interdependent make noncooperative, independent decisions.

The inefficiencies associated with noncooperative behavior among landowners confronted with spatial scope economies in meeting a compulsory collective habitat goal extend as well, though with less force, to trade in habitat preservation credits and, separately, to landowner wealth redistributions coerced by the central authority.

In an ideal, fully efficient setting where no owner can improve his well-being without reducing the well-being of some other owner (a Pareto optimum), each owner would equate the marginal benefits he *and* all other owners obtain from his provision of additional habitat to his marginal cost of providing that habitat, where the marginal cost is his foregone commodity production. This follows from the impure public good implication that the private provision of habitat produces benefits for other landowners. In each ideal case, each parcel owner acts as if he and he alone must bear the habitat consequences that commodity production on his parcel has for all parcels.

Given adequate biological knowledge and citizen trust in the authority, habitat preservation credits can be defined, accepted as legitimate, and defended from intruders. They may even be sufficiently transparent to eliminate all slack in trade. But trade in them cannot, by itself, meet the nonrival condition for the impure public good that constitutes local collective habitat. Certainly if different owners have different preferences for or different opportunity costs from habitat preservation, economic efficiency requires that they end up with differing combinations of habitat and commodity production. With tradable habitat preservation credits, as earlier argued, trade will take place among owners until each source of utility for each owner is equal at the margin to each source of utility for every other owner. Also, the money equivalent of each of the utility sources will be equal to the marginal opportunity costs of providing them. These outcomes exhaust all gains from trade: they eliminate all slack among owners. The tradable credit market clears and all owners attach exactly the same value to a little bit less or a little bit more habitat on their individual ownerships. This admittedly substantial invisible-handlike achievement does not speak to the biological fact that local collective habitat is not strictly rival. Each owner gains from the provision of habitat by his peers because he then has to provide less habitat on his land to enable the local collective habitat objective to be met. His private habitat optimal decisions are contingent on what he expects his peers to contribute to the collective. Economic efficiency for the impure public good that constitutes collective habitat requires that an additional condition be met beyond the standard condition of "marginal benefits equal marginal private costs." In particular, the sum across parcel owners of the rate at which they are willing to substitute their own and collective habitat provision for own-commodity production (their individual marginal rates of substitution between habitat provision and commodity production) must equal the marginal cost of habitat provision, and this marginal cost must be equal across parcel owners. Fulfillment of this summing condition avoids the free-rider problem. It is necessary because additional collective habitat benefits each and every parcel owner with the spatial scope economies it provides. Taking advantage of these economies means that each owner has to contribute less habitat to the collective habitat goal, reducing his opportunity costs and, incidentally, making him less averse to implementing the goal.

Wealth redistribution alone, in the form of central authority taxes on commodity production or payments for habitat provision, is also unable to achieve the equality and the summing conditions for economic efficiency in meeting a given collective habitat goal. This would be true even if the authority has perfect information on the structures and the behaviors of the relevant biology. Under command-and-control the individual owner would select that level of own-habitat provision that maximizes only his narrowly conceived private well-being, given his expectations about the habitat provision activities of other owners. He would have no incentive to account for the impact of his decisions on other owners, since the absence of trading opportunities means that these other owners have no way to register their wants with him and to make these wants an opportunity cost for him. The baseline habitat states on which the authority would levy its taxes and make its payments would therefore be states established in settings where potential gains from trade have not been realized. Though taxes and payments might be structured to equate the sum of own and collective marginal rates of substitution to marginal costs, the levels of taxes and payments necessary to achieve this condition would be calculated from an inefficient baseline habitat configuration among parcels.

Given the collective habitat goal, achievement of the efficient habitat configuration requires that all gains from trade among parcel owners be exhausted *and* that the sum of own and collective marginal rates of substitution between commodity production and habitat provision be equated to the marginal opportunity costs of habitat provision. These two conditions can be achieved in a sequence of four steps. Initially the central authority specifies and makes compulsory its habitat conservation goal; it then sets up, legitimates, and enforces a set of habitat preservation credits; makes a market in these credits; and then, after having observed the realized collective habitat, levies taxes on and makes payments to landowners. That these taxes and payments are to be made would be conveyed to landowners prior to any credit trading. Habitat preservation credits are to be initially assigned to a landowner in direct proportion to the habitat the owner has created prior to trade in credits (his original habitat). After landowner gains from trading credits are exhausted, the authority then levies these taxes on and makes those payments to landowners that cause each landowner's net marginal private benefit of original and additional (through trade) habitat provision to be equal to the contribution additional collective habitat provision makes to the commodity production in which other owners can engage. Both efficiency conditions would then be achieved, in accordance with the Tinbergen (1967) principle, one policy instrument per condition to be met. The baseline on which taxes and payments are calculated would be efficient, and the appropriate taxes and payments would assure that the sum of the private and the collective marginal benefits of habitat provision to landowners and interested others equals its marginal opportunity costs to landowners.

Some Practical Issues

A reader with only a casual interest and background in economic analysis might suggest that practical matters can easily scuttle the proposal idealized in the previous section for establishing property rights in habitat credits, allowing the trading of those credits, and then taking or paying landowners according to the state of their habitat after they have traded credits. Paeans about the efficiency and the fairness in the invented world of the proposal fail to impress this reader. He correctly asserts that true attention to efficiency must consider nuanced questions of implementation in real, not idealized, settings. Though this practical stance may be fully appropriate, it cannot properly be used to justify inertia about changes in the command-and-control procedures that currently dominate implementation of the ESA. One must instead compare the severity of command-and-control implementation issues to the severity of those issues for the proposal. This section attempts a qualitative comparison of the costs of implementing these two alternative regimes for conserving habitat. These implementation costs accrue to efforts to define habitat units; to monitor, assess, and enforce performance; to inform and complete transactions; and to identify participants.

Habitat Units

Habitat, defined as the biotic and the abiotic attributes of landscapes, constitutes the fundamental unit of analysis for the biodiversity the ESA aims to conserve. Habitat attributes feed into individual species populations, thence into these species' likelihood of survival, on to the biological benefits of biodiversity, and finally into the values society places on these benefits (C. Montgomery et al. 1999). Whether the current command-and-control regime or the tradable credit and wealth redistribution regime applies, some measure of what habitat means must be developed and used. Exactly what constitutes a unit of habitat is left implicit in the management injunction and the one-on-one consultations that form the ESA authority's current dealings with private landowners. This implicitness has two not mutually exclusive consequences: the unit the authority employs to assess the same conservation objective can differ across landowners; and the interactions of the ESA authority and the landowners become less transparent to outside observers. In effect, the ambiguity under the current regime of what constitutes a habitat unit provides the authority with an informational advantage in its dealings with private landowners since the owner is less able to compare his treatment from the authority to the treatment his neighbor receives. This informational advantage gives the authority additional bargaining leverage that it may use, if the authority is not fully benevolent, to divide and conquer landowner coalitions directed at debating the authority's goals and procedures. Moreover, the lack of transparency inherent in the current regime makes any nonbenevolent activity more difficult to specify and to evaluate. Also, in the presence of spatial scope economies, ambiguities about the specification and the evaluation of habitat units can defeat habitat conservation objectives. One owner can less readily ascertain whether another owner is adhering to a habitat preservation agreement. Owner observations of the behavior of other owners can provide a valuable monitoring service to an authority that has limited monitoring and enforcement resources. In sum, an authority that operates a command-and-control regime has less accountability when habitat is ambiguously defined.

In contrast, a regime based on tradable credit and wealth redistribution requires a clear, unambiguous definition of habitat units. Efficient market definitions of property rights are clear and refer to all economically scarce dimensions of a commodity. People do not engage in trade unless they think they know what they are getting and giving up. Efficient wealth redistribution obliges a similarly clear specification of the baseline distribution of habitat units. Otherwise the authority cannot determine if redistribution causes the aggregate (summing) efficiency condition to be met. The point here is that the connection between distribution of responsibilities among owners and parcels to provide habitat and the efficient provision of collective habitat cannot be systematically approached in the absence of a definition of habitat units that all parties understand in exactly the same fashion (i.e., in the sense that all agree what a loaf of bread is). No plausible replacement for the current ESA command-and-control regime can be developed until agreement is reached as to what constitutes a habitat unit.

This is not the place to suggest what the dimensions of a habitat unit might be. Four points are, nevertheless, worth making. First, the choice of a measure for a unit has an economic as well as a physical side. For example, according to the purpose, water is measured in acre-feet, H_2O molecules, or cubic meters per second; Canada uses the metric system, and the United States generally sticks to the English system. Second, it is the stock of habitat, and not the flow of activities that alter habitat, that is properly the focus of concern. The rate of activities that alter the stock is much less important than the size of the stock, especially if the habitat exhibits threshold properties, where once the threshold is crossed, recovery of the stock is impossible or extremely costly. Third, assertions that habitats are not like grains of sand and are therefore not susceptible to standardized measures appears protective of the ESA status quo. Biologists (and economists) who build mathematical or simulation models of landscapes must assign measurement units (scalar or vector valued) to their variables and parameters. Also, it is not self-evident that on-ground habitats are any more complex than the meteorological systems for which a substantial literature exists (e.g., Rodriguez 2000) on the design of units for tradable emission permits. Fourth, if limited resources and knowledge force the use of habitat proxies, a proxy consistent in measure across a large number of possible outcomes of random events is to be preferred.

Monitoring, Assessment, and Enforcement

Shifting from the current administrative command-and-control regime to a more marketlike regime implies the transfer of significant power from the ESA authority to landowners. The shift may also relieve the authority of a fair portion of the considerable investments it must now make in monitoring, assessment, and enforcement. A more marketlike regime can shift some of the costs of these investments to landowners. Again, the extent to which either shift can occur depends on the prior development of a clear, common consensus on what a habitat unit involves. Any marketlike regime requires such a consensus: owners who would monitor and assess each other's uses of habitat must be able to recognize the meaning of what they see.

Under an administrative command-and-control regime, the authority is no more likely to be able to exercise perfect enforcement of its dictates than it is likely to be omniscient. Landowners likely have information about the structure and behavior of the habitats on nearby lands they do not own. An owner can therefore make informed judgments of the habitat preservation efforts being made on these other ownerships. Moreover, the ESA authority can only observe habitat alteration ex post. Given the quasi-irreversible nature of much habitat alteration, its enforcement response will then be too late. The authority's alternative is to review any land use practice that might lead to habitat alteration, but landowners who see their neighbors' activities on a daily basis provide a ready review. These owners have an incentive to watch each other under a marketlike regime, since the likelihood that an individual owner will have to provide additional habitat to meet the collective habitat objective is inversely related to the habitat preservation efforts of all owners. Alternatively put, a marketlike regime gives owners an incentive to cooperate in meeting the collective habitat objective. Problems of monitoring, assessment, and enforcement are therefore reduced below those incurred by an ESA authority who must deal one on one with owners who do not cooperate in habitat provisions.

Transaction Costs

Whether the regime uses command-and-control or tradable credits and wealth redistribution, considerations of wealth distribution and efficiency are not independent when dealing with habitat issues involving multiple owners and parcels. Spatial economics of scope economies make them interdependent. If habitat is completely rival, such that no spatial scope economies exist, trade in habitat credits alone would assure the achievement of an economically efficient outcome. To repeat the earlier refrain, each owner would trade credits to equate his private marginal benefits of habitat provision to his private marginal costs of provision and all slack would be removed from the system. The distribution of habitat credits would not affect the outcome and would not affect efficiency.[3] However, spatial scope economies introduce an element of nonrivalry, implying that the distribution of credits will influence the configuration of trading opportunities among owners and across parcels. These trading opportunities will determine the set of trades that occur and the realized contours of collective habitat. Some of these realized contours may be inefficient in the sense that they fail to meet the condition wherein private plus collective marginal benefit equals marginal cost. For example, if credits were granted a wealthy owner already blessed with plentiful habitat, a poor owner may not be able to pay the wealthy owner enough to acquire any credits even when the use of the credits by the poor person would result in greater aggregate benefits from habitat provision.

The ESA authority currently relies on case-by-case, one-on-one consultations and negotiations with landowners to transact its habitat preservation objectives. Aside from the fixed costs of maintaining the ability to recruit a staff, nearly all of the transaction costs of the current regime appear to be variable to the authority and to landowners. The desired staff for the authority varies with the number and the complexity of consultations and negotiations undertaken.

Landowners call on expert and legal help only if they expect to be visited by the authority. In contrast, fixed costs appear to dominate the transaction feature of the tradable habitat credit and wealth redistribution regime this chapter proposes. The costs of establishing and maintaining any single market in habitat credits is largely independent of the number of participants and the volume of trade taking place.[4] The up-front cost for the authority of developing and putting in place a legal framework for making and enforcing contracts (making a market) on clearly defined habitat units is likely to be large. Once this is done, however, such that conditions of trade are transparent to all potential participants, authority costs increase only with the difficulty of enforcing the contractual obligations landowners and others who acquire habitat credits have voluntarily chosen. A well-structured legal framework makes it likely these costs will not be great. Because fixed costs dominate in a trading regime, costs per transaction decline with the volume of transactions and with accumulated experience in making markets. This contrasts sharply with the behavior of costs per transaction in the current administrative command-and-control regime. Declining costs per transaction with a trading regime imply gains from making the spatial and temporal domain of the market in habitat credits as large as political, legal, and biological circumstances will allow. Thick markets work better than thin markets.

This declining cost feature of market operation for the ESA authority extends as well to those immediately impacted by the habitat objective the authority sets—the landowners. The costs of participating in a market decline as its spatial and temporal scope and its liquidity increase. Brokers who reap rewards from bringing buyers and sellers together become less necessary. A well-structured legal framework for the market reduces participant risks, increasing the number of market participants and increasing the scope of the market. In turn, increases in market scope reduce participant risks because of the increase in potential transactions. "Take it or leave it" stances have less force.

Participants

The more participants in a market, the greater its scope, with all the attendant benefits. This implies that the costs of operating the market will decline and that the gains from trade it can generate will increase when those who have an interest in land use but who are not yet landowners can participate. Landowners who engage these nonowners can then be compensated for providing habitat by those who desire habitat protection. This contrasts with the current regime where outsiders who desire local habitat protection often find it less costly or even free to have the

ESA authority carry forward their desires. Goods supplied free to the individual that are costly for the society to provide reward selfishness.

Conclusion

In the 1970s, public concern about the capacities of markets and the willingness of local communities to take care of landscapes spurred the concentration of extensive authority over matters of habitat conservation and commercial, industrial, and residential development in the hands of national bureaucracies and biological technicians. The ESA manifested this concern. Now, for habitat conservation to move beyond often inscrutable criteria narrowly focused on biological principles, linkages between landowner incentives and habitat effects must be systematically established. The proposal for tradable habitat credits and wealth redistribution advanced here might help reconcile conservation objectives with landowners' interests.

This hybrid tradable habitat credit and wealth redistribution proposal is not meaningful by virtue of specific, plug-in algorithms of trade-offs between commodity production practices and socially valued habitat. The proposal instead allows the authority and landowners to target least-cost parcels for habitat protection, as opposed to an economically undiscriminating selection that can appear enigmatic and arcane—even arbitrary and capricious—to landowners and to the general public. Inattention by the ESA authority to economic means and criteria for site targeting has plausibly squandered opportunities for both conservation and commercial development and has inflamed tensions among landowners, bureaucracies, and others interested in habitat conservation. Agents for the public beneficiaries of habitat conservation cannot abdicate complete authority and responsibility for local landscapes to landowners, but these agents can do considerably better at improving the incentives for these landowners to accept, to create, and to monitor habitat conservation. The tradable credit and wealth redistribution proposal set forth here provides these incentives because it allows landowners to share in the benefits of habitat conservation while spreading its costs out to owners who degrade habitat and to others who purchase habitat credits.

Appendix

Let there be two private landowners, $i = 1, 2$, in a given period whose mutually exclusive land parcels take up all of an area that a central ESA authority has autonomously dedicated to habitat conservation. Nothing but additional notation is gained by extending the results to follow to more than two landowners. Both landowners must participate in the conservation effort, and their identities do not change. Owner decisions in one period have no effect on their decisions in subsequent periods.

Define habitat preservation credits, h_i, in accordance with whatever set of underlying biological principles and units are to apply to the area in question. The total credits the ESA central authority makes available are $H = h_1 + h_2$. Suppose each landowner can produce a marketable commodity, y_i, that requires some irreversible destruction of habitat on his parcel and a permanent sacrifice of habitat preservation credits. This marketable commodity is sold at an exogenously fixed price. It can therefore be defined in pecuniary terms and serve as a numeraire. The landowner's wealth, W_i, in the period is the arithmetic sum of the numeraire and the scarcity rent, ν_i, he receives from the habitat preservation credits in his inventory. This scarcity rent is an opportunity cost since an owner can either sell the credits or sacrifice them by producing marketable commodities on his ownership, that is, $\nu_i = \nu_i(h_i)$, where $\nu_i' > 0$, $\nu_i'' > 0$.

Each landowner has a strictly concave, continuous, and everywhere twice differentiable utility function, $U_i = U_i(y_i, H, h_i)$, increasing in the first and second arguments. The third argument can be of either sign. Additional habitat may give the owner more outdoor recreational opportunities he enjoys, or he may find his sense of identity and community in surroundings that are more natural. Alternatively, he may be a pecuniary maximizer who regrets the unaffordability of a cabin on the biggest and newest cruise ship that provision of more habitat on his land causes him. In either case, he takes pleasure in whatever habitat the other owner provides because that provision either gives him more recreational opportunities and nestlike surroundings or relieves him from having to provide as much habitat on his own land. The form of the utility function then implies that habitat states are an impure public good (Cornes and Sandler 1986): they appear twice in an owner's utility function, once as a private good and again in combination with the quantity of habitat supplied by the other owners.

The Social Optimum

Presume the ESA control authority is omniscient and clairvoyant such that, once it has determined the level of habitat conservation it wants, it assigns those positive levels of commodity production and habitat preservation credits to each owner that maximize the sum of the owners' well-beings. The authority's problem is then to

Maximize: $U_1(y_1, H, h_1)$ (1)
(y_1, y_2, h_1, h_2)

subject to:

$$U_2(y_2, H, h_2) \geq \overline{U}_2, \tag{2}$$

where $\overline{U}_2$ is the reservation utility level of the second owner, and subject to:

$$y_1 + y_2 + \nu_1(h_1) + \nu_2(h_2) \leq W_1 + W_2. \tag{3}$$

Expression (3) says that the sum of values, $W_1 + W_2$, of the marketable commodities produced on the owners' lands is the owners' incomes less the opportunity costs of the habitats they provide.

The first-order conditions from the Lagrangian for this problem are

$$y_1: \partial U_1/\partial y_1 - \lambda = 0, \tag{4}$$

$$y_2: \theta(\partial U_2/\partial y_2) - \lambda = 0, \tag{5}$$

$$h_1: \frac{\partial U_1}{\partial H} + \frac{\partial U_1}{\partial h_1} + \theta\left(\frac{\partial U_2}{\partial y_2}\frac{\partial y_1}{\partial h_1} + \frac{\partial U_2}{\partial H}\right) \tag{6}$$
$$- \lambda\left(\frac{\partial y_1}{\partial h_1} + \frac{\partial y_2}{\partial h_1} - \nu_1'\right) = 0,$$

$$h_2: \frac{\partial U_1}{\partial H} + \theta\left(\frac{\partial U_2}{\partial y_2}\frac{\partial y_2}{\partial h_2} + \frac{\partial U_2}{\partial h_2} + \frac{\partial U_2}{\partial H}\right) \tag{7}$$
$$- \lambda\left(\frac{\partial y_1}{\partial h_2} + \frac{\partial y_2}{\partial h_2} + \nu_2'\right) = 0,$$

and expressions (2) and (3). The θ and the λ terms are the Lagrangian multipliers (shadow prices) attached to the constraints in expressions (2) and (3). Upon substitution of expressions (4) and (5) into (6) and (7) and then simplifying, these last two expressions become:

$$h_1: \frac{\partial U_1/\partial H}{\partial U_1/\partial y_1} + \frac{\partial U_1/\partial h_1}{\partial U_1/\partial y_1} + \frac{\partial U_2/\partial H}{\partial U_2/\partial y_2} = \nu_1' \tag{8}$$

and

$$h_2: \frac{\partial U_2/\partial H}{\partial U_2/\partial y_2} + \frac{\partial U_2/\partial h_2}{\partial U_2/\partial y_2} + \frac{\partial U_1/\partial H}{\partial U_1/\partial y_1} = \nu_2'. \tag{9}$$

Expression (4) says economic efficiency requires that the first owner expand commodity production until his marginal utility from doing so is equal to the marginal contribution that more of the limited resources in expression (3) will make to his utility. Expression (5) implies that while fulfilling expression (4), the utility level of the second owner must be maintained. It is expressions (8) and (9) that are of primary interest, however, because they refer to the economically efficient interactions via habitat preservation required of the two owners. The expressions require that each owner equate the sum of both owners' marginal rates of substitution between overall collective habitat preservation and own-commodity production to the marginal opportunity cost of own-habitat provision less that owner's marginal rate of substitution between own-habitat provision and own-commodity production. That is, the aggregate marginal benefits of local collective habitat preservation for each owner must equal the marginal costs he bears by contributing to this collective preservation. Each owner's commodity production generates a positive private benefit for him and a negative collective cost in lost habitat, where he is part of the collective.

Tradable Habitat Preservation Credits

Presume a noncooperative setting in which each landowner takes the other landowner's activities as given. Let h_i^0 be the level of habitat preservation an owner produces and the habitat credits he accumulates prior to any trading of credits. In addition, let t_i be the net result in terms of his habitat credit inventory of credit trading by owner i. Thus $t_i > 0$ indicates that the owner purchases credits, and $t_i < 0$ says that he sells credits. Explicitly writing out the components of y_1, the first owner's optimization problem is characterized as

$$\text{Maximize: } U_1[w_1 - v_1(h_i^0 + t_1) - pt_1, H, h_1^0 + t_1], \tag{10}$$

where p is the market price of a credit, and $h_1 = h_1^0 + t$.
The first-order conditions include

$$h_1^0: \ -\frac{\partial U_1}{\partial v_1}v_1' + \frac{\partial U_1}{\partial H} + \frac{\partial U_1}{\partial h_1} = 0, \tag{11}$$

$$t_1: \ -\frac{\partial U_1}{\partial v_1}v_1' - \frac{\partial U_1}{\partial t_1}p + \frac{\partial U_1}{\partial h_1} = 0. \tag{12}$$

Because v_1 is the only component of the numeraire that can vary in expression (10), the v_1' in expressions (11) and (12) can be replaced by y_1. When rewritten, these expressions then became

$$\frac{\partial U_1/\partial h_1}{\partial U_1/\partial y_1} + \frac{\partial U_1/\partial H}{\partial U_1/\partial y_1} = v_1', \tag{13}$$

and

$$\frac{\partial U_1/\partial h_1}{\partial U_1/\partial y_1} = v_1' - \frac{\partial U_1/\partial t_1}{\partial U_1/\partial y_1}. \tag{14}$$

The same exercise for the second owner would yield similar expressions.

Exhaustion of all gains from trading credits results in

$$v_1' = v_2' = -\frac{\partial U_1/\partial h_1}{\partial U_1/\partial y_1} = -\frac{\partial U_2/\partial h_2}{\partial U_2/\partial y_2} = p = \frac{\partial U_1/\partial H}{\partial U_1/\partial y_1} = \frac{\partial U_2/\partial H}{\partial U_2/\partial y_2}. \tag{15}$$

That is, trade in habitat preservation credits leads only to the equality and neglects the summation of the various marginal rates of substitution that expressions (8) and (9) require for an economically efficient outcome.

Wealth Redistribution

Each owner tries to supply that level of habitat that maximizes his well-being, given the habitat he expects other owners to provide. The first owner solves

Maximize: $U_1(y_1, H, h_1)$. \tag{16}

This owner's first-order conditions include

$$h_1: \frac{\partial U_1}{\partial H} + \frac{\partial U_1}{\partial h_1} = 0 \equiv \frac{\partial U_1/\partial H}{\partial U_1/\partial y_1} + \frac{\partial U_1/\partial h_1}{\partial U_1/\partial y_1}. \tag{17}$$

Similar results are obtained for the second owner. A comparison of expression (17) to expression (8) shows that the $(\partial U_2/\partial H)/(\partial U_2/\partial y_2)$ term appearing in (8) is absent in (17). Therefore, the basis in habitat for the authority's calculation of taxes and payments is inefficient, implying that the wealth redistribution instrument cannot be efficient.

Credit Trading and Wealth Redistribution

As before, allow the central authority to create habitat preservation credits and permit landowners to trade these credits. Presume now that subsequent to owner credit trade and commodity production decisions for the period, the authority uses taxes and payments to redistribute wealth between the landowners. This makes sense because the authority can only ex-post observe the realized local collective habitat. Owners know before trading that the authority will impose taxes and make payments subsequent to trading.

Given that credits can be traded, the rational expectations optimization problem of the first owner is

Maximize: $U_1(y_1, h_1^0, h_2^0, \bar{t}_1, H, h_1)$, \tag{18}

where $H = h_1^0 + h_2^0$, $h_1 = h_1^0 + \bar{t}_1$, and $\bar{t}_1$ is the first owner's net trade in credits. This owner's first-order conditions are

$$h_1^0: \frac{\partial U_1}{\partial H} + \frac{\partial U_1}{\partial h_1} \equiv \frac{\partial U_1/\partial H}{\partial U_1/\partial y_1} + \frac{\partial U_1/\partial h_1}{\partial U_1/\partial y_1} = 0 \qquad (19)$$

and

$$\bar{t}_1: \frac{\partial U_1}{\partial H_1} = 0 \equiv \frac{\partial U_1/\partial h_1}{\partial U_1/\partial y_1}. \qquad (20)$$

Parallel expressions are easily derived for the second owner.

Expression (19) says that if the central authority adopts an after-trade redistribution policy known to the landowners that will set

$$\frac{\partial U_2/\partial H}{\partial U_2/\partial y_2} = v_1', \qquad (21)$$

then the condition set forth in expression (8) for the social optimum will be fulfilled. That is, if the authority lets it be known before trade that at the end of the period it will tax or pay each owner that amount which equates the owner's marginal rate of substitution between collective habitat and his commodity production to the other owner's marginal opportunity cost of contributing to collective habitat, the well-being of both owners will be maximized given the central authority's conservation goal. The tax or payment from the central authority equates the marginal benefits one owner obtains from the collective provision of habitat to the other owner's marginal opportunity costs of providing habitat. Again making use of expression (21), expression (20) suggests owners will trade credits to make the marginal opportunity costs of habitat provision equal across landowners. This follows from expression (15).

Notes

1. Environmental protection is viewed by some as inequitable because it burdens a narrow group, such as a few landowners, with the costs of implementation while spreading the benefits to a much larger public. By not analyzing criteria for designation of a general area within which habitat conservation is to occur, this chapter sets aside this dimension of the equity or burden-sharing issue.

2. Private interests may include the desire to conserve nonmarketable habitat. Individual efforts to conserve may be for naught, however, if owners of nearby parcels fail to conserve. The ESA potentially provides an institutional vehicle whereby voluntary conservation efforts among landowners become feasible.

3. This is the famous Coase (1960) theorem, in which the economic efficiency of exchange outcomes is independent of to whom property rights are assigned.

4. These fixed costs would, however, become variable as the number of markets thought appropriate increases. Admitting multiple markets raises a host of

questions about criteria for market segmentation, arbitrage among market segments, and so on.

Acknowledgments

Greg Parkhurst, David Finnoff, and the editor have contributed insightful comments.

References

Ando, A., J. Camm, S. Polasky, and A. Solow. 1998. Species distributions, land values, and efficient conservation. *Science* 279:2126–2127.

Arthur, J., M. Hachey, K. Sahr, M. Huso, and A. Kiester. 1997. Finding all optimal solutions to the reserve site selection problem: Formulation and computational analysis. *Environmental and Ecological Statistics* 4:153.

Bayon, R. 2002. A bull market in . . . woodpeckers? *Milken Institute Review* 4, no. 1: 30–39.

Bellandi, R. L., and R. B. Hennigan. 1977. The why and how of transferable development rights. *Real Estate Review* 7, no. 2: 60–64.

Boyd, James, Kathryn Caballero, and R. David Simpson. 1999. The law and economics of habitat conservation: Lessons from an analysis of easement acquisitions. Discussion paper 99-32. April. Washington, D.C.: Resources for the Future.

Coase, R. 1960. The problem of social cost. *Journal of Law and Economics* 3:1–44.

Cornes, R., and T. Sandler. 1986. *The theory of externalities, public goods and club goods.* Cambridge: Cambridge University Press.

Crocker, T. 1966. The structuring of atmospheric pollution control systems. Pp. 61–86 in *The economics of air pollution,* edited by H. Wolozin. New York: Norton.

Csuti, Blair, Stephen Polasky, Paul H. Williams, Robert L. Pressey, Jeffrey D. Camm, Melanie Kershaw, A. Ross Kiester, Brian Downs, Richard Hamilton, Manuela Huso, and Kevin Sahr. 1997. A comparison of reserve selection algorithms using data on terrestrial vertebrates in Oregon. *Biological Conservation* 80:83.

Danner, J. 1997. TDRs: Great idea but questionable value. *Appraisal Journal* 65, no. 2: 133–142.

Erickson, O. 1996. Regional dynamics of plants: A review of evidence from remnant, source-sink, and metapopulations. *Oikos* 77:248–258.

Frey, B., F. Oberholzer-Gee, and R. Eichenberger. 1996. The old lady visits your backyard: A tale of morals and markets. *Journal of Political Economy* 104: 1297–1310.

Johnston, R., and M. Madison. 1997. From landmarks to landscapes: A review of current practices in the transfer of development rights. *Journal of the American Planning Association* 63, no. 3: 365–378.

Levinson, A. 1997. Why Oppose TDRs? Transferable development rights can increase overall development. *Regional Science and Urban Economics* 27, no. 3: 283–296.

Merrifield, J. 1995. A market approach to conserving biodiversity. *Ecological Economics* 16:217–226.

Montgomery, C., R. Pollak, K. Freemark, and D. White. 1999. Pricing biodiversity. *Journal of Environmental Economics and Management* 38:1–19.

Montgomery, D. 1972. Markets in licenses and efficient pollution control programs. *Journal of Economic Theory* 5:395–418.

Panayotou, T. 1994. Conservation of biodiversity and economic development: The concept of transferable development rights. *Environmental and Resource Economics* 4:91–110.

Potts, E. R. 1999. A proposal for an alternative to the private enforcement of environmental regulations and statutes through citizen suits: Transferable property rights in common resources. *San Diego Law Review* 36:547–583.

Pruetz, R. 1997. *Saved by development: Preserving environmental areas, farmland, and historical landmarks with transferable development rights.* Burbank, Calif.: Arje Press.

Rodriguez, F. 2000. On the use of exchange rates as trading rules in a bilateral system of transferable discharge permits. *Environmental and Resource Economics* 9:379–395.

Stavins, R. 1989. Harnessing market forces to protect the environment. *Environment* 31:5–7, 28–35.

Swallow, S. 1996. Economic issues in ecosystem management: An introduction and overview. *Agricultural and Resource Economics Review* 25:83–100.

Taylor, B. L. 1995. The reliability of using population viability analysis for risk classification of species. *Conservation Biology* 9:235–251.

Thorsnes, P., and G. P. W. Simons. 1999. Letting the market preserve land: The case for market driven transfer of development rights program. *Contemporary Economic Policy* 17, no. 2:256–266.

Tinbergen, J. 1967. *Economic policy: Principles and design.* Amsterdam: North-Holland Publishers.

Turner, J., and J. Rylander. 1998. The private lands challenge: Integrating biodiversity conservation and private property. Pp. 92–137 in *Private property and the Endangered Species Act: Saving habitat, protecting homes,* edited by J. Shogren. Austin: University of Texas Press.

UNESCO. 1996. *Biosphere reserves: The Seville strategy and the statutory framework of the World Network.* Paris: UNESCO.

CHAPTER 8

The Role of Private Information in Designing Conservation Incentives for Property Owners

JASON F. SHOGREN, RODNEY B. W. SMITH,
AND JOHN TSCHIRHART

Most people interested in protecting endangered species would agree that imperfect information about population biology and the role of species in ecosystems confounds the design of preservation policy. In like manner, imperfect information about economic behavior and preferences further complicates preservation policy design and implementation. For instance, a private landowner might be the only individual who knows a listed species is on his or her land. In such a case the government would need landowner cooperation to gain the information necessary to administer conservation policy. If, however, regulation leads to an unattractive economic outcome, the landowner will likely withhold the biological information from government officials. Hence, information asymmetries between landowners and the government can potentially introduce an additional set of issues revolving around the landowners' incentives to reveal information.

Asymmetric information problems are pervasive in the economy, both in private transactions and government policies. Economists typically are interested in two types of asymmetric information: hidden action and hidden information. In hidden action problems one economic agent takes an action that affects the well-being of another, and the action of the former is unobservable to the latter. Under hidden information the parties to a transaction have different information about an important aspect of the transaction. Both problems can manifest in different ways and are especially problematic when policies designed in their presence need to be voluntary.

As an example of hidden information, assume that to protect a listed species the government is willing to purchase landholder use rights. Typically only the landowner will know his or her true land valuations. If so, and if the government is concerned with containing costs, then the land-holder's private information may present the government with a problem. The landowner will typically want as large a payment as possible for his use rights, while the government will typically want to purchase the land as cheaply as possible. In such a case we say the landowner and the regulator's incentives are incompatible, or we have an incentive compatibility problem. A likely result of this incentive compatibility problem is that at the margin the government's payment to the landowner will be greater than the landowner's actual valuation. Absent asymmetric information over land values the government may have been able to purchase the land more cheaply, so that at the margin payments received by landowners would be equal to their true land valuations. Under asymmetric information resources will likely be wasted and the benefits of market exchange not fully realized (Stiglitz 1996, p. 35).[1]

Although information occupies a central role in any economy (Hayek 1945), only in the last three decades has the field incorporated the consequences into our formal models. We know well that information about prices, about production processes, about consumer preferences, or, more to the subject at hand, about the impact of economic activity on the habitat that shelters endangered and threatened species is critical to market exchanges and successful policymaking. Now economists have begun to address the importance of information explicitly ("about time," some might say), by moving it to the forefront of economic analyses, a move that arguably represents one of the most important advances in the economics discipline over the period.

This chapter explores how the lack of information about economic behavior affects the design of economic incentives to protect endangered species on private land. We begin with a general discussion of asymmetric information and why it matters. Our goal here is to convince the reader that asymmetric information is not just some academic exercise but is a real problem. We offer as two examples the insurance industry, where the consumer and the company have different information, and the public utility industry, where the company and the government regulator have different information. Then we look at how asymmetric information affects the design of incentives for private landowners to preserve endangered species. The fourth section discusses whether the data needed to implement the economic prescriptions are, or ever will be, available. We conclude by arguing that imperfect information about economic behavior is as fundamental to effective species protection policy on private land as is dealing with imperfect information about natural systems.

Pervasiveness of Asymmetric Information

Before delving into examples of problems, some definitions and organizing themes will be helpful. As it turns out, most problems can be categorized within a simple framework. Think of two parties in a transaction, broadly defined, and call them the principal and the agent. In the case of endangered species, the principal would be the U.S. Fish and Wildlife Service and the agent would be the landowner. The principal wants the agent to reveal some characteristic or to perform some task, and there is asymmetric information in that only the agent knows either the characteristic or how to perform the task.

In the first example, the characteristic is the landowner's true land valuation. Note that the asymmetric information would not be a problem for the principal except that the agent has a different goal from the principal's (i.e., the principal's and the agent's incentives are incompatible). In the context of our example, the principal wants to find an economic incentive mechanism that induces the landowner to reveal his or her true land valuation. Viewed another way, the principal would like to develop a mechanism that would purchase land-use rights as cheaply as possible. This framework defines the basic features of what has come to be called a principal-agent problem.

Table 8.1 lists examples of principal-agent problems. Two types of problems typically discussed are those of adverse selection and moral hazard. From the perspective of most, adverse selection and hidden information problems are viewed as one and the same; they are both situations in which the agent possesses some characteristic (like managerial ability or raw intellectual ability) that the principal cannot observe. Strictly speaking, the moral hazard problem is a special type of hidden-action problem that has several ingredients. First, an agent takes actions that are unobservable to the principal. Second, the action, combined with a random event also unobservable to the principal, determines an outcome that is observed by both principal and agent. The final ingredient is that the actions taken by the agent are good from the principal's perspective but costly for the agent: the incentive compatibility problem.[2]

Purchasing insurance is the classic example of the principal-agent problem, because both adverse selection and moral hazard exist in the industry. Adverse selection results in insurance companies' going through a process to determine whom to insure and what types of premiums to charge. Suppose an insurance company is offering auto insurance to people with bad driving records. These people have bad driving records

Table 8.1. Principal-Agent Problems

Principal: Principal's Objective	Agent: Agent's Objective	Asymmetric Information	Adverse Selec- tion	Moral Hazard
Manager: Maximize mana- gerial salary	Worker: Maximize worker salary	Worker knows more about per- forming the task		X
Firm owners: Maximize firm profit	Managers: Maximize mana- gerial salary	Managers know more about running the firm		X
Client: Win a lawsuit	Attorney: Earn an income, not work too hard	Attorney knows more about the law		X
Insurance company: Maximize profit	Policyholder: Pay low premiums for good coverage	Policyholder knows more about the risks she faces	X	
Insurance company: Maximize profit	Policyholder: Pay low premiums for good coverage	Policyholder may not take precautions to avoid danger		X
Government agency: Have a private firm pro- vide a quality service at low prices while earning a reasonable profit	Private firm: Maximize profit	Firm knows more about the true costs of the service	X	
Fish and Wildlife Service: Have a private land- owner provide habitat to protect species for the public good	Private landowners: Maximize profits	Landowners know more about the true productivity of their skill	X	

because either they are careless drivers or they have had a string of bad luck. The company would like to separate the bad drivers from the un-lucky ones. A priori the company cannot tell the difference between the two types of drivers because all it has to go on are past driving records and they appear to be the same. This is an adverse selection problem, with the private information being the driver's true driving habits and ability. One way the insurance company separates the different driver types is by offering insurance policies with different deductibles. An unlucky driver, knowing he or she is actually a good driver, will typically choose a policy with higher deductibles than will a bad driver.

The auto insurance company may also encounter moral hazard problems with its policyholders. Most people dislike facing risks and will insure against large losses, like a stolen car. Whether a car is stolen will depend in large part on the vigilance of the owner in terms of where the car is parked, whether it is locked, whether a steering wheel lock is used, and so on. If the car owner is fully insured against theft, the incentive to be vigilant is reduced. After all, if the car is stolen, insurance will cover it. This lack of vigilance is the moral hazard. Insurance companies also use deductibles to make the owner share in the expense of a stolen car and hence induce the car owner to be more vigilant.

Because we are concerned with endangered species and the role government plays in preservation policy, consider another example that involves government intervention in a private market. Historically in the United States, electric, telephone, and natural gas companies have been regulated by state and federal public utility commissions. The justification was that these companies were natural monopolies; that is, the average cost of delivering electricity and telephone services decreased as the number of people serviced increased. As such, a single company could provide, say, 1 million units of natural gas more cheaply than two identical companies, suggesting it is in society's best interest to have these utilities be monopolies. In this case the government is the principal and the investor-owned public utilities are the agents.

The conundrum was that a competitive market environment usually serves society better because prices are relatively low and amounts of service relatively large. In the case of the public utilities, however, competition would lead to wasteful redundancy of production capacity. Furthermore, if the utilities were allowed to be monopolies without restrictions, to maximize profits, they would have an incentive to charge relatively high prices and provide relatively small amounts of service. Government took on the role of franchising these utilities, protecting them from competition in their service areas, and setting the prices the utilities charged.

The regulatory process, called rate-of-return regulation (RORR), involved a request from the utility for a rate hike from the commission, which would set into motion a rate hearing. To make its case at the hearing, the utility would present to the commission its costs of production and its capital base. The commission would then set prices so the utility would earn enough revenue to cover its costs and earn a reasonable return on the capital base.[3] A huge economics literature blossomed in the 1960s and 1970s decrying RORR for providing utilities no incentive to hold down production costs, particularly with respect to their capital base. Various remedies were proposed to reduce the built-in inefficiencies of RORR, but they ignored the fact that the utilities had superior information about their costs. Any policy that did not take into account the asymmetry of information would be fraught with potential problems. Starting in the 1980s, asymmetric information moved to the fore of the economic analyses of regulation. This next round of literature contributed to the sea change in utility regulation in the 1990s, marked by competition in the electric and telecommunication industries, utility divestitures, and government abandonment of RORR.

Let's consider how adverse selection creates a problem for regulators, and some specific remedies developed in the economics literature. For simplicity, suppose the regulated utilities have one of two cost structures: high-cost or low-cost. The regulator is in charge of setting the prices the utilities will charge their customers. In the absence of asymmetric information, the regulator would set output prices so that the utilities earn enough revenue to cover their costs (and earn a reasonable return on their capital investments) and consumers realize the maximum possible net benefits from the services provided. We will refer to this solution as charging efficient prices and earning normal profits. As one might suspect, typically, to earn a normal profit, a high-cost utility will need higher prices than a low-cost utility.

Under private information, however, each utility knows its own cost structure but the regulator does not, and the regulator must rely on each utility to report its cost as high or low. Therein lies the problem. A high-cost utility will report its cost as high. A low-cost utility, however, may not necessarily report its cost as low. By reporting that its cost is high, the low-cost utility would be allowed to charge the high price instead of the low price, giving the low-cost utility excess profits. If both types of utilities charge high prices, society is worse off because, with a low-cost utility, at the margin consumers' benefits (which equal the prices they pay) are higher than the cost of providing those benefits. Society would be better off if output were increased until at the margin consumers' benefits and the prices they pay for the service equal the cost of delivering that service. Of course, the regulator could set low prices for both utilities, but doing so might drive the high-cost utilities out of business.

The regulator's challenge then, is to devise a mechanism that provides incentives for the low-cost utilities to admit to being low-cost, and hence charging low prices and produce output levels that are close to the low-cost utility's socially efficient levels of output. At the same time, the mechanism must provide high-cost utilities an incentive to charge high prices and produce output levels that are close to their efficient levels of output.

A mechanism for implementing efficient or close to efficient outcomes is to announce a menu of prices and combinations of rewards and penalties to the utilities. The utilities review the menu and choose the price-reward pair that is in their best interest.[4] Because there are only two utility types in this example, the menu is simple and consists of two contracts, both of which include a price and a tax. One contract is targeted to low-cost utilities; the other is targeted to high-cost utilities. The contract designed for the high-cost utilities, or high contract, contains a price that is higher than the efficient price, plus a tax that confiscates the excess profit the high-cost types would earn using the higher price. The contract designed for the low-cost utilities, or low contract, contains the efficient low price, plus a negative tax, or subsidy. The subsidy is chosen so that a low-cost utility is indifferent to the choice between a low or high contract. Such a scheme will leave the low-cost utilities earning more profit than they would if they did not have superior information.

The crux of the price menu is as follows. The regulator wants to charge the efficient prices, but this essentially requires knowing the true cost structures. The regulator can induce the low-cost utilities to behave appropriately by offering a reward equal to the profit a low-cost utility would realize when choosing the high contract. This reward can potentially be quite costly and comes at the expense of consumers. Such behavior must be made unattractive, and this can be accomplished by distorting output prices. Because there is more net benefit to be had from the low-cost utilities than from the high-cost utilities, it makes more sense to distort high prices rather than low prices. Accordingly, the regulator sets the price for high-cost utilities at the efficient level, which cuts back on demand and the high-cost utilities' output. In addition, the excess profit induced by the inefficiently high price is taxed away. Hence, we have the schedule of output prices and taxes-subsidies.

Now, if the low-cost utilities choose a high contract so they can charge the higher price, the excess profit they earn is smaller than before because output is smaller than before. Plus, they have to pay the tax. This implies that the reward the regulator must pay to induce proper behavior (i.e., elicit the truth about a utility's cost structure) is smaller because the payoff from choosing the high contract is smaller. The regulator sacrifices some of the net benefits associated with a high-cost utility's production, to reduce the reward she must pay the low-cost utilities for choosing the low contract. Once the low costs are reported, the efficient low-cost price is charged and the large net benefits associated with low-cost utility production is preserved. In the end, high-cost utilities produce less and earn normal profit, while low-cost utilities produce the efficient output and earn some excess profit.

As we will see in the next section, on endangered species, these results are quite general. The more valuable the agent is to society, the more important it is not to distort the agent from his efficient output, but the more he must be rewarded to report truthfully.

Asymmetric Information and Land Preservation

Numerous examples exist of contracts to protect species on private land. In 1890 the first private land trust in the United States was founded in Massachusetts, and many other land trusts followed in the Northeast. As people and development moved westward, the land trusts followed. For example, the Jackson Hole Land Trust in Wyoming was founded in 1980 by a few local citizens and now protects more than 9,000 acres of private land. Currently about 250 private land trusts in the West collectively preserve more than one million acres (Nijhuis 2000). Government has also become involved in land preservation. Cities and counties in the United States have introduced taxes with the sole purpose of funding the preservation of undeveloped land. In Colorado alone, at least ten cities and counties have open space sales taxes. In 1999 the citizens of Larimer County in northern Colorado voted by a 60-percent majority to extend a quarter-cent sales tax. Much of the preserved property is farm- and ranchland, with some private trusts such as the Colorado Cattlemen's Agricultural Land Trust specializing in these parcels.

Preservation is accomplished through purchasing either the land or the development rights to the land. With development rights, the landowner retains the land but cannot develop it further. For instance, a rancher can continue working and living on the land, but the land must be maintained as a ranch. Asymmetric information between landowners and the trusts or the government complicates the design of compensation policies to preserve land and protect endangered species. The question is whether these private contracts have been as efficient as they could have been and, had we accounted for the presence of asymmetric information, whether society could have garnered more species protection with fewer resources.

We introduce the basic problem by considering an example.[5] Suppose the government is the potential preserver, and there are two landowners with private property, any portion of which can be sold for development. Each acre has both a development value associated with developing the land and a social value associated with preserving the land, and these values are common knowledge. Assume the social value exceeds the development value. The government can purchase the development rights on a portion of land at a price above the development value but below the social value, and society would then enjoy gains. Nevertheless, raising funds through taxes to pay landowners may be politically unpopular, as well as causing inefficiencies in the economy owing to the distortionary nature of taxes.

Recognizing this, if possible the government would like to pay the landowners even less than the development rights. Since the landowners enjoy some value from keeping the land as it is and not developing, they are willing to take less than the development value per acre. How much less they are willing to take is private information, and each landowner has an incentive to claim that they derive no pleasure at all from the undeveloped land. The government is assumed to know that one type of landowner, which we call the preserver, places a higher total and marginal value on each acre retired from development than does the other type of landowner, the developer, but because these values are private information, the government does not know who is a preserver and who is a developer.

Once again, this situation can be viewed as a principal-agent problem, in which a principal (the government) must design an economic incentive scheme to elicit information from an agent (the landowner), given that the principal and agent have different objectives and the agent has private information unavailable to the principal.[6] In this example, the government designs and offers a menu of contracts to the landowners; each contract specifies a per-acre payment and a number of undeveloped acres. The government recognizes that the landowners must be willing to participate in the selling of development rights to the government and that the contracts must be incentive compatible (that is, each landowner must prefer her contract to the contract designed for the other type of landowner). This is like the regulator's problem in the last section, wherein the utility commission had to design a menu that would lead low-cost utilities to reveal their true costs, because they preferred the low contract to the high contract. Assuming a benevolent government, its objective is to maximize the sum of benefits from undeveloped and developed acres, plus the receipts of the landowners, minus the total cost of payments to the landowners. Here, the total cost of payments to the landowner includes the direct payment to the landowner, which is equal to the landowner's receipts, plus the deadweight cost of raising tax revenues.[7]

To appreciate the solution to this problem, consider the benchmark case where raising public funds through taxes is not distortionary, and there is full information. In such a case the government can retire acreage by paying each landowner the minimum the landowner is willing to accept for selling. From the perspective of the regulator, the exact amount paid is immaterial, because if raising funds through taxes costs nothing, the payments are just transfers without any efficiency implications. Consider now the case where public funds are costly, but full information remains intact. Here efficiency calls for the government to purchase development rights on each parcel such that the social benefit of preserving one more acre, net of the forgone benefits of development, is equal to the additional cost of raising tax revenues plus the additional transfer to the landowner. The government gets by with paying the landowners less than what he could obtain from developing, because we assume the landowners also get some value from preservation. In both cases, the developer receives a higher payment per acre than does the preserver, because the personal loss of not converting is higher for the developer, and the government takes this information into account in the payments it offers.

Now consider the case in which information is private. The preserver has an incentive to claim to be a developer and, in doing so, collect the higher payments potentially received by the developer. In response, the government takes two actions. One action is to make the developer's contract less attractive to the preserver by both decreasing the total number of acres retired by the developer and decreasing the corresponding payment. The other action is to make the preserver's contract more attractive by increasing the payment while maintaining the socially efficient level of retired acres. In the most interesting cases under asymmetric information, efficiency loss is unavoidable. But this sort of plan reduces the preserver's profits and government payouts associated with privately held information, while purchasing the efficient amount of the relatively cheap land of the preserver and still paying the developer what is necessary.

Smith and Shogren (2002) take the question a step further. They examine the properties of two types of voluntary incentive mechanisms to protect endangered species on private land. One mechanism, loosely referred to as an ex-ante mechanism, offers each landholder a set of contracts that are independent of other landholders' types. The other mechanism, called an ex-post mechanism, offers contracts that are type-contingent: a landholder's actual payment and retirement levels depend on both his own type and the other landholders' types. They also presume that the government has selected a probabilistic safe minimum standard for species survival, called the minimum acceptable probability of survival (MAPS), which serves as a safety net by determining the minimum number of acres to set aside to guarantee survival of the species.

Their model suggests several results worth considering. First, if the MAPS constraint binds because social gains for less-known and less-favored species fall below the MAPS constraint (e.g., historical pests like the black-tailed prairie dog), then the habitats created by both ex-ante and ex-post mechanisms will be the same size. Plus, the ex-ante mechanism will bunch the landholders. By bunching, we mean the regulator asks each landholder to retire the same number of acres and pays each landowner the same amount for each acre retired. In this case each landowner receives an amount equal to the lost rent of the landholder with the most expensive land. Landowners with less-known but protected species capture top dollar irrespective of their type.

If the MAPS constraint does not bind, the choice of mechanism leads to different habitat sizes. Nonbinding MAPS constraints are more likely when the regulator confronts more well-known and charismatic species like the bald eagle and the grizzly bear. People will support programs for species they understand. They also note that the social welfare associated with an ex-post allocation is greater than the social welfare associated with the corresponding ex-ante allocation. This is because the ex-post mechanism makes use of more information than the ex-ante mechanism, linking contracts to type combinations. This suggests that policymakers should seek ways to address the feasibility of the more efficient ex-post compensation plans for those species that surpass the minimum level of survival as specified by the MAPS constraint.

The Smith and Shogren results show that it is quite reasonable to expect the size of the ex-post habitat to be smaller than the corresponding ex-ante habitat. This is especially true if the deadweight losses associated with raising tax revenues are relatively small. Hence, environmentalists might prefer that the government implement the simpler ex-ante mechanism.

There is an additional caveat to the willingness to trade off habitat size for information rents. Controlling information rents requires smaller reserves, which in turn increases the chance of bumping into the MAPS constraint. If so, fights over the stringency of the MAPS constraint may begin to dominate the debate over the Endangered Species Act, with concerns over information rents being of second-order concern. Compensation schemes, if implemented, could consist of paying top dollar to each landholder to hit the fixed MAPS target, regardless of one's rental structure. As such, policymakers should be prepared for the likelihood that fewer acres may be retired than expected or that retired acres will be more costly than expected.

Finally, Smith and Shogren discuss the plausibility of implementing an efficient voluntary habitat scheme, and when it might make sense to implement nonlinear retirement schemes. If the private habitat reserve can be noncontiguous, designing an efficient nonlinear voluntary retirement scheme could be worth the trouble. The value of such a scheme might be limited, however, if the desired habitat reserve cuts across the entire landholdings of many landholders. Here the regulator must compare the relative pros and cons of a voluntary versus command mechanism. Landholders are likely to prefer a voluntary scheme, but regulators run the risk of paying top dollar if they are unable to separate landholder types.

Issues in Implementation

A government wanting to implement a voluntary ex-ante or ex-post mechanism requires specific information. The ability to minimize information rents depends on the quantity and quality of the information one can secure. An ideal set of information would include: the expected species survival function, a level for the MAPS constraint, the deadweight costs to society, the distribution of land types across landholders, the basic structure of a landowner's profit function, and the expected social benefits of species protection.

First, using input from wildlife ecologists, conservation biologists, and others, policymakers will have to choose the level of the MAPS constraint. Given a MAPS constraint, the minimal requisite set of information is the distribution of landholder types and knowledge of the structure of landholder rents. Such information helps the regulator design a least-cost voluntary ex-ante or ex-post mechanism. Acquiring data on the distribution of land values should be a relatively routine matter. For instance, data sources like the Farm Service Agency of the Department of Agriculture maintain county-level data on the distribution of agricultural land values for most counties in the United States.

If the government cannot measure the social benefits of habitat size, then the regulator's problem is to minimize the cost of creating a habitat at least as large as that dictated by the MAPS constraint (see, for instance, Smith 1995). Furthermore, if landholder rents are linear in acres, then the optimal mechanism will be one in which the government picks a single price to offer and lets each landholder retire as many acres as the landholder wants at that price. The practical implication is that when choosing one price to offer two or more landholders, if the habitat reserve needs to be contiguous, the regulator might have to pay everyone top dollar. This is especially true if the regulator wants all of a particular landholder's land and is forced to pay that landowner top dollar. Because all landholders are treated the same, everyone receives top dollar for the acres retired.

Alternatively, if rents are nonlinear in acres, then the government should be able to implement a nonlinear voluntary habitat reserve scheme in which prices received are more closely linked to each landholder's true underlying rental values. Implementing the nonlinear scheme, however, involves two challenges: correctly inferring the distribution of types, and estimating the landholder rent function. Given a reasonable approximation of the landholder rent function and the distribution of landholder rents, the social scientist can derive the optimal acreage retirement and transfer combinations using readily available software like Mathematica.

If the regulator also knew the social benefit associated with a given habitat, then it might be able to improve social welfare by choosing retirement levels so the marginal benefit of retiring land is equal to the marginal lost rents of retiring the land. To date, however, the current state of the art on species valuation has opportunities for improvement. Taking the reported values from several species-specific contingent valuation surveys suggests that people would pay 1 percent of gross domestic product to save less than 2 percent of the listed species (see Brown and Shogren 1998). Many people will see that value as high and will downplay the usefulness of such values to guide the implementation of a voluntary incentive scheme. Other people are likely to focus on using the nonmonetized species survival function for implementation.

Concluding Remarks

Policymakers have proposed using economic incentives to protect endangered species on private lands, but imperfect information confounds the design of preservation policy. Herein we have focused on how to design economic incentives that account for the private information problem, because a truly voluntary program must present landowners with alternatives and allow them to choose from among the alternatives freely. Landowners must be allowed to self-select. Also, landowners usually must be offered the same set of choices. Therefore, even if the regulator knew each landowner's ability to make profits, if forced to implement a voluntary program she would be unable to exploit such information. The incentive compatibility and participation constraints tell us that we can get away with paying the developer-type landowner his preservation value. They also tell us we will have to give the preserver-type landowner some information rents, and the least amount of those rents he must be given.

We examine the theory and practical limits of designing voluntary incentive schemes to induce private landholders to create habitat reserves, in which the regulator wants the habitat reserves to meet minimum size restrictions. In doing so we find effective conservation policy may need to buy information rather than sell fear with permits and fines. The agency should lower the payment to lessen the incentive for some landowners to take advantage of their private information, but smaller subsidies result in fewer acres set aside for habitat. On net, the realized habitat will be less than desired, or the desired habitat will be more expensive than justified. Research on the economics of imperfect information suggests that a combination of mechanisms might be needed to help society reach a better level of species protection. Compensation, government or conservation group purchases of land or development rights, insurance programs, tax breaks, and tradable rights in habitat conservation might all be needed.

We consider briefly two types of incentive schemes under asymmetric information. The ex-ante incentive scheme offers each landholder a contract that depends only on that landholder's reported rental values. In contrast, the ex-post incentive scheme offers each landholder contracts that are type-contingent—the contract received by each landowner depends on the rental values reported by him and all other landholders. Our results suggest that if the expected marginal benefit of species survival is too small, the minimum size restriction will force the regulator to offer all landholders the same contract. Those accepting contracts will retire the same number of acres, and each will be paid top dollar. This result holds for both incentive schemes. But if the marginal benefit of species survival is large enough, cases exist in which the state-contingent incentive scheme implements the full-information habitat. The ex-ante incentive scheme never implements a full-information habitat, and the expected size of the ex-ante habitat is no greater than the ex-post scheme.

Notes

1. Stiglitz, a Nobel laureate, has written numerous seminal theoretical papers on the economics of information and has served on the President's Council of Economic Advisors. Partha Dasgupta has referred to Stiglitz as one of the "most significant social thinkers of our time." Stiglitz argues that the basic economic thinking underpinning neoclassical economic models "provides little guidance for the choice of economic systems, since once information imperfections are brought into the analysis, as surely they must be, there is no presumption that markets are efficient" (p. 13).

2. Note that some economic problems contain both moral hazard and adverse selection. An example would be when a regulator wants to regulate irrigation water use but is unable to observe any individual farmer's water use (moral hazard) and does not know the farmer's profit structure (adverse selection).

3. Rate-of-return regulation is a special case of cost-plus regulation, which is more or less the method used in many situations where the government must procure goods from the private sector (e.g., military procurement).

4. Equivalently, the utility could review the contracts and report a type to the government.

5. Some of the material in this section is based on Innes et al. (1998). Smith and Shogren (2002) introduce a more complex version of the following example wherein species survival is greatly enhanced by preserving contiguous parcels from multiple private properties. The regulator designs contracts to retire acres and allows bonuses to promote agglomeration across landowners.

6. For other examples of the principal-agent problem in environmental problems see Lewis (1996). He extends the theory of principal-agent problems into environmental economics, offering a model of an environmental protection agency (principal) and polluting firms (agents) who have private information about their production and abatement costs.

7. The idea here is that a potential deadweight loss is associated with each dollar transferred to a landowner. On the surface it would appear that although some people have lost income through taxation, the gains by landowners would

exactly offset those losses. Raising the dollar through taxes, however, causes inefficient behavior, and this is a cost above and beyond the one dollar. In fact, this deadweight loss plays an important role in principal-agent models of regulation. With deadweight loss the government cannot acquire private information for free (see Laffont and Tirole 1993).

References

Brown, Gardner Jr., and Jason F. Shogren. 1998. Economics of the Endangered Species Act. *Journal of Economic Perspectives* 12:3–20.

Hayek, Friedrich A. 1996. The use of knowledge in society. Pp. 77–91 in *Individualism and economic order.* Reprint edition. Chicago: University of Chicago Press.

Innes, Robert, Stephan Polasky, and John Tschirhart. 1998. Takings, compensation, and endangered species protection on private lands. *Journal of Economic Perspectives* 12, no. 3: 35–52.

Laffont, Jean-Jacques, and Jean Tirole. 1993. *A theory of incentives in procurement and regulation.* Cambridge, Mass.: MIT Press.

Lewis, Tracy R. 1996. Protecting the environment when costs and benefits are privately known. *RAND Journal of Economics* 27 (winter): 819–847.

Nijhuis, Michelle. 2000. Acre by acre: Can land trusts save the West's disappearing open space? and A land trust toolbox. *High Country News,* 28 February.

Polasky, S., and H. Doramus. 1998. When the truth hurts: Endangered species policy on private land with imperfect information. *Journal of Environmental Economics and Management* 35:22–47.

Shogren, J. F., J. Tschirhart, T. Anderson, A. W. Ando, S. R. Beissinger, D. Brookshire, G. M. Brown Jr., D. Coursey, R. Innes, S. M. Meyer, and S. Polasky. 1999. Why economics matters for endangered species protection. *Conservation Biology* 13:1257–1261.

Smith, R. B. W. 1995. The Conservation Reserve Program as a least-cost land retirement mechanism. *American Journal of Agricultural Economics* 77: 93–105.

Smith, Rodney B., and Jason F. Shogren. 2001. Protecting species on private land. Pp. 326–342 in *Protecting endangered species in the United States: Biological needs, political realities, economic choices,* edited by J. Shogren and J. Tschirhart. New York: Cambridge University Press.

———. 2002. Voluntary incentive design for endangered species protection. *Journal of Environmental Economics and Management* 43:169–187.

Stiglitz, Joseph E. 1996. *Whither Socialism?* Cambridge, Mass.: MIT Press.

PART III

ECONOMIC INCENTIVES
FOR ESA REAUTHORIZATION

CHAPTER 9

Evaluating the Incentive Tools

GREGORY M. PARKHURST AND JASON F. SHOGREN

A U.S. senator once said in private conversation that "if we pay land-owners to grow endangered species, we will have more critters than we know what to do with." The question is how to do this in the most cost-effective manner such that biological needs are met, landowner concerns are addressed, and government budgets are solvent. We have presented the practical pros and cons of each incentive mechanism in Chapter 3, and the other authors have raised numerous concerns about these methods in the chapters following it. We conclude by evaluating each economic incentive based on three broad criteria that reflect the general concerns raised throughout the volume: (1) biological-land tar-gets, (2) landowner interests, and (3) government or regulatory con-cerns. Each criterion is examined in turn, and the incentives are ranked in the matrix in Table 9.1. We offer our evaluation of each criterion as a broad starting point. Specific applications of each incentive mechanism will have different success rates depending on the specific combination of species, landowners, and habitat type. A complete dissection of the anatomy of successes and failures in the use of economic incentives is the next step in our long-run research agenda.

Before we consider how these incentives match up with the practical criteria, consider first how incentives fit into the broader issues raised by Debra Donahue over the need for a new land ethics and Frieda Knob-loch and Greg Cawley over the desire for a tighter social fabric. Obvi-ously these elements of humanity matter for endangered species protec-tion. These honorable concerns raise the issue of what one should expect to get out of an economic incentive system. If the goal is to change the ethic, either by example or by moral suasion, economic incentives are not necessarily the tool of choice. Education is the tool. Policymakers

Table 9.1. Matrix of Economic Incentive Mechanisms and Evaluation Criteria

				Economic Incentive Mechanisms				
Criteria	Regulation Zoning	Impact Fee	Subsidy	TDRs	Conservation Banking	Fee Simple Purchase	PDR Easement	Donated Easement
Biological								
Odds of targeting specific habitat characteristics:								
Satisfying species-specific requirements	VH	L	M	VH	VH	M	M	L
Permanency	L-M	VL	VL	L-M-H	VH	L-M	L-M-H	L-M-H
Active habitat management	VL	VL	VH	VL	VH	VH	M-H	M-H

Landowner

Voluntary participation	VL	L	VH	VL	VH	VH	VH	VH
Privacy maintenance	VH	VH	L-M-H	H	H	L	L-M-H	L-M-H
Stewardship recognition	VL	VL	M	VL	VH	VL	L-M-H	L-M-H
Government								
Administration costs	L-M	M	H-VH	H	VH	L-M	H	L-M
Monitoring and enforcement costs	H-VH	H-VH	M	H	L-M	L	H-VH	H-VH
Acquisition costs	VL	VL	H	VL	VL	VH	M-H	L-M
Information rents (DWL)	VL	VL	H-VH	VL	VL	H-VH	M-H	M
Risk of habitat destruction	VH	VH	VL	H-VH	VL	VL-L	VL	VL

Note: VH, very high; H, high; M, medium; L, low; VL, very low who have what Thomas Sowell (1987) calls an "unconstrained vision" believe people have a sizable untapped morality buried within, just waiting to emerge once pointed in the right direction. Solutions like the compulsory rules and regulations are primary; the tradeoffs involved are secondary. As Sowell puts it, "every closer approximation to the ideal should be preferred. Costs are regrettable, but by no means decisive."

People do learn to take more care and might be moved by a sense of public spirit, but incentives per se are not designed to make these fundamental changes in inward personality to be a better citizen. Rather, incentives affect outward behavior in the short term, not the internal personality traits. Behavior changes because the relative price of neglecting critical habitat has increased to the point at which species protection is the least-cost option. Incentives are not designed to change the underlying character of the person. People are people, as they are today and were yesterday, here and around the globe; incentives do not corrupt them. Policymakers who have this constrained vision of people weigh ideals against the costs of achieving them. Real incentives are needed to get people to take on the goals of species protection intentionally. We hold the constrained vision in our evaluation below.

Biological Needs

We consider three policy-oriented biological needs aimed at retiring and enhancing habitat on private property that shelters endangered species. We first address the ability of a mechanism to target specific characteristics of the land, whether it be to create one large preserve with minimal edge, to preserve a specific type of vegetation or key species, or to preserve several small preserves for metapopulation management; second, the likely permanence of the protected habitat; and third, the ability of the mechanism to implement active habitat management techniques. We follow Terborgh's (1976) observation that "logic calls for a strategy that minimizes extinctions, and this . . . is best accomplished with large preserves." Biologists seem to agree with the view that habitat requirements are species-specific, and species that are more land sensitive need larger habitat remnants for survival (see, for example, Saunders et al. 1991). Fragmentation increases the risk to species when it alters the microclimate of the habitat and when each fragment remains isolated. We make the presumption that biologists have identified and targeted the private land most suitable to guarantee the safe minimum standard, or the maximum viable population, or the minimum acceptable probability of survival. We then use the likelihood of satisfying species-specific habitat requirements (accomplished through targeting specific land characteristics and compelling landowners to undertake active habitat management) and the probability that the habitat reserve will be retired and protected permanently as the proxies for the basic biology at work behind these land use decisions.

Odds of Targeting Specific Habitat Characteristics: Satisfying Species-Specific Requirements

Most scientists agree that habitat requirements are species-specific, and species that are more land sensitive need larger habitat remnants for survival (Saunders et al. 1991; Willis 1984; Gilpin and Diamond 1980; Whitcomb et al. 1976; Higgs and Usher 1980). Unfortunately, for most listed species, habitat destruction has reduced the amount of remaining habitat to a level below that necessary for species survival. In most cases, the remaining habitat is fragmented in several smaller reserves. Although some species thrive on the edges between habitats, biologists believe most endangered species do not. New evidence has overtaken the Leopold (1933) "law of interspersion" (more edge, more population density) with the proposition that edge effects cause extinction (Mills 1995). Edge effects arise from nest parasitism and the penetration of light and wind into the habitat. Species move away from the edge and farther into a forest, causing a reduction in total area and lower population persistence (e.g., Vickery et al. 1994).

   For other endangered and threatened species, a large threat to survival is disease. For example, the black-footed ferret is affected by canine distemper and sylvatic plague, among other diseases. The black-tailed prairie dog, the primary diet of the black-footed ferret, is also susceptible to canine distemper. If infected by these diseases, an entire colony can be wiped out (BFFRIT 2002). For species sensitive to disease the biological goal would include preserving several isolated populations as well as meeting a minimum population size or habitat core area. Management of several metapopulations would be necessary to meet some minimum probability of survival, because as the number of individual populations is reduced, the probability that an epidemic will wipe out the species is increased.

   Another biological concern that needs to be addressed when planning and designing habitat reserves is the preservation of land that possesses key habitat characteristics that the listed species need for survival. For example, the red-cockaded woodpecker requires roughly 100 acres of open pine stands for foraging and roosting. For foraging, pines need to be at least thirty years old, while roosting cavities are typically dug into older pines (more than sixty years) that are infected by red-heart disease (USFWS 2002). A second example is the black-footed ferret, which primarily preys on prairie dogs, so it requires habitat that provides for its dietary needs (BFFRIT 2002). Each species has its own set of habitat and dietary needs, which must be considered in conjunction with the minimal size of the habitat reserve, when designing mechanisms for protecting species.

An effective conservation strategy needs to address these biological needs and, in doing so, should view the landscape as a whole. Targeting species-specific habitat requirements and coordinating landowner conservation efforts to create larger preserves, for most listed species, will increase the species' probability of survival. Therefore, coordinating conservation across landowners, so that two or more fragmented habitats of insufficient size are connected to make one large reserve, may also have the added benefit that in meeting the ESA objective of conserving imperiled species "to the extent practicable," fewer total acres are required. By coordinating conservation into larger reserves, especially if the edge-to-core ratio is minimized, the minimum acceptable probability of survival for a listed species will be met with fewer total acres than if conservation is fragmented.

Zoning, TDR, and conservation banks have a very high potential for targeting species-specific habitat needs and coordinating conservation into larger habitat reserves. The regulator, when employing either a zoning or TDR policy, restricts the land desired for conservation from being used for any purpose other than conservation. The regulator can target specific land and land attributes, which include the edge-to-core ratio of the habitat reserve.

Unlike the command-and-control approaches of zoning and TDR, conservation banking is effective at preserving specific land attributes and at creating one single large habitat reserve, because the bank owner is presented with incentives to create the most effective conservation reserve. The number of credits the conservation bank owner can earn per acre is dependent on the quality of the habitat of the conservation bank, the rarity of the species, and the number of listed species that the bank can support. To maximize the number of credits available for sale, the bank owner has an incentive to create a conservation bank with the smallest possible core-to-edge ratio.

Subsidies, fee simple acquisition, and PDR easements are all voluntary incentive mechanisms, and as a result, the regulator's ability to target specific land for conservation is reduced. Some landowners may not want to participate in the program at any price; other landowners may value their land at a higher price than the regulator is willing to pay. Landowners unwilling to participate may limit the effectiveness of these policy instruments in designing one large habitat reserve.

The regulator has the least control over the land that is set aside for habitat protection when a donated easement or impact fee policy is used. When an impact fee policy is used, the land that remains undeveloped or conserved is the land with a development value less than the impact fee. It is unlikely that the conserved land is the land with the highest-quality habitat or that the configuration of the habitat reserve would be such that edge effects are minimized.

The problem with donated easements is that they appeal only to owners who place a high conservation value on their land, because typically landowners are not fully compensated for the lost land productivity. Although it is possible that all landowners that find donated easements appealing live in the same area, and that their properties border each other in a manner that creates the largest possible core, it is unlikely. The case more likely to occur with donated easements is that habitat reserves will remain fragmented.

Permanency

Land worth conserving today because of the biodiversity benefits that the land provides for species protection is likely to be land worth preserving indefinitely. This concept holds if the regulator is seeking to meet the ESA objective at least cost, where the minimum acceptable probability of survival is just satisfied. A loss of a relatively small portion of the conserved land could send a delisted species back to an imperiled status. Three potential pitfalls for permanency in conservation are (1) short-term contracts, because successive negotiations may not be successful; (2) oversight and future land uses are subject to political whims; and (3) contracts are subject to conflict, future litigation, and possible reductions in conservation requirements.

A mechanism does best at avoiding conflict when three conditions are met: when agreements are mutually beneficial to all participating parties, when contracts are of shorter duration, and when the number of participating parties is kept relatively small. Intuitively, the smaller the number of participants involved in the agreement, the more likely it is that agreements will be mutually beneficial. Furthermore, shorter contracts reduce the number of participating parties by decreasing the probability that land will be transferred to another party.

The incentive mechanism that is best able to guarantee that the land will stay in conservation in perpetuity is conservation banking. Conservation banks, prior to approval by the regulator and the sale of the first bankable credit, are required to establish a conservator for the bank and fund the management and maintenance of the bank in perpetuity. If the conservation bank falls short of its conservation goal, the banking instrument specifies the corrective actions that are to be taken.

PDR easements, donated easements, and TDRs with zoning are designed to conserve land in perpetuity, but they may be shrouded in uncertainty. The easement contract specifies that the conservation requirements are forever. Easements, however, are susceptible to the scrutiny of subsequent landowners in search of loopholes that will increase their personal return on the land. The agreements may have to be renegotiated, or the conservator may have to force the landowner to comply by taking legal action. It is likely that the landowners will gain more flexibility in using their land, and conservation commitments will be reduced as a result. Over time, conservation commitments may be reduced sufficiently to render the conservation commitment inadequate to achieve its initial goal, much the same as if the land had been developed completely.

Fee simple acquisition and zoning are less likely to conserve land permanently than easements. The ability of these two mechanisms to conserve land in perpetuity depends on whether the goals of the government remain constant across time. If the objectives of the government change and species protection becomes less important, the land could be reassigned to other uses or sold to fund other government projects. Fee simple acquisition and zoning are subject to lobbying by special interest groups, interest groups which represent a relatively small portion of society. If the interest groups are successful in influencing the government's objectives, it is likely that the costs to society will outweigh the benefits to the select few that the interest group represents.

The least effective means of preserving land in perpetuity are subsidies and impact fees. Impact fees in and of themselves do not restrict land to conservation; they only keep it from being developed. Subsidies are generally paid on an annual basis, so landowners have the opportunity to develop their land without repercussion every year. Also, funding the subsidy may prove to be problematic. If the necessary funding is not available, landowners may revert to developing their land.

Active Habitat Management

The ESA prohibits landowners from undertaking activities that harm listed species, either directly or indirectly through habitat modification. The act does not require landowners to improve the quality of the species habitat on their land. The act serves to conserve habitat, but for many species, deterring productive uses of the land is insufficient to ensure that a minimum acceptable probability of survival will be met. Species recovery plans require landowners to restore or create habitat, or implement active management practices, such as prescribed burns, alien species control, reduced use of the land for grazing, or reduced use of pesticides on the conserved land to maintain habitat suitable for species recovery. For example, the leading threats to the California red-legged frog are fragmentation of habitat, degradation of water quality, and the introduction of an alien species, the bullfrog. The recovery plan for the California red-legged frog calls for the restoration and creation of habitat as well as control of the threat posed by the bullfrog. A second example, the black-capped vireo, requires an open brushy area of young small trees and shrubs for its habitat. In the absence of natural fires, landowners must maintain suitable habitat for the vireo through prescribed burns. In a study of 305 listed species, better than 60 percent required active habitat management or habitat restoration (Environmental Defense Fund 2000).

Active habitat management techniques are best incorporated into an incentive mechanism when participation is voluntary, each contractual agreement can be negotiated independently, contracts are of short duration, and assurances are included in the agreement. Voluntary participation ensures that the landowner is being fully compensated for the habitat management requirements set forth in the agreement. Negotiating contractual agreements allows the contract to be tailored to each individual landowner and to each specific species. Negotiations allow greater flexibility in designing an incentive package that satisfies both landowner and species-specific needs. Shorter contracts necessitate frequent renegotiations, which subsequently permit the provisions of the contract to be altered to meet changing landowner and species needs.

Furthermore, the regulator can monitor the landowner's compliance with previous agreements prior to negotiating new agreements. Assurances provide legal remedies in the event that the landowner does not fulfill the agreement. Assurances can require the landowner to set aside funding sufficient to ensure the long-term active management of habitat.

The biggest deterrent to active habitat management is involuntary participation. Involuntary participation is the current approach to endangered species protection and does not necessarily provide landowners with the incentives to manage the habitat on their land in the species' interest. In contrast, the landowner might have an incentive to eliminate the species and its habitat to avoid the costs of protecting species. The second deterrent is long-term contracts, because the longer the elapsed time between the present and the initiation of the management agreement, the greater the likelihood that the landowner or a subsequent landowner will violate the agreement in an attempt to increase economic rents. Active habitat management is costly, so landowners can increase their economic rents by violating the agreement.

The mechanisms that have a very high potential for implementing active habitat management are subsidies, conservation banking, and fee simple acquisition. Subsidies are voluntary short-term contracts, typically negotiated between the landowner and the regulator. Subsidies can be tailored to a specific species and to each individual landowner. Because subsidies are short-term contracts, the regulator can ensure that the landowner has fulfilled the habitat management requirements prior to renewing the subsidy.

Conservation banks are also voluntary and negotiated on a case-by-case basis. The number of credits a conservation bank earns for resale depends partly on the quality of the habitat. Conservation bank owners are required to maintain the habitat in perpetuity. To ensure that conservation bank owners fulfill the terms of their contract, the banking agreement requires that financial assurances are set aside to pay for the management of the habitat in perpetuity. Financial assurances can counter the negative effect of long-term contracts.

A fee simple acquisition mechanism purchases the land outright, placing ownership and responsibility for managing the land on the government. Implementing habitat management is straightforward and requires that the appropriate government agency be notified of the management requirements.

Easements, both PDR and donated, are voluntary long-term contracts negotiated between the landowner and the regulator. In evaluating the ability of the mechanism to implement active habitat management, easements are similar to subsidies except that easements are long-term contracts. Unlike conservation banking, easements do not have built-in assurances to offset the negative effects of the long-term aspect of the incentive mechanism. Landowners receive payment in full at the time of contract initiation and must satisfy the terms of the agreement in perpetuity. Fulfillment of the active habitat management required in the contract will depend on the integrity of the landowner, the landowner's conservation value, and the regulator's monitoring and enforcement of the agreement. As time passes, active habitat management is likely to diminish as the encumbered land changes ownership, or the opportunity cost of habitat management increases, or as the regulator relaxes the monitoring and enforcement of agreements.

TDRs, zoning, and impact fees all have a very low ability to require landowners to undertake active habitat management, because they force landowners to conserve their land involuntarily. Involuntary participation creates resentment and disincentives for landowners to undertake activities that enhance the habitat on their land. Zoning and impact fees both require landowners to conserve habitat without being compensated for lost productivity; any habitat improvements undertaken by such a landowner will only increase his out-of-pocket expenses, costs the landowner is unlikely to incur.

Landowners receive some compensation with a TDR incentive mechanism, but the compensation is independent of the opportunity cost of the land. Improving the quality of the habitat only increases the landowner's opportunity cost without affecting his compensation. A landowner incurs fewer opportunity costs by not undertaking active habitat management.

Landowner Interests

We consider three basic landowner concerns identified over the years in informal and formal discussions with ranchers, developers, and farmers. Landowners want their participation to be voluntary, they want their privacy maintained, and they want their stewardship toward the land recognized and acknowledged.

Voluntary Participation

Mechanisms that allow landowners to participate voluntarily, rather than forcing landowners to participate through some type of command-and-control mechanism, alter the landowners' incentives. When landowners are coerced into conserving their land to protect species and habitat without compensation, the landowners are faced with incentives to destroy the species and habitat before government regulation is imposed. Alternatively, if the landowner is compensated for habitat conservation, and the compensation is dependent on the quality of the habitat, then landowners are provided the incentive to conserve their land and to do so without force.

Zoning and TDR policies predetermine which land will be conserved and then force those landowners into conserving their land. For these mechanisms, voluntary participation is almost nonexistent. Fee simple acquisition can also be nonvoluntary when the government uses its power of eminent domain to force the landowner to sell his or her land. Fee simple acquisition can also occur in situations in which the landowner voluntarily sells his or her land to the government agency or other conservator.

When an impact fee policy is used, landowners who choose to develop their land are required to pay an impact fee. A landowner does have the choice not to pay the impact fee, but that entails an opportunity cost of forgoing development of the land. Only landowners with a conservation value in excess of the opportunity cost of forgone development will choose to conserve their land voluntarily.

Regulatory policies using subsidies, conservation banking, and PDR and donated easements all rank very high on the scale of voluntary participation for landowners. Landowners that create conservation banks do so voluntarily with the expectation of turning a profit.

Subsidy programs typically require landowners to apply for the subsidy and then to satisfy specified criteria. The number of applications often exceeds the accepted conservation projects. If the incentives are not sufficient for the landowner, the landowner need not apply. PDR and donated easements require landowner and conservator to negotiate contracts, which specify the obligations and requirements of both the landowner and the conservator. If the contract is not satisfactory to the landowner, the landowner can abort negotiations and not conserve his or her land.

Maintenance of Privacy

Most landowners in the United States want to preserve their right to exclude persons from trespassing on their land. Also landowners want to minimize the rights of a third party to enter their land legitimately, through contractual agreement or other arrangement. Policies that do not alter or split the property rights to the land are more effective at maintaining privacy. When the property rights remain intact, confusion over who has what rights is avoided. Impact fees maintain the right to privacy most effectively because, on payment of the impact fee, compliance to the policy is satisfied for developed properties. For properties not developed, landowners maintain the right to exclude government regulators from entering their property. Zoning, like an impact fee policy, also maintains a very high level of privacy. The landowner maintains all rights to the land and therefore can restrict access to the land.

Conservation banking and TDR instruments for conserving habitat are highly effective at maintaining the landowner's privacy. Both instruments allow the government regulator access to the land to monitor and enforce the contractual agreements; however, the access is typically specific. For subsidies, PDR easements, and donated easements the ability to maintain privacy is dependent on the negotiated contracts or the rules of the program. Some subsidy programs require the landowners to permit access to their land to the general public, although the landowner does have the ability to exclude specific individuals. With easements, the property rights are severed and split between the two parties. The landowners' ability to protect their privacy will hinge on the contractual agreement and may be low, medium, or high. When the government purchases land through fee simple acquisition, the land becomes the property of the public. The ability to deny the general public access to the land may be limited.

Recognition of Stewardship

Is the landowner's effort to preserve or enhance the habitat on the land acknowledged? Acknowledgment can take many forms, including public or financial rewards, but it must create an incentive for the landowner to preserve or enhance the habitat on the land. Conservation banking rewards bank owners for good stewardship by increasing the number of credits that the bank owner can sell to offset development. The bank owner enhances the property, increasing the quality of the habitat or the number of listed species, and as a result increases the number of credits that can be sold, which increases the revenue to the bank owner. Subsidies also reward stewardship, but less effectively. The subsidy policy can entail that the landowner restore or create habitat, or it might serve only to keep the land from being developed.

PDR and donated easement contracts may or may not specify that the landowner undertake habitat management techniques. If the contract specifies that the landowner maintain the habitat on the land, the extent to which the landowner meets his or her contractual obligations will likely depend on the conservator's diligence in monitoring and enforcing the contract. Also, because the landowner receives full payment when the contract is negotiated, the conservator has no leverage to ensure that the landowner holds up his or her end of the agreement.

Impact fees, zoning, and TDR policies do not provide landowners with any incentive to enhance and maintain the habitat on the land. In many cases the opposite holds true, to avoid being forced to conserve the land, the landowner may choose to destroy the habitat. Fee simple purchase also offers very low stewardship rewards, because the land is in public hands and individuals may see the responsibility of maintaining the land as the government's problem.

Government Concerns

We consider five general categories of governmental concerns associated with implementing an incentive scheme: administrative costs, monitoring and enforcement costs, acquisition costs, information rents, and risk of habitat destruction. Consider each in turn.

Administrative Costs

Administrative costs are expenditures for the staff necessary to establish the conservation plan, process applications, establish markets to facilitate trades between suppliers and demanders of tradable development rights and bankable credits, process and maintain records for property right transfers and land use restrictions, and staff and fund programs that maintain government-owned conservation lands. Administrative costs increase as the needed staff, reporting requirements, and other various accounting needs increase.

Administrative costs are lowest for the status quo, zoning. Zoning ordinances have been used to control the shape of growth for a century. The infrastructure necessary to administer a zoning conservation policy is already in place. Fee simple acquisitions also have low to medium administrative costs, which primarily result from the need to manage and maintain land once acquired. Government agencies responsible for managing these lands are largely intact and, therefore, only a minimal increase in staff may be necessary. Like fee simple acquisition, donated easements also have low to medium administrative costs because the infrastructure necessary to oversee a donated easement policy is already in place. A large portion of the administrative responsibility for donated easements rests in the IRS, which has the economies of scale to deal with the responsibility of oversight of donated easements at a minimal or zero impact on staffing requirements. Although donated easements must still be negotiated between the landowner and a conservator, the administrative costs to the regulator are small because the conservator can be an IRS-approved nonprofit conservation organization.

Conservation banks are at the other end of the spectrum, exhibiting high administrative costs. Conservation banks require the regulator to staff the oversight of an extensive application process as well as establishing a market for and tracking the transfer of bankable credits. Also having high administrative costs are policies for PDR easements, subsidies, and TDR. For PDR easements, contract negotiations constitute the bulk of the administrative costs. The costs of contract negotiations are high because PDR easements result in the landowner and the regulator having joint ownership in the property. Some agreements on how to split the property rights may require complex and costly negotiations.

Subsidy policies also have high to very high administrative costs, because subsidy programs typically require the landowner to submit an application and to satisfy specific requirements. The regulator incurs administrative costs to evaluate applications and to insure that the specified requirements are met. For TDRs land is allocated for conservation through zoning. Administration costs center around the need to establish a market to facilitate trades and to record transfers of TDRs. Records must be kept to ensure that once a landowner has traded (sold) away the development rights in the land, that the land is designated for conservation thereafter. If records are not maintained, the landowner could lobby for zoning changes in the future and, if successful, develop the land.

Monitoring and Enforcement Costs

Monitoring costs are the costs that the regulator accrues in insuring that land use restrictions are not being violated and that contractual conservation agreements are being upheld. When violations of land use restrictions or contractual agreements occur, enforcement costs accrue in correcting the situation. Monitoring and enforcement obligations are perpetual and therefore must be funded annually.

Fee simple acquisition has low monitoring and enforcement costs. Inherent in the purchase of the land is the right to control acceptable land uses, and the costs of monitoring and enforcement may be limited to preventing the public from misusing the land. Conservation banking has low to medium monitoring and enforcement costs. The costs to monitor and enforce agreements are low because the banking agreement stipulates reporting and monitoring criteria, establishes a bank manager, and specifies remedies for violations of the agreement. Furthermore, because the sole purpose of a conservation bank is to earn profits through the provision of conservation, bank owners are unlikely to undertake activities that diminish their potential profits.

Incentive mechanisms that allow the landowner to remain on the land and retain complete or partial property rights have higher monitoring and enforcement costs. The magnitude of the costs to monitor and enforce conservation requirements is related to many factors, including the time frame in which conservation payments are made to the landowner, the length of conservation agreements, and the landowner's range of permissible land uses. Spreading landowner compensation payments over many periods, rather than paying the landowner one lump sum, is likely to reduce the costs of monitoring and enforcing agreements. The landowner must prove compliance at regular time intervals to receive the periodic conservation payment. Likewise, the shorter the contract duration, the lower the monitoring and enforcement costs are likely to be. Monitoring and enforcement costs tend to increase as the time that has lapsed between the present and the time of the agreement initiation increases. Furthermore, with longer contracts, the probability that the land will transfer ownership increases. As subsequent landowners take control of the land, the likelihood that conservation agreements will be upheld decreases, and the costs of monitoring and enforcing agreements increases. A larger set of permissible land uses can have either a positive or negative effect on the magnitude of monitoring and enforcement costs. On the positive side, as the landowner's freedom to use her land increases, the need to violate the agreement decreases. More acceptable land uses, however, provide the landowner with more opportunities to misinterpret the agreement, intentionally or unintentionally. Whether the positive or negative effect of landowner freedom is of more significance is uncertain. Longer contracts that compensate landowners with a one-time lump sum payment, as is the case with both donated and PDR easements, tend to have larger costs to monitor and enforce agreements. Subsidies, which are shorter-length contracts with periodic (typically annual) payments, have lower monitoring and enforcement costs but still exceed the costs of conservation banking and fee simple acquisition.

Involuntary incentive mechanisms also have high monitoring and enforcement costs. Involuntary incentive mechanisms, such as zoning, TDRs with zoning, and impact fees, force strict rules on landowners. Some restricted land uses that require government permits, like the construction of an office building or house, may be easily monitored. Other restricted land uses, such as cultivating crops or clear-cutting trees, may require the regulator to engage in more active and costly monitoring and enforcement activity.

The main point is that both voluntary and involuntary incentive mechanisms that allow the landowner to stay on the land require the regulator to incur monitoring and enforcement costs. Compensation paid in short-term intervals is possibly the only method of reducing these costs.

Acquisition Costs

Acquisition costs are the actual cash outlays required to purchase or otherwise retire land for species protection. Land can be retired through purchase of either full or partial interest in the land, or by a payment that retires the land for a specified term. Both subsidies and fee simple acquisition have very high costs of retiring land for conservation purposes. Fee simple acquisition has very high costs, because acquiring land in its entirety, with all its rights intact, is expensive and requires the greatest amount of financial resources initially.

The acquisition costs associated with subsidies are less than the acquisition costs of fee simple acquisition in the short run. In the long run, however, subsidy acquisition costs may exceed those of fee simple acquisition. The primary reason for lower short-run and higher long-run acquisition costs is that subsidies generally restrict land activities for only a limited time period. As such, the annual payment of the subsidy is less than the cost of purchasing the land fee simple. If the land is continually conserved through subsidies, the sum of payments over time is likely to exceed the cost of purchasing the land outright. The increased cost for a subsidy mechanism is the price of flexibility. Subsidies provide more flexibility to both the government regulator and the landowner. At the fruition of the subsidy, both the regulator and the landowner can reevaluate their options and determine their best course of action for the next time period. The regulator may prefer a subsidy if limited funds make it impossible to meet the ESA goal with other incentive mechanisms. The landowner may prefer more flexibility if she is uncertain about future opportunities. Regardless of who prefers more flexibility, the cost to conserve the land in perpetuity using a subsidy incentive scheme is likely to be greater than the cost of fee simple acquisition.

PDR easements require the regulator to incur acquisition costs, but those acquisition costs are less than for fee simple acquisition, because the regulator is purchasing only a partial interest in the land. PDR easement acquisition costs have been estimated to be in the range of 30 to 70 percent of the costs of fee simple acquisition. Donated easements are funded through federal tax deductions, which means the landowner typically receives less than the fair market value. Therefore, donated easements require less actual cash outlay than do PDR easements. The tax deduction represents a decrease in the federal government's annual budget, funds that must be spread across all worthy projects. Therefore, funding a donated easement program reduces the funds available for all federal government programs. A local regulator, using a donated easement mechanism, can conserve land with minimal cash outlay.

Zoning, TDRs with zoning, conservation banking, and impact fees all have relatively low acquisition costs. Under an impact fee scheme, a government funds the acquisition costs by requiring developers to pay a fee to offset the impact of their development. Likewise, TDR with zoning and conservation banking have conservation funded by developers through the purchase of development rights or bankable credits. Zoning forces the costs of conservation on the landowner, incurring acquisition costs in the rare event that a Fifth Amendment property taking has occurred.

Information Rents

Information rents occur when landowners are paid more than their opportunity cost of the lost land simply because the landowners know more about themselves than the regulator does (see Chapter 8). Information rents are most prominent when the regulator is confined to conserving specific land parcels and required to use voluntary incentive mechanisms. Landowners can act strategically. The landowner, knowing that the regulator must acquire his land to satisfy the conservation objective, is able to extract from the regulator an extra payment that exceeds his or her actual opportunity cost. The landowner would have sold for less. When the landowner earns information rents, society pays too much for its conservation. The incentive mechanism can be perceived as inequitable from society's point of view.

For zoning, impact fees, conservation banking, and TDRs with zoning, information rents are very low or nonexistent. Information rents are absent for zoning and impact fees because landowners are not compensated for conserving land. With conservation banking and TDRs with zoning, compensation is determined by the market. The landowner's private information is reflected in the market price, and therefore information rents are eliminated.

Of the four completely voluntary incentive mechanisms, donated easements have the smallest potential for information rents. Subsidies and fee simple acquisition have high to very high potential for information rents, and PDR easements have a medium to high potential for information rents. The ability of landowners to earn information rents is dependent on the value of the compensation paid to the landowner and the ability of the landowner to act strategically in negotiating for compensation. Donated easements have the lowest compensation, and the rules regulating the use of donated easements are well defined, reducing the possibility for the landowner to act strategically. Compensation under a PDR easement is greater than under a donated easement, and because compensation is negotiated on a case-by-case basis, the opportunity for the landowner to strategically overstate his or her asking price is present. Like PDR easements, the fee simple acquisition incentive mechanism provides the landowner with the opportunity to act strategically. Unlike PDR easements, under a fee simple acquisition, because full interest rather than partial interest in the land is being purchased, landowners receive greater compensation. Because compensation is greater and the opportunity for strategic behavior is equal, information rents are greater.

With a subsidy incentive mechanism, unlike the other three, contracts and payments are negotiated on a regular basis. Furthermore, the opportunity for strategic behavior is present for subsidies just as it is for PDR easements and fee simple acquisition. If subsidies are negotiated annually, the landowner has the opportunity to earn information rents every year. The accumulation of information rents over time could be substantial, and in present value it may exceed the information rents of fee simple acquisition.

Risk of Habitat Destruction

When involuntary incentive mechanisms are used, government regulation imposes uncompensated out-of-pocket expenses on landowners. To avoid incurring the regulatory costs of conserving their land, landowners are faced with the incentive of destroying the habitat on their land prior to regulation. Landowner destruction will reduce the amount of land available for species preservation. The quality of land available for conservation will also be affected if the landowner perceives that the probability of being regulated increases with land quality, which is likely the case.

Zoning has high deadweight loss if landowners develop their land hastily to escape the high costs that a potential zoning rule would impose. Development that supersedes zoning on environmentally rich land can create a loss of conservation benefits. Landowners who are subject to TDRs with zoning may also face the incentive to develop their land prematurely. Because landowners zoned for conservation under a TDR with zoning incentive scheme are at least partially compensated, the incentive to destroy land is less than that for zoning alone. The deadweight loss of landowner destruction associated with impact fees depends on whether the magnitude of the impact fee is set on the habitat quality of the land. If the impact fee is set in conjunction with the conservation value, landowners will have an incentive to destroy habitat to escape expensive impact fees. For voluntary incentive mechanisms, landowners are fully compensated, and therefore the incentive to destroy habitat is low to very low.

Conclusion

When markets have many buyers and sellers, such that the developmental pressure in the region is strong, conservation banking is the preferred mechanism for species protection. Conservation banking consolidates the conservation requirements of many landowners and places them in the hands of one individual or organization, whose sole objective is to make money by providing conservation. Furthermore, because their profits depend on the quality of the conserved parcel, as well as minimizing the costs of conservation, conservation reserves will likely satisfy the biological criteria and reduce many of the long-term government costs.

When markets have few buyers and sellers, no incentive mechanism stands out as the clear favorite. Each mechanism has its own strengths and weaknesses. If we assume that the government prefers a voluntary incentive mechanism over a command-and-control mechanism, then the field of potential policies is limited to easements, fee simple acquisition, subsidies, or any combination thereof. In comparing the three on the basis of government costs, it appears to be a wash. The landowner requirements are very similar as well. However, the biological criteria have one important difference—the conservation reserves permanency. Subsidies are by far the least permanent, whereas easements have the potential for the greatest permanency. The problem with easements is that there is no guarantee; landowners may lack sufficient incentives to continue to uphold the contract in the future. A possible remedy to this situation would be to create a policy that combined easements (both PDR and donated) with subsidies.

The conservator could purchase the development rights in the land initially and negotiate other land use restrictions. Some of these restrictions, in particular land management and maintenance requirements, could be tied into an annual subsidy that is negotiated periodically. The easement portion would provide permanence, while the subsidy would give the landowner and the conservator some flexibility. The number and types of landowners that this policy would appeal to would likely be more than each mechanism appealed to independently. The potential to create a larger preserve should increase as a result, and because landowners are being paid an additional annual subsidy for which they can negotiate, the permanence of the conservation should be more secure.

Considering government costs, monitoring and enforcement costs are likely to be smaller, for the same reason that the conservation reserve is likely to be more permanent. Acquisition costs are likely to increase, however, and the cost of the easement initially may decrease because of the stream of subsidy payments that will follow. Administration of the policy would maintain an approach similar to a subsidy policy, and costs will continue to be very high. Information rents will be higher; the landowner has two pieces of private information for which to extract rents: the personal value of the easement and the personal value of the annual subsidy.

References

Black-footed Ferret Recovery Implementation Team (BFFRIT). 2002. Black-footed ferret: Ferret facts. www.blackfootedferret.org/ [cited 20 May 2002].

Environmental Defense Fund. 2000. Progress on the back forty: An analysis of three incentive-based approaches to endangered species conservation on private land. www.edf.org/ [cited January 2000].

Gilpin, M. E., and J. M. Diamond. 1980. Subdivision of nature reserves and the maintenance of species diversity. *Nature* 28:567–568.

Higgs, A. J., and M. B. Usher. 1980. Should nature reserves be large or small? *Nature* 285:568–569.

Leopold, A. 1933. *Game management.* New York: Charles Scribner's Sons.

Mills, L. 1995. Edge effects and isolation: Red-backed voles on forest remnants. *Conservation Biology* 9:395–403.

Saunders, D. A., R. J. Hobbs, and C. R. Margules. 1991. Biological consequences of ecosystem fragmentation: A review. *Conservation Biology* 5:18–27.

Sowell, Thomas. 1987. *A conflict of visions.* New York: Wm. Morrow & Co.

Terborgh, J. 1976. Discussion in "Island biogeography and conservation: Strategy and limitations." *Science* 193:1027–1032.

U.S. Fish and Wildlife Service (USFWS). 2002. Species accounts: Red-cockaded woodpecker. http://endangered.fws.gov/i/b/sab4a.html [cited 23 May 2002].

Vickery, P., M. Hunter Jr., and M. Scott. 1994. Effects of habitat area on the distribution of grassland birds in Maine. *Conservation Biology* 8:1087–1097.

Whitcomb, R. F., J. F. Lynch, P. A. Opler, and C. S. Robbins. 1976. Discussion in "Island biogeography and conservation: Strategy and limitations." *Science* 193:1027–1032.

Willis, E. O. 1984. Conservation, subdivision of reserves, and the anti-dismemberment hypothesis. *Okios* 42:396–398.

About the Authors

STEVE W. BUSKIRK is a professor in the Department of Zoology and Physiology at the University of Wyoming.

R. MCGREGGOR CAWLEY is a professor in the Department of Political Science at the University of Wyoming.

THOMAS D. CROCKER is the J. E. Warren professor in the Department of Economics and Finance at the University of Wyoming.

DEBRA DONAHUE is a professor of law in the College of Law at the University of Wyoming.

FRIEDA KNOBLOCH is an assistant professor in the Departments of American Studies and Women's Studies and the School of Environment and Natural Resources at the University of Wyoming.

GREGORY M. PARKHURST is an assistant professor in the Department of Agricultural Economics at the Mississippi State University.

JASON F. SHOGREN is the Stroock Distinguished Professor of natural resource conservation and management and a professor of economics in the Department of Economics and Finance at the University of Wyoming.

RODNEY B. W. SMITH is an associate professor in the Department of Applied Economics at the University of Minnesota.

JOHN TSCHIRHART is a professor in the Department of Economics and Finance at the University of Wyoming.

SAMANTHA M. WISELY is a graduate student in the Department of Zoology and Physiology at the University of Wyoming.

Index